IMAGES
of America

BATH

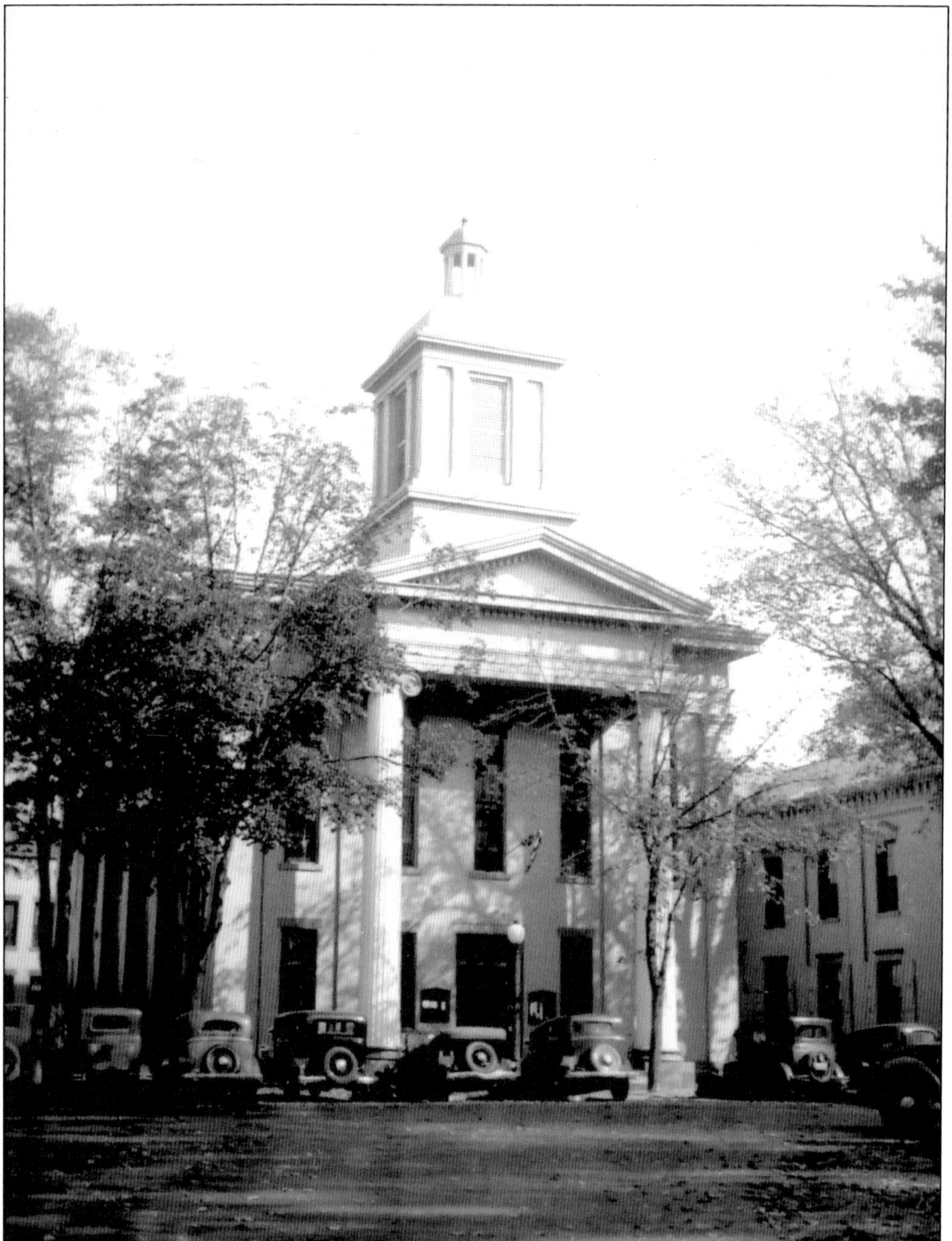

The Steuben County Courthouse is a Bath landmark.

IMAGES
of America

BATH

Kirk W. House and Charles R. Mitchell

ARCADIA
PUBLISHING

ISBN 978-0-7385-3575-3

Published by Arcadia Publishing
Charleston, South Carolina

Printed in the United States of America

Library of Congress Catalog Card Number: 2004102489

For all general information contact Arcadia Publishing at:
Telephone 843-853-2070
Fax 843-853-0044
E-mail sales@arcadiapublishing.com
For customer service and orders:
Toll-Free 1-888-313-2665

Visit us on the Internet at www.arcadiapublishing.com

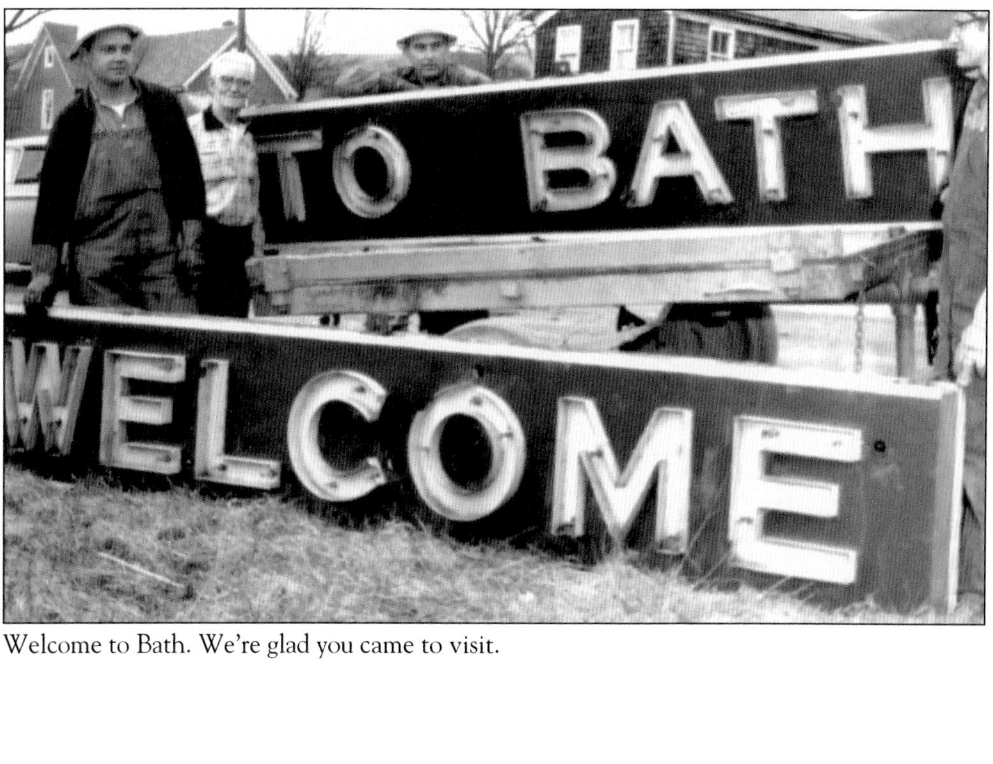

Welcome to Bath. We're glad you came to visit.

Contents

ACKNOWLEDGMENTS

Most of the photographs we have used came from the collection of the Steuben County Historical Society at Magee House in Bath. While it is always risky to single out individuals when many people have made a work like this possible, we are going to take a chance and specifically thank Ron Wyatt, who helped us through the archives, and Joe Paddock, who remembers more about Bath than most people will ever learn. President Martha Treichler kindly arranged permission to use the collection, and the society as a whole has been a real encouragement.

Quite a number of our images were originally created by George Atanesian, who for many years worked as a professional photographer in Bath. Anyone interested in county history owes a debt not only to Atanesian but also to Ruth and Gary Waldo. The Waldos preserved much of Atanesian's work, donating it to the historical society along with Gary's own voluminous collection.

Another significant set of photographs came from the Steuben County Historian's Office (also in Magee House), for which we thank the historian and assistant historian. Historian Twila O'Dell unexpectedly helped by asking us to print a set of glass-plate negatives, many of which became terrific additions to this book. Assistant historian Marion Springer, among other services, unhesitatingly opened a file drawer and pulled out the image of the ark that heads the first chapter.

Levi Weaver and Betty Langendorfer graciously lent photographs, as did the Dormann Library. Carrie Fellows of the Corning-Painted Post Historical Society gave us a chance to use an image from the collection of Isabel Walker Drake; this collection was the basis of *Corning*, our earlier book in the Images of America series.

Chris Geiselmann and Trafford Doherty of the Glenn Curtiss Museum allowed us to use images of early aviation history in Bath, and Carol Mozes of the Liberty Street Café gave us background on her father's time as mayor. Joshua House helped with photograph identification and with railroad history. Melissa Mitchell once again provided technical support with the layout.

It should not surprise anyone in Bath that we need to thank the Davenport and Dormann families. Decades ago, the Davenports gifted the community with their Cameron Street home, originally built by John Magee. This served as the Davenport Library until 1998, when Henry and Alice Dormann funded the creation of the new Dormann Library on the same property, now renamed the Dormann-Davenport Learning Campus. The old library of the Magee House became home to the historical society, the county historian, and Elm Cottage Museum. We needed the facilities and collections of all four institutions to prepare this book.

Anyone interested in the history of Bath and Steuben County owes a big debt to Dick Sherer, Jim Hope, and John Ormsby. They have each held various official positions over the years, but those positions have only been public recognition of their lives as collectors, preservers, researchers, interpreters, and, what every community needs most, rememberers. We thank the three of them—and we will remember them, too.

INTRODUCTION

Bath might have been the great metropolis of western New York.

It was Iroquois country once, and the Longhouse People maintained their independence not only by force of arms but also by skillfully counterbalancing competing French and British ambitions.

The Iroquois League fell apart in the Revolutionary War; some groups siding with their traditional allies the British, some helping out the upstart Americans, and others trying desperately to stay neutral. Iroquois-British-Loyalist raids into Pennsylvania provoked George Washington to dispatch Gen. John Sullivan with the largest independent command ever created by the Continental army. Sullivan devastated the Iroquois towns. America won the Revolution, and the long Iroquois independence ended.

Eager as Americans were to exploit this newly opened territory at last, they had first to settle other issues. New York and Massachusetts both claimed the land, based on conflicting royal charters issued a century before—a conflict moot until then. A Solomon-like decision gave sovereignty to New York and real estate title to Massachusetts. Massachusetts then promptly set about selling off land for profit.

The region quickly passed through several hands, including those of Revolutionary War financier Robert Morris and those of speculators Phelps and Gorham. However, America was still an underdeveloped country. Most available development capital was back in the old mother country . . . a fact not lost on Sir William Pulteney, who put together an investment group.

Contemporary laws forbade the alienation of such property to foreign owners, prompting the Pulteney group to turn to Charles Williamson. A Scottish royal army captain who had been captured during the Revolution, Williamson had since acquired an American wife, American citizenship, and a colonel's commission. He was quickly pressed into service as frontman and owner of record.

Since the Susquehanna-Chemung-Conhocton chain of rivers joined the Genesee Country with Chesapeake Bay, Williamson saw the "first families" of Virginia and Maryland as the natural purchasers in his new territory, where they could establish vast estates of pristine wilderness, shipping the land's increase by the river highway. Ascending the Conhocton River, he cleared land on its banks where the east–west river met the north–south vale of Keuka Lake and Pleasant Valley, already a crossroad of Iroquois trails.

Here, "Charles the Magnificent" laid out his city of broad boulevards, named for Sir William Pulteney's lady, the Countess of Bath. Despite the crankiness of pioneer prophetess Jemima Wilkinson, who grumped about his worldliness from the north end of Keuka Lake, Williamson was soon sponsoring horse races, fairs, and even a permanent theater. From Bath, he could see, all of western New York would be settled. Steuben County was fissioned from Ontario County in 1796, making Bath a seat of government as well as a transportation hub and a fine center for the growth of wheat. Gentleman owners from the Tidewater brought in their slaves, and the future dawned bright.

Clouds gathered quickly. Not long after clearing its first lot, Williamson dug Bath's first grave, for his three-year-old daughter who had died of Genesee fever—probably malaria. Her headstone, and many more, may be found in the Pioneer Cemetery on Steuben Street.

The colonel's marriage broke down under the weight of his chronic infidelity. Sales never met expectations, and eventually Pulteney, taking advantage of a change in American law, retrieved direct control. Williamson's Springfield estate, near Salubrious Lake, was sold off and started to slide downhill.

The opening of the Erie Canal shattered any dreams that may have lingered in memory of Williamson. Syracuse, Rochester, and Buffalo became the region's great cities, and Albany and New York (rather than Baltimore and Norfolk) became its trading partners. Steuben's agricultural focus passed from wheat to potatoes to grapes.

No longer was Bath a frontier boomtown, but it still had its history, its county seat, its lovely prospects, and its spacious layout, inherited from Williamson's vision. Bath is now in the early years of its third century. The broad streets, many of them still tree lined, connect the town with bygone days. We hope that they will still do the same in days long to come.

One

The Birth of Bath

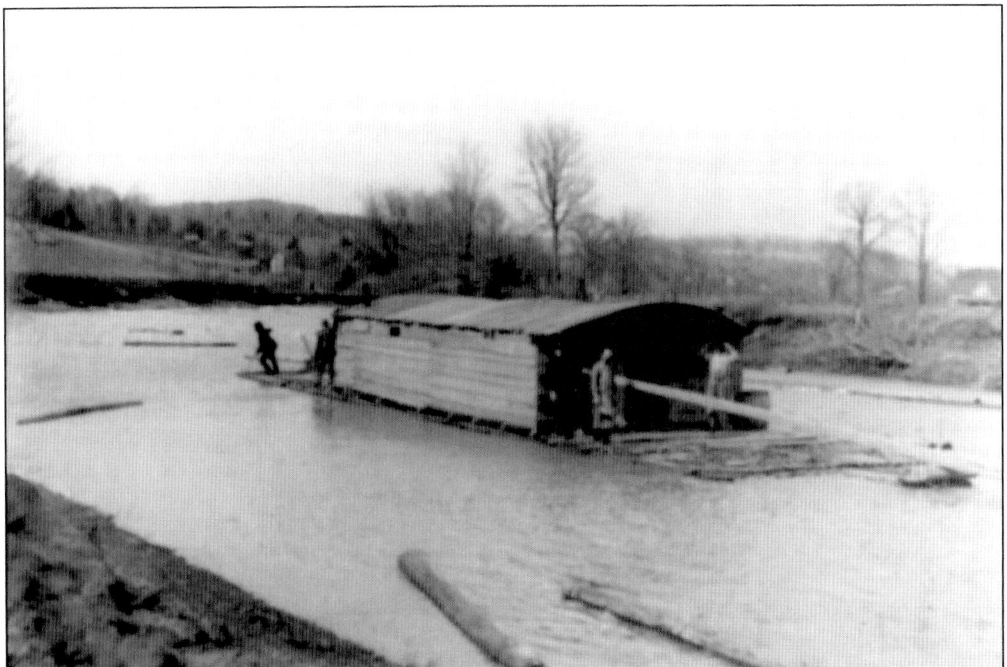

Col. Charles Williamson followed the Conhocton River to the site of his new metropolis, recognizing in the river system an ideal wilderness highway, naturally (and lucratively) connecting Bath with the Tidewater region. Steuben folks knocked together "arks" and rafts to carry their produce down the Conhocton . . . into the Chemung . . . south on the Susquehanna to Havre de Grace . . . and along Chesapeake Bay to Baltimore. Produce disposed of, they sold their arks for lumber and walked back home. The Erie Canal, undreamed of in Williamson's day, shifted the focus of western New York from the Southern Tier to a northern axis. When railroads came in a little later, the remaining river traffic quickly evaporated. Given the fact that railroads and photography arrived at just about the same time, the ark pictured here must have been one of the very last. (Courtesy Steuben County Historian's Office.)

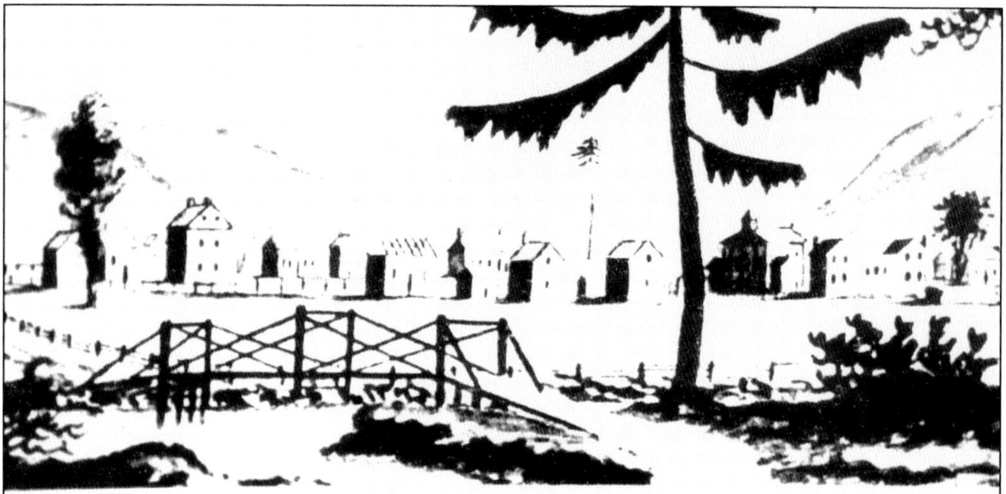

BATH DANS LA GENESEE ÉTABLISSEMENT DE C. WILLIAMSON

THE VILLAGE OF BATH, NEW YORK, 1798

Five years after the felling of the first tree, two years after its designation as seat of the newly erected Steuben County, Charles Williamson's *etablissement* was taking on an impressive appearance. *Dans la Genesee* does not suggest that Bath lay along that river; the whole region was known as the Genesee Country.

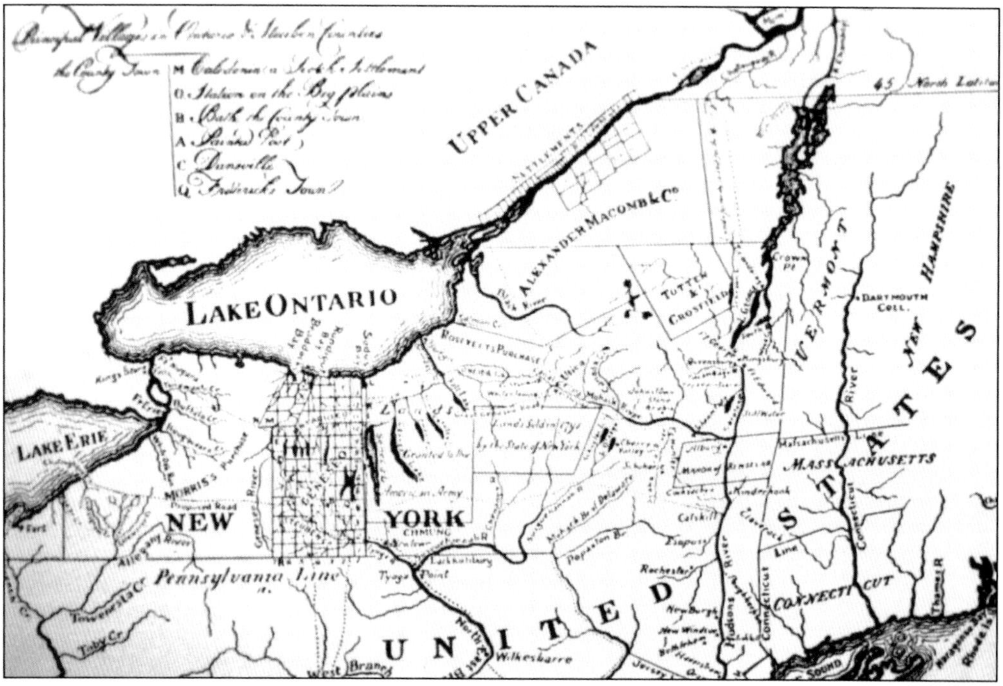

The gridded area between the state line and Lake Ontario is Williamson's wilderness empire—the Phelps and Gorham Purchase, running roughly from the Pre-Emption Line (now Pre-Emption Road) to the Genesee River, including the site of present-day Rochester. Notice the Conhocton River's strategic position as a highway. Notice also that the Y-shaped Crooked (or Keuka) Lake has unaccountably become X-shaped.

No one ever accused "Charles the Magnificent" of thinking small.

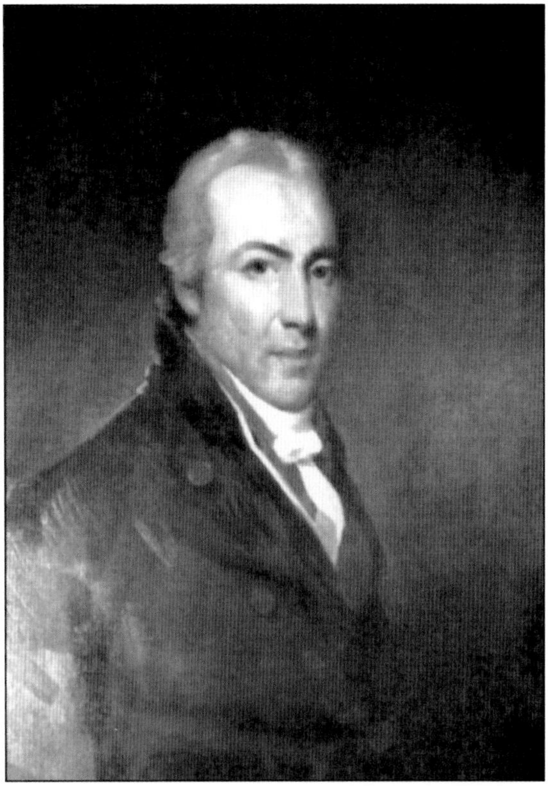

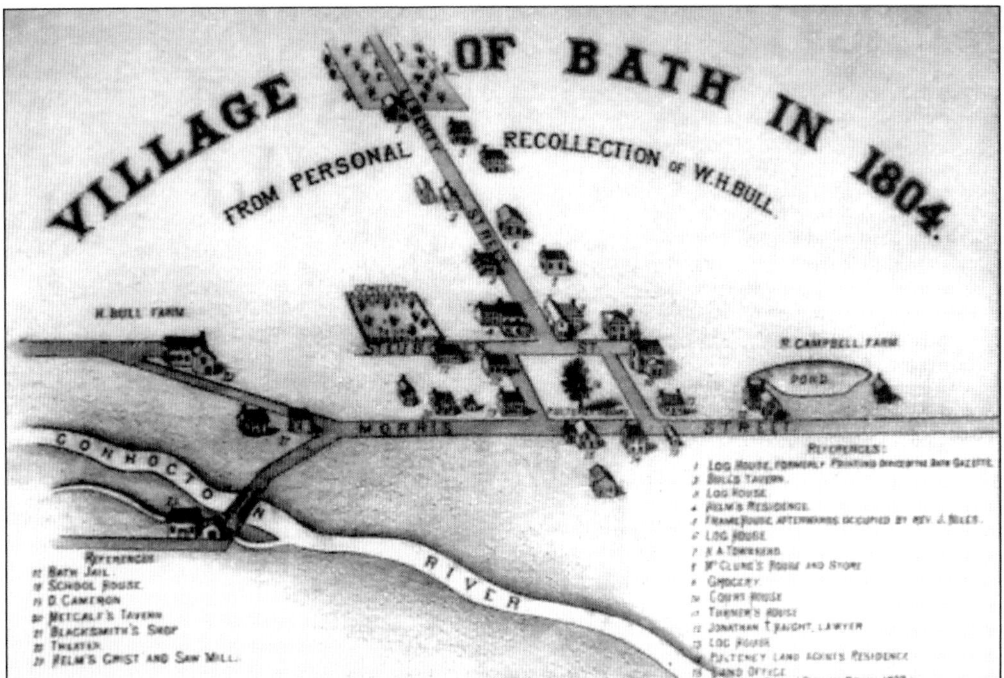

By 1804, an impressive town was thriving. Charles Williamson's vision graced Bath with the broad avenues and squares that still define the village.

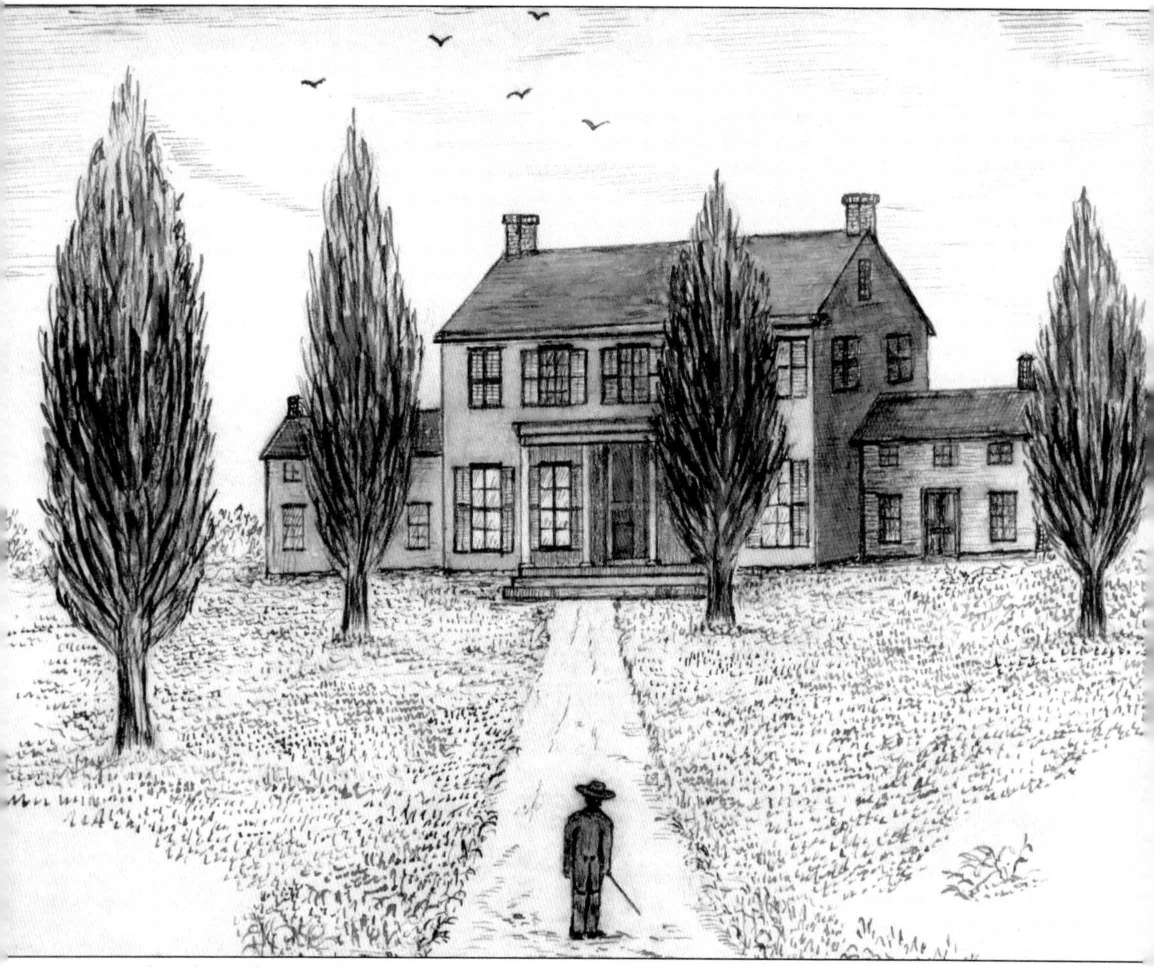

Finding his cabin on the courthouse square insufficiently grandiose, Charles Williamson built a home, which he called Springfield, between what is now Babcock Hollow Road and the shores of tiny Lake Salubria (the official name of Lake Williamson never caught on). Another contemporary sketch shows the now vanished house with an extra half story in the main section, a more grandiose front stairway, and a sort of circular pavilion in the left foreground. Williamson also had several other houses scattered across the Pulteney Purchase.

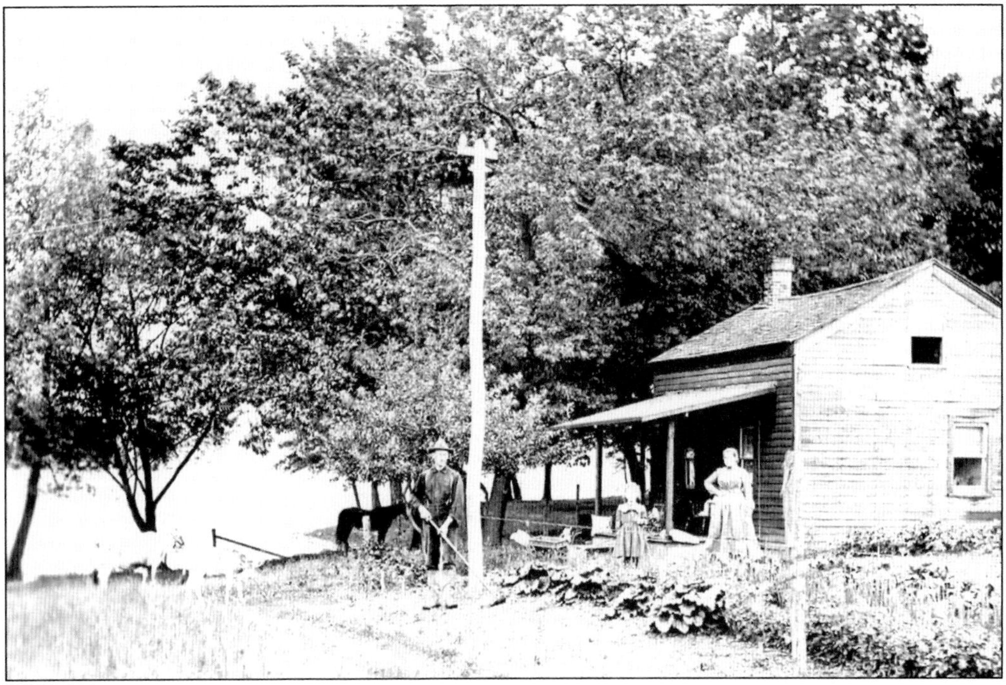

Despite the success of his 1796 World's Fair, Charles Williamson had dreams for Bath that never bore the fruit he had hoped for. A few decades later, one wing was all that survived of Springfield. Apparently, that portion survived long enough to get either electricity or telephone.

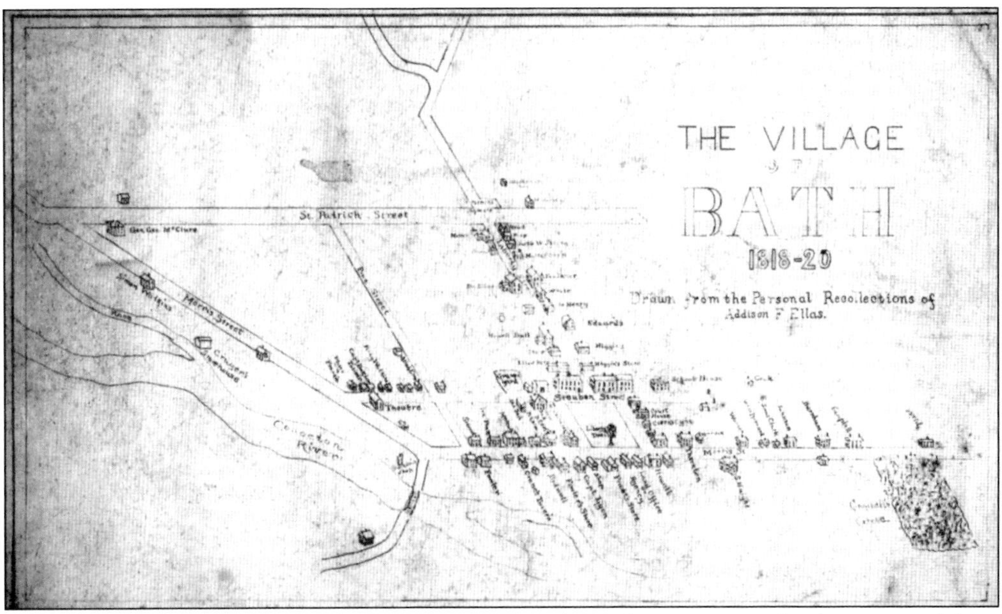

Two decades into the 19th century, new growth made Bath even more clearly recognizable to 21st-century residents. St. Patrick Street is now Washington Street.

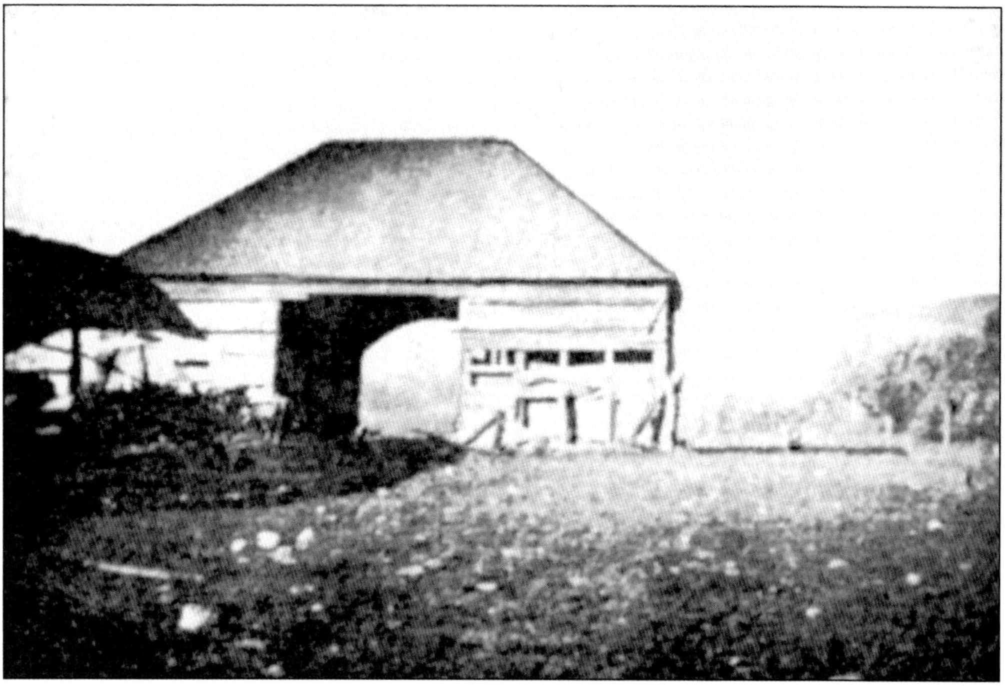

A fair population of slaves remained in Bath into the 1820s. Some of them lived in this cottage, shown here in its later version as a barn, on the Wilkes (originally Williamson) place.

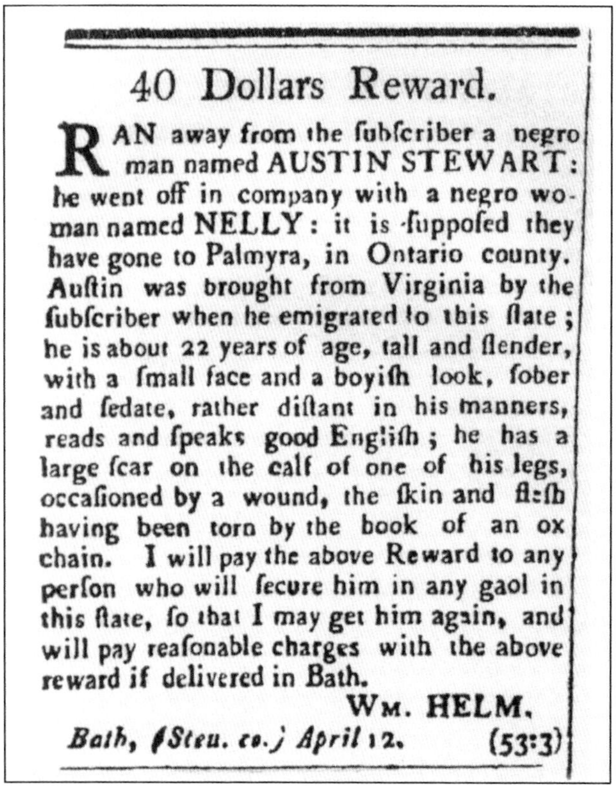

40 Dollars Reward.

RAN away from the fubfcriber a negro man named AUSTIN STEWART: he went off in company with a negro woman named NELLY: it is fuppofed they have gone to Palmyra, in Ontario county. Auftin was brought from Virginia by the fubfcriber when he emigrated to this ftate; he is about 22 years of age, tall and flender, with a fmall face and a boyifh look, fober and fedate, rather diftant in his manners, reads and fpeaks good Englifh; he has a large fcar on the calf of one of his legs, occafioned by a wound, the fkin and flefh having been torn by the hook of an ox chain. I will pay the above Reward to any perfon who will fecure him in any gaol in this ftate, fo that I may get him again, and will pay reafonable charges with the above reward if delivered in Bath.

WM. HELM.

Bath, (Steu. co.) April 12. (53:3)

Austin Steward (misspelled in the advertisement), after surreptitiously consulting a Bath attorney, walked away from slavery one night and hiked to Manchester, where he found work.

Austin Steward became a prominent Rochester businessman in grocery, meats, and real estate. He was also a leader in Canada's Wilberforce community of ex-slaves, an associate of Frederick Douglass, and an Underground Railroad conductor.

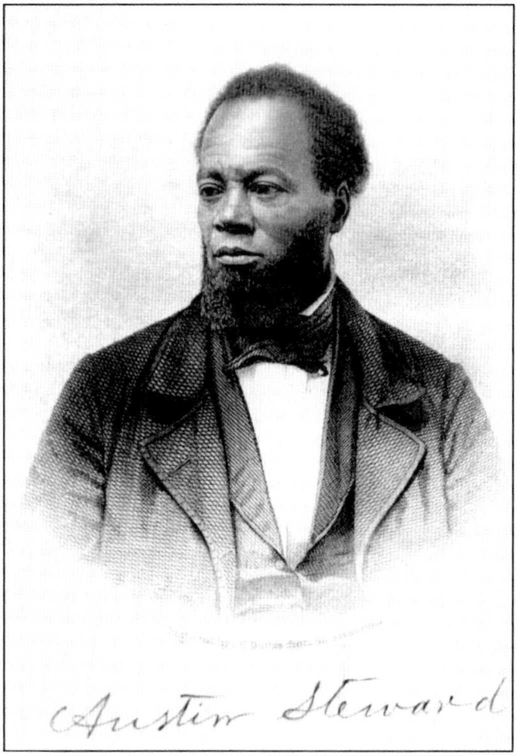

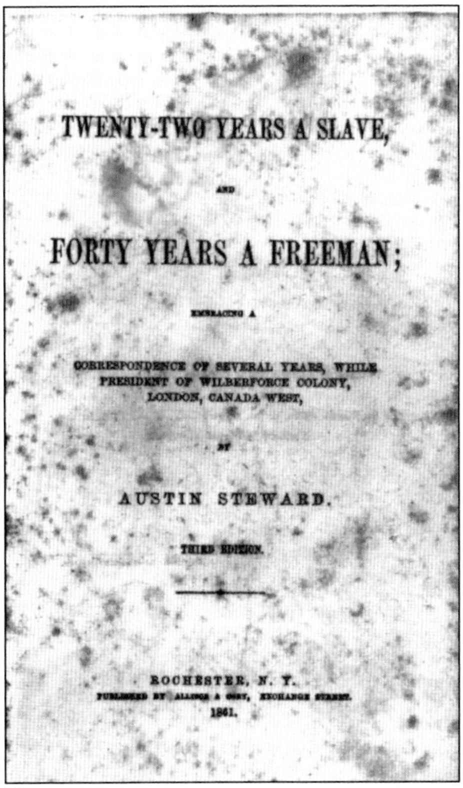
TWENTY-TWO YEARS A SLAVE,

AND

FORTY YEARS A FREEMAN;

EMBRACING A

CORRESPONDENCE OF SEVERAL YEARS, WHILE
PRESIDENT OF WILBERFORCE COLONY,
LONDON, CANADA WEST,

BY

AUSTIN STEWARD.

THIRD EDITION.

ROCHESTER, N. Y.
PUBLISHED BY [illegible], EXCHANGE STREET.
1861.

Austin Steward's book was one of many first-hand accounts unveiling the injustice of slavery.

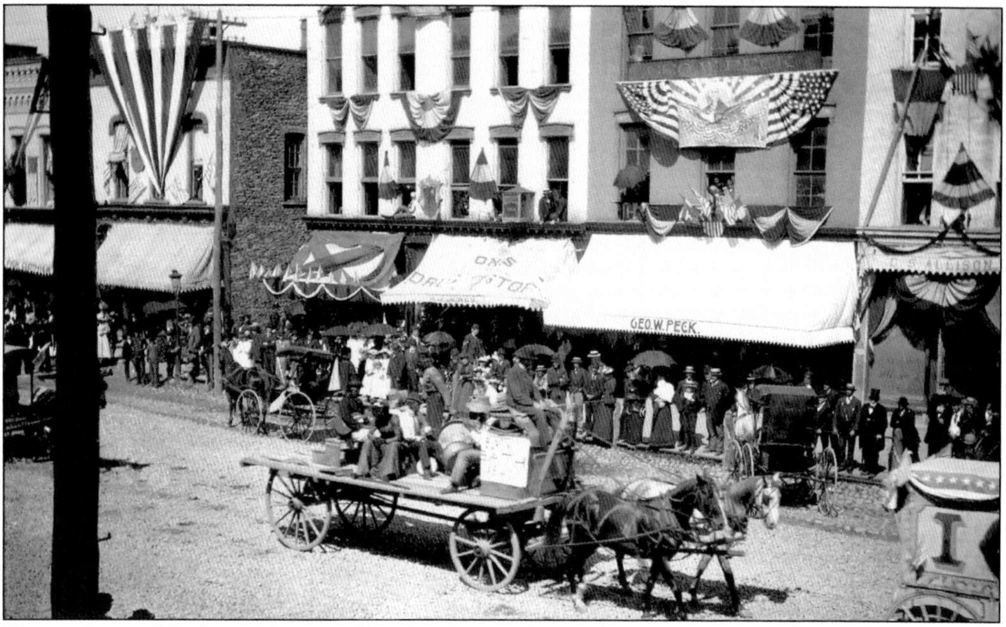

The enduring black population of Bath supported an African Methodist Episcopal church for generations. However, an enlargement of this photograph of the 1893 centennial parade bizarrely demonstrates that the figures on the commemorative float are white folks in blackface.

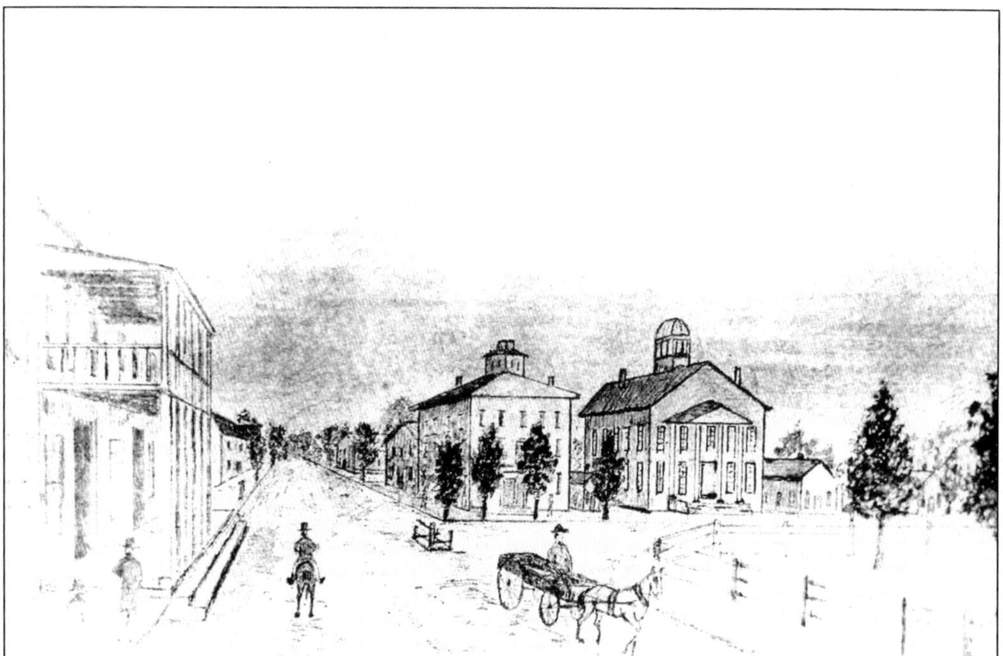

Court of Common Pleas first sat in the original courthouse on July 21, 1796.

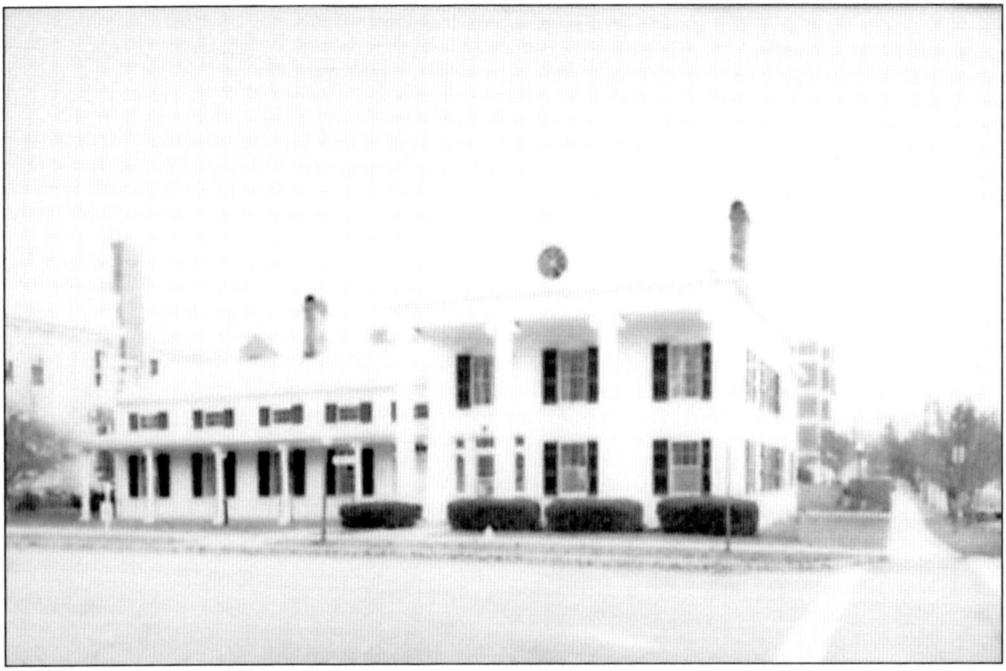

The Balcom House, now judicial chambers, was built in 1819; it is probably the oldest house in Bath still on its original site. Citizens of the new republic were enthusiastic about the Greek Revival style.

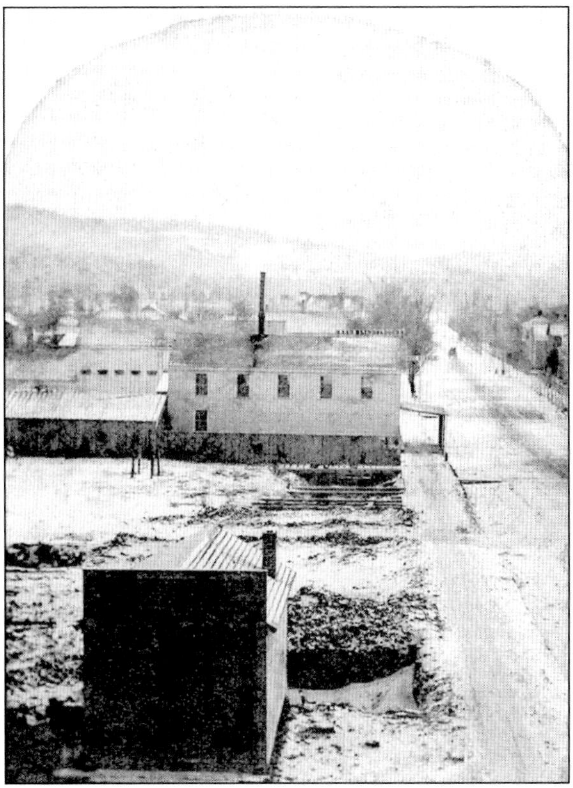

An 1859 fire devastated East Steuben Street from Liberty to Gansevoort. As this stereograph shows, the Beekman Sash, Blinds and Doors factory was quickly rebuilt.

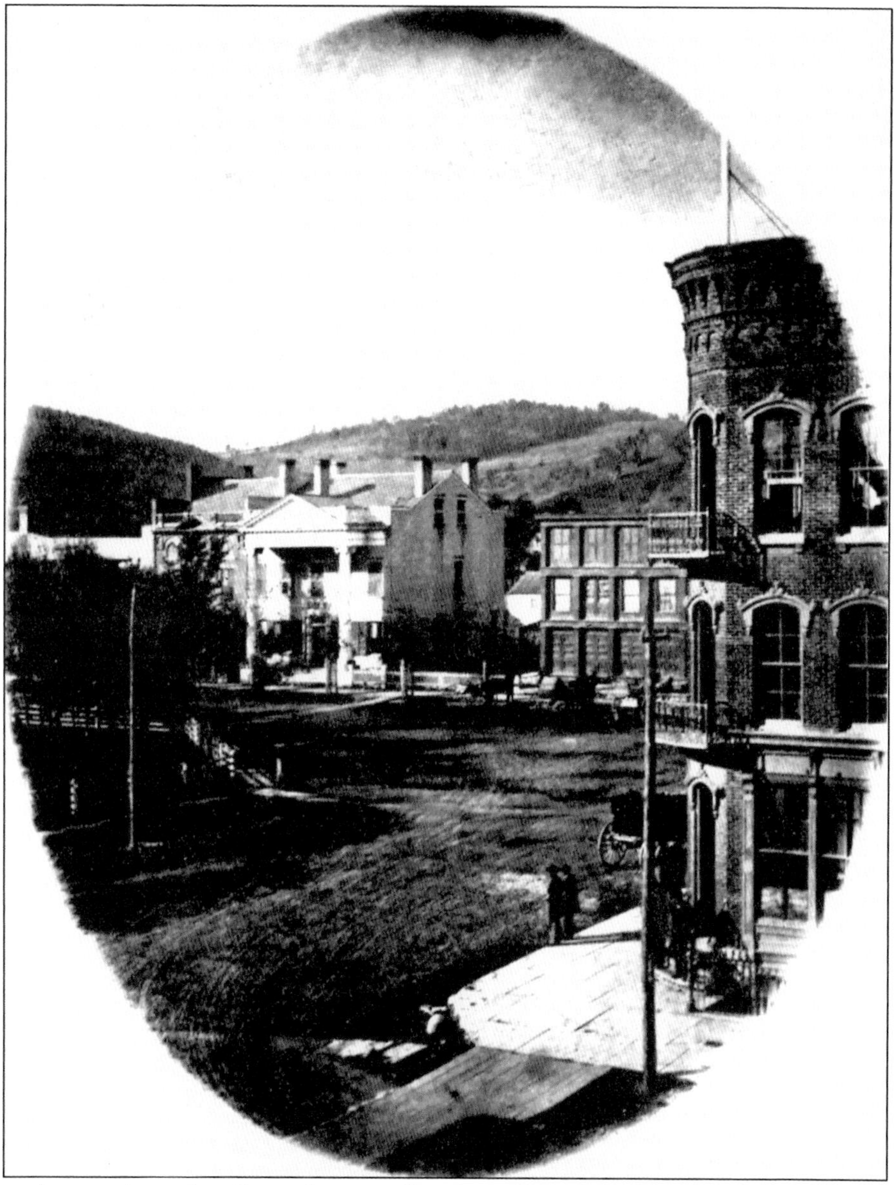

Notice the wooden sidewalks and crosswalks along the unpaved streets. The pillared 1832 building on the left, built by John Magee as the Steuben Bank, now serves as Masonic Hall, the chamber of commerce, and Susan Narby's audiology office. The walk-in vault is still inside. Just left of the bank is the Robert Gansevoort home, built at the same time and still standing. The corner building on the right (1 Liberty Street), also remaining today, was constructed after an 1862 fire.

Twice captured in the War of 1812, John Magee started his career in Bath cutting wood at 25¢ a cord. Elected to Congress for several terms beginning in 1826, he turned down a cabinet appointment from Pres. Andrew Jackson. In 1864, Magee moved to Watkins Glen, where he concentrated on his coal and rail interests, notably the Fall Brook Line.

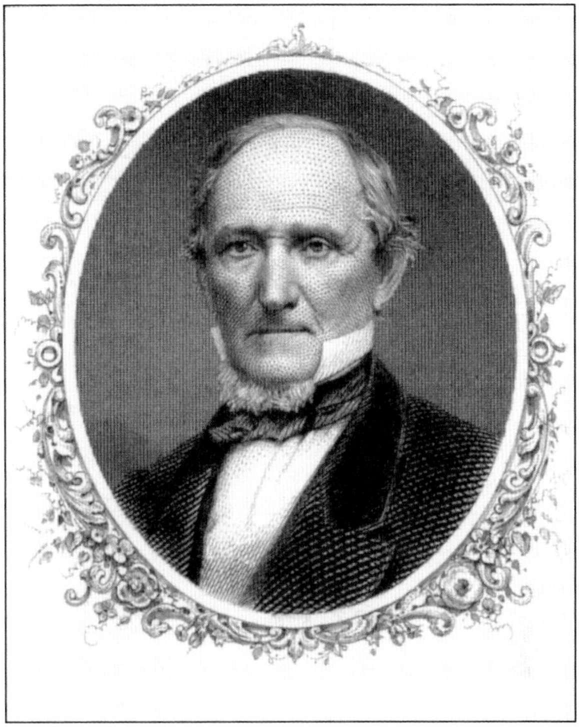

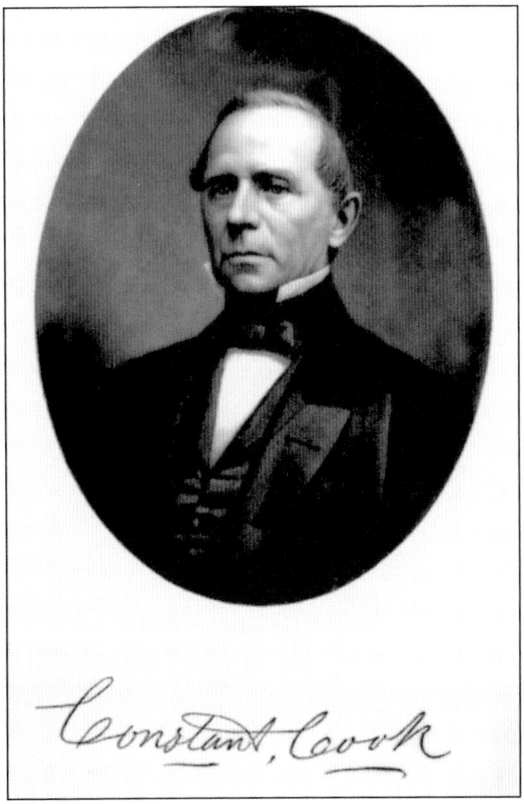

Constant Cook joined John Magee in financing a major portion of the Erie Railroad's route through the Southern Tier.

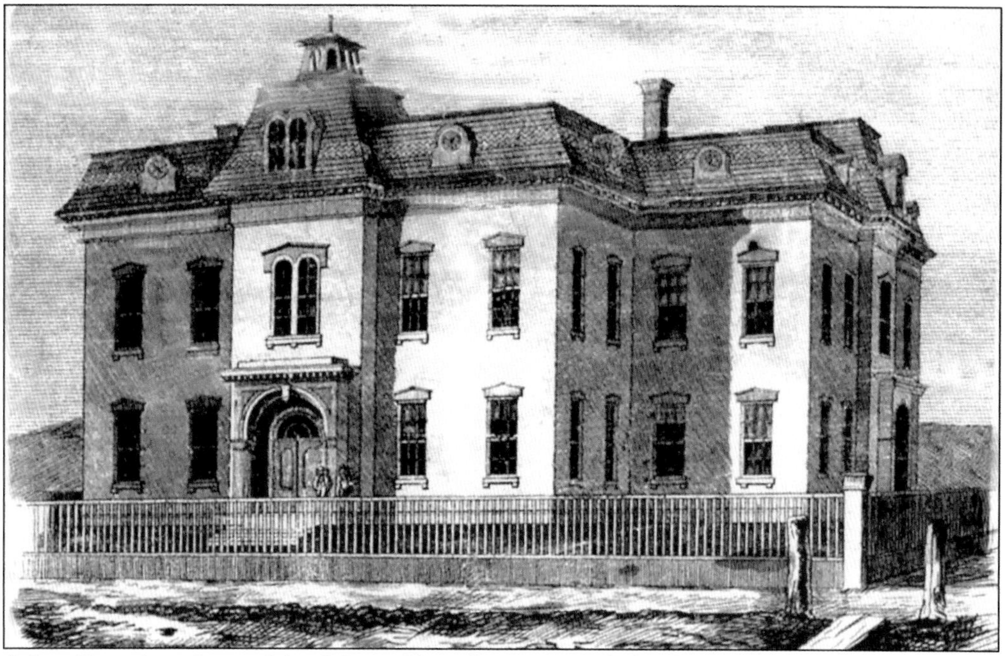

Adam Haverling donated land for public education, and the first Haverling School, erected in 1847, served until 1866. The district used newer structures on the St. Patrick Square (or Washington Square) site, most recently the Dana Lyon Elementary School, until 2002.

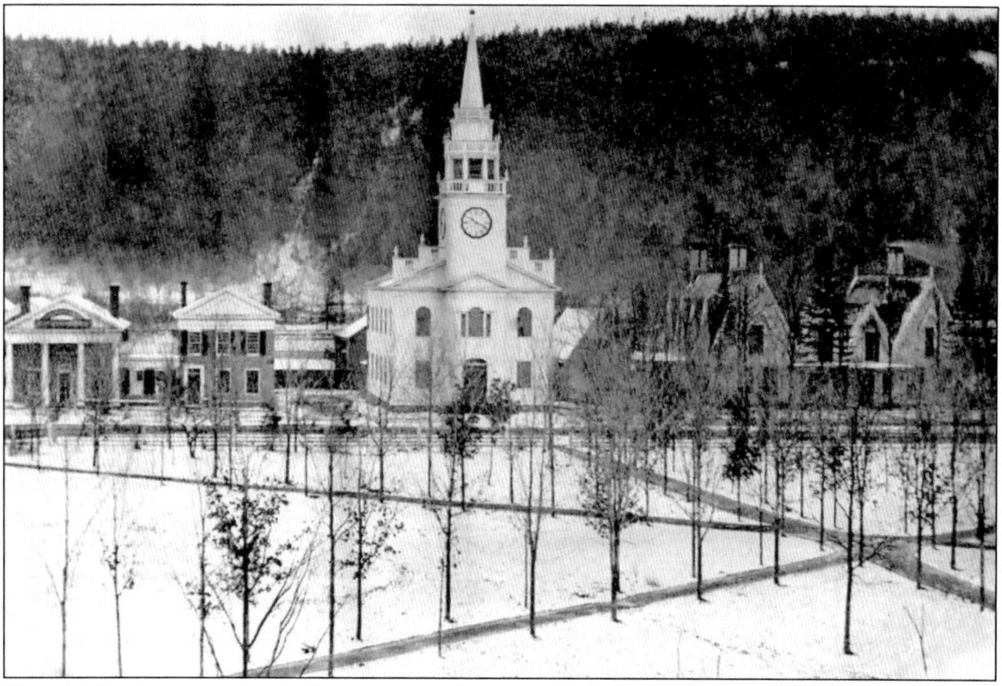

The old Presbyterian church featured a traditional, if lavish, design. Just right of the church is the old Pulteney Purchase (or Pulteney Estate) Land Office, later site of the first Bath Hospital. Pleasant Valley and Bath had both been gouged out by the last glacier before the upright wall of Mossy Bank, South Hill, and Davenport Hill, just past the river to the back, had stopped it dead.

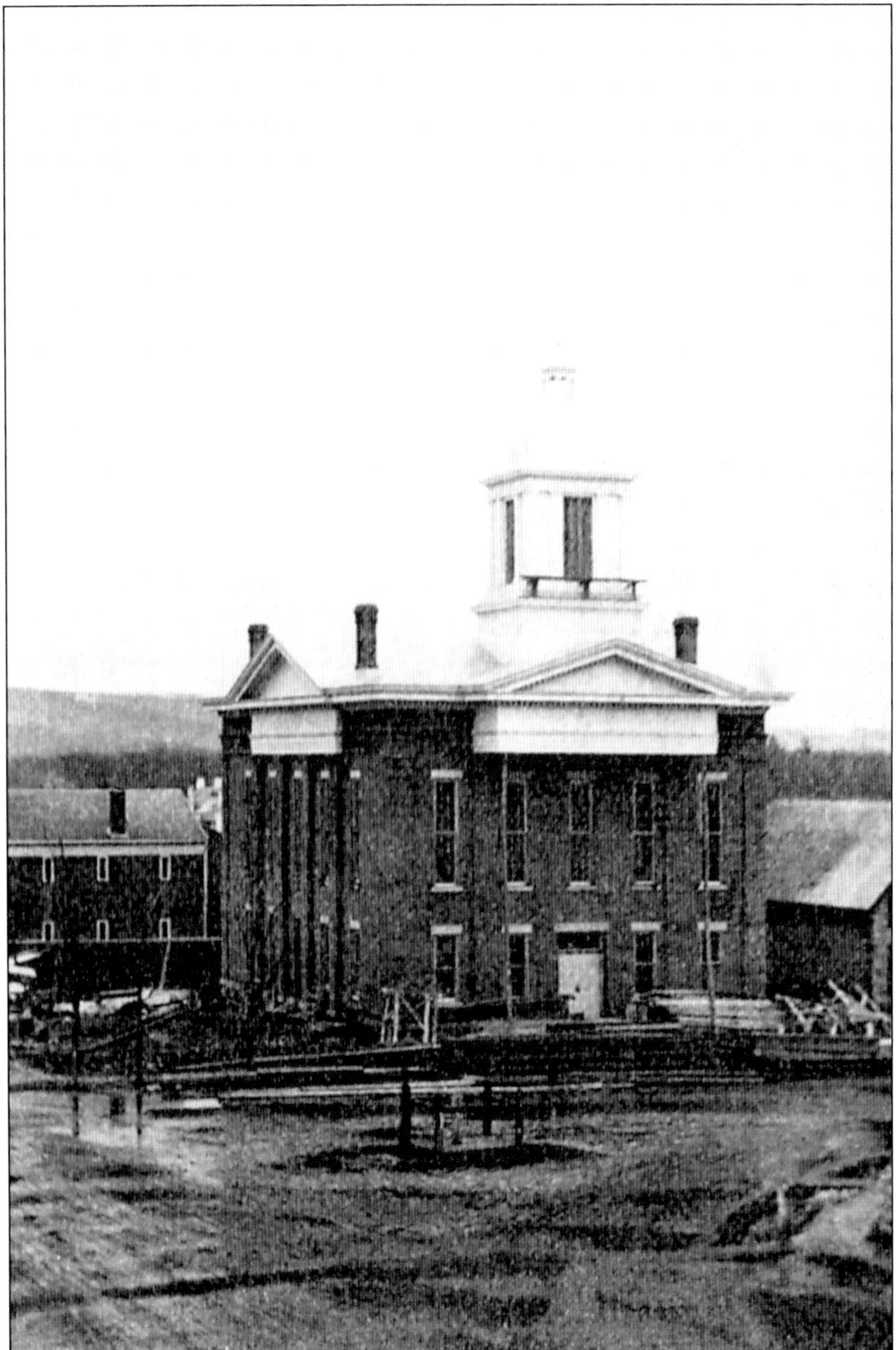

The new courthouse, here under construction in 1860, was built largely of brick salvaged from the second courthouse after a disastrous fire. Well into Bath's third century, it continues to anchor Pulteney Square, as well as the new Steuben County office building campus.

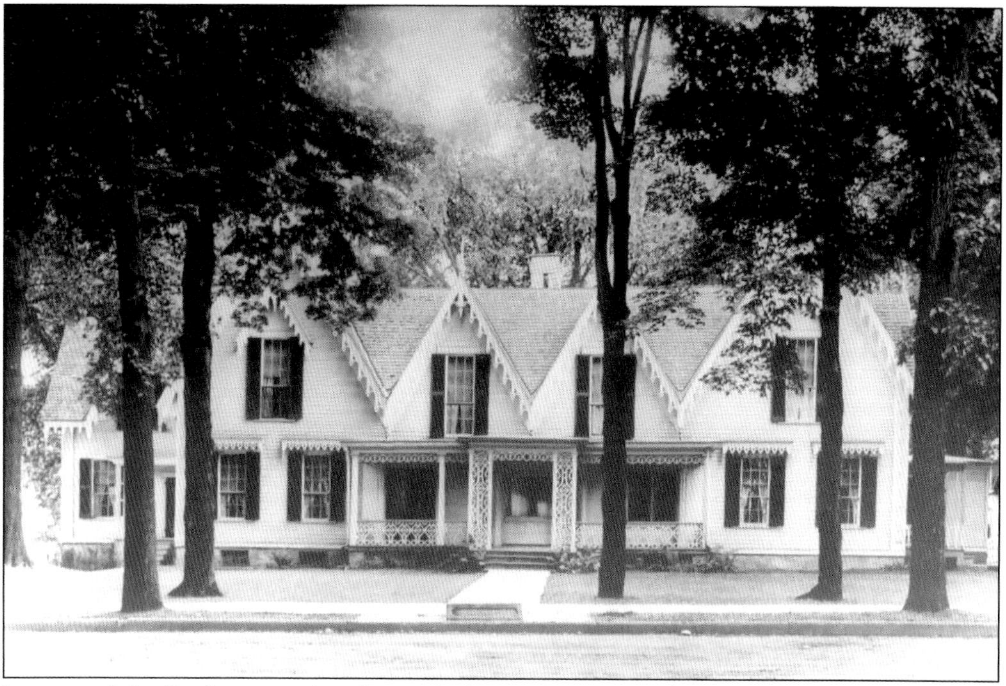

Just east of the Presbyterian church, at 8 Pulteney Square, on the site of Charles Williamson's first home, Col. Levi C. Whiting built an impressive gabled home in 1852. It stood until 1920.

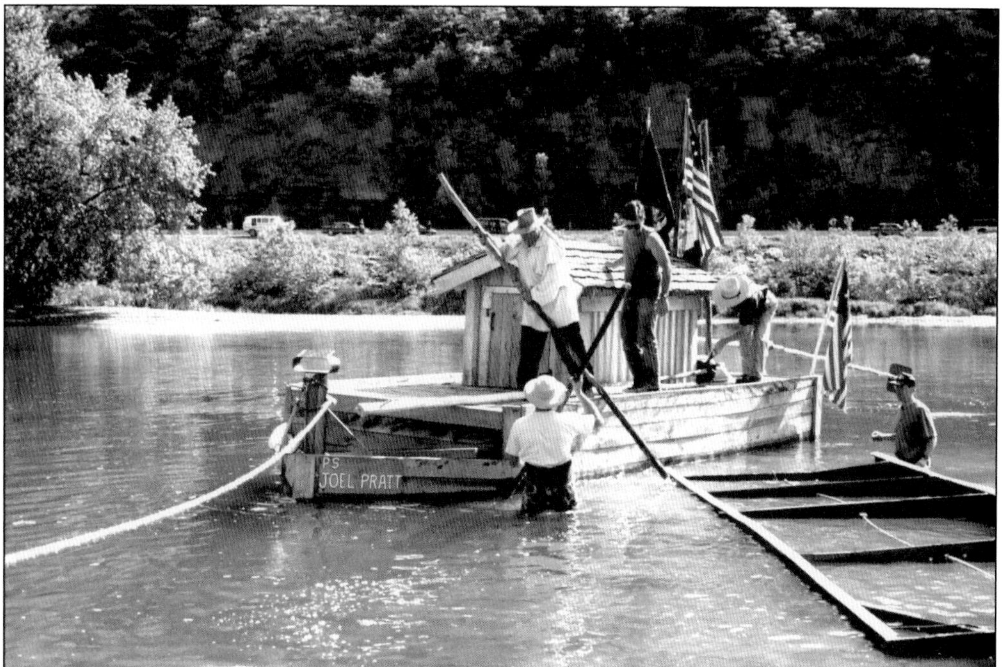

In 1996, Steuben enthusiasts built a brand-new ark (on a smaller scale) and once again poled all the way to salt water. Their celebration of the county bicentennial stirred hundreds of miles of dreams.

Two

IN THE VILLAGE

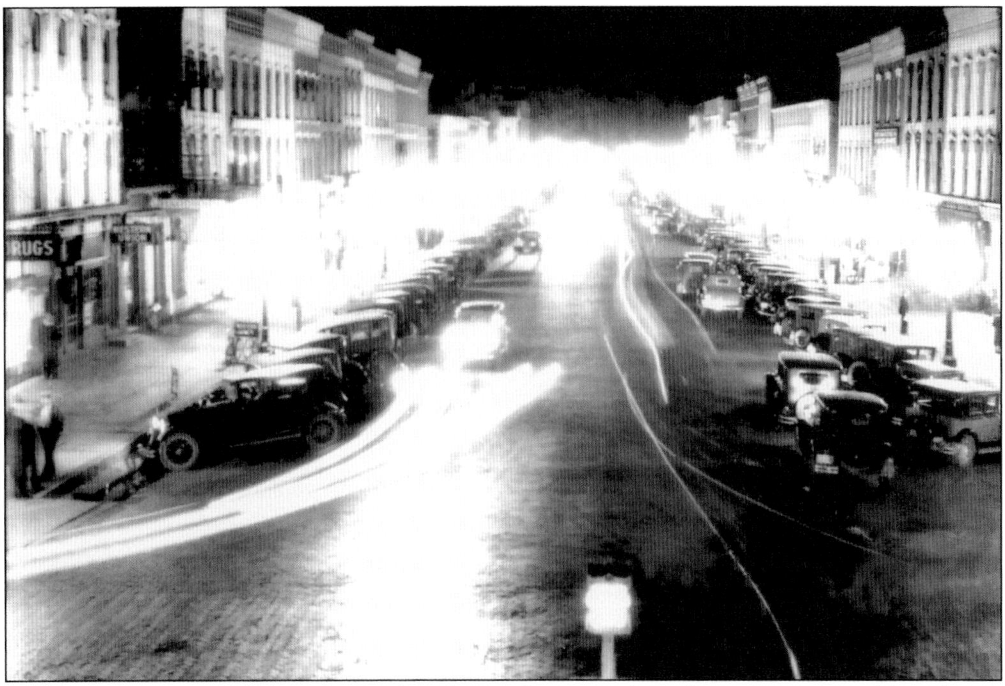

Bath's broad boulevards actually predate those of Paris and Washington, D.C.—although it is unlikely that Bannecker, L'Enfant, or Haussmann turned here for inspiration. For centuries the downtown shopping and business district was a magnet for clients and customers from miles around. Avoca historian Grace Fox recalled being in New York City at Christmastime with a group of children, one of whom remarked, "You know, it's really just like Bath." If South Liberty Street and Pulteney Square form the heart of Bath's public life, North Liberty and Washington Streets set the tone for the residential district. And how many other towns this size have a county fairground right at their very heart?

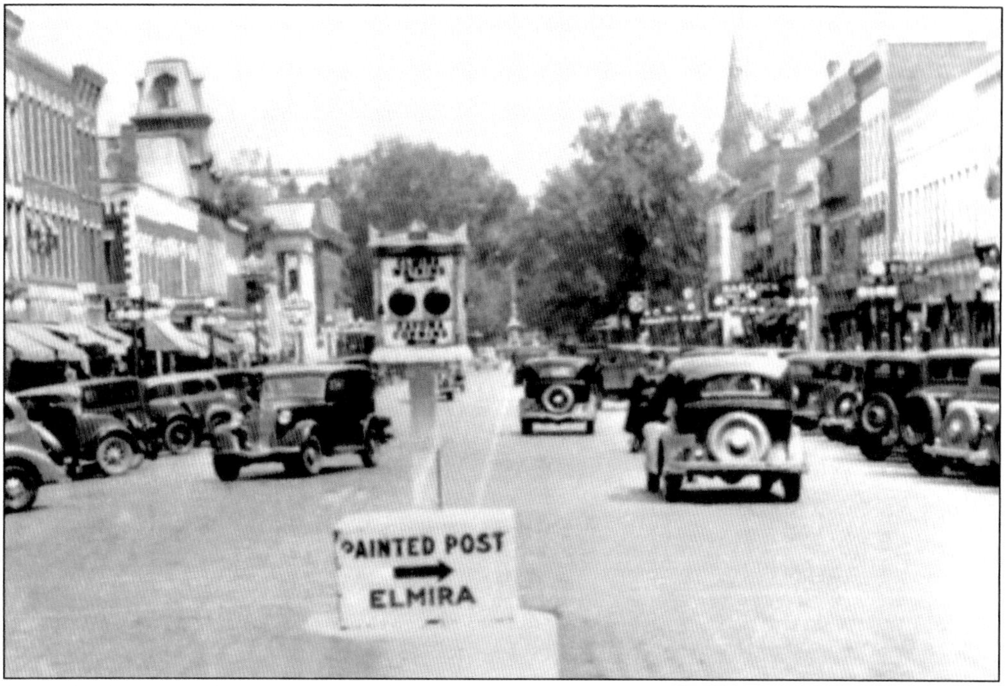

Until the Southern Tier Expressway (now Interstate 86) was built, the region's main artery ran along South Liberty Street.

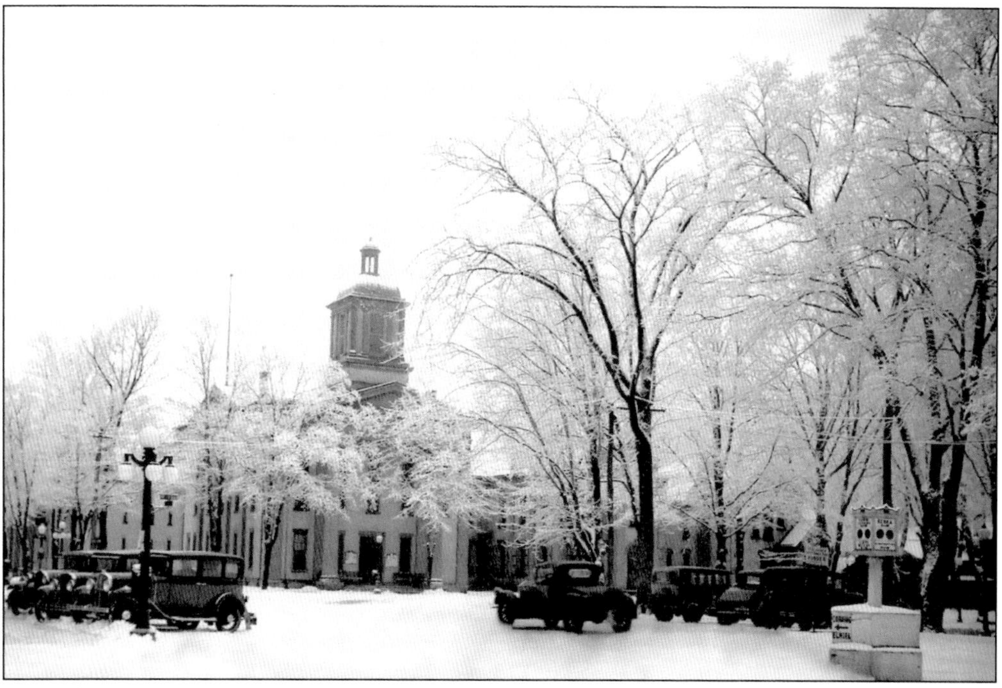

Most photographs of the courthouse seem to be taken from this vantage point, looking east from 1 Liberty Street.

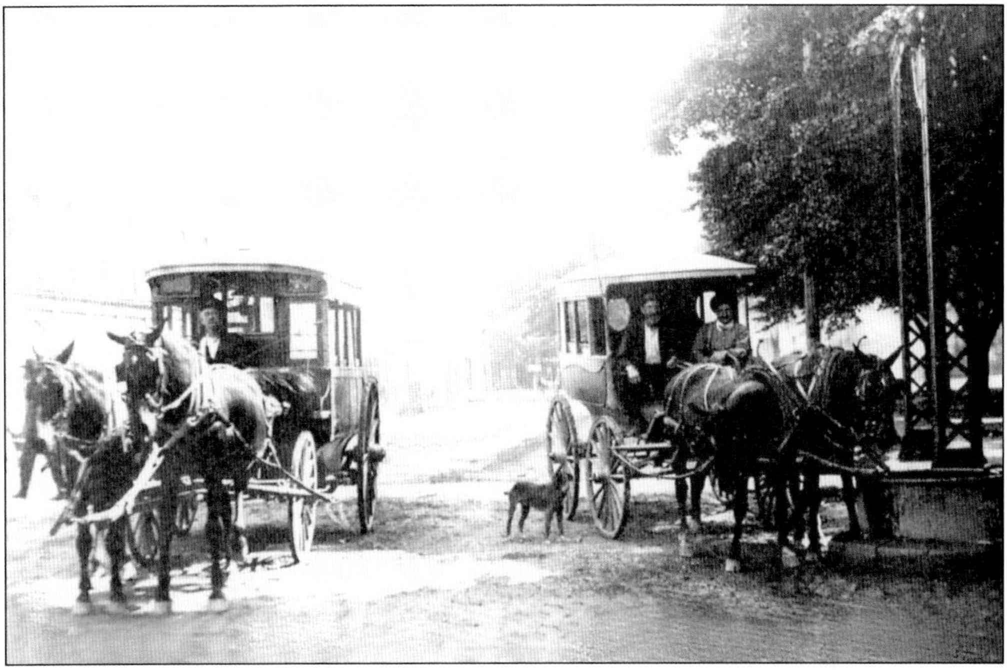

Before automobiles crowded the streets, horse-drawn conveyances ruled the road. Notice the public drinking trough at the right.

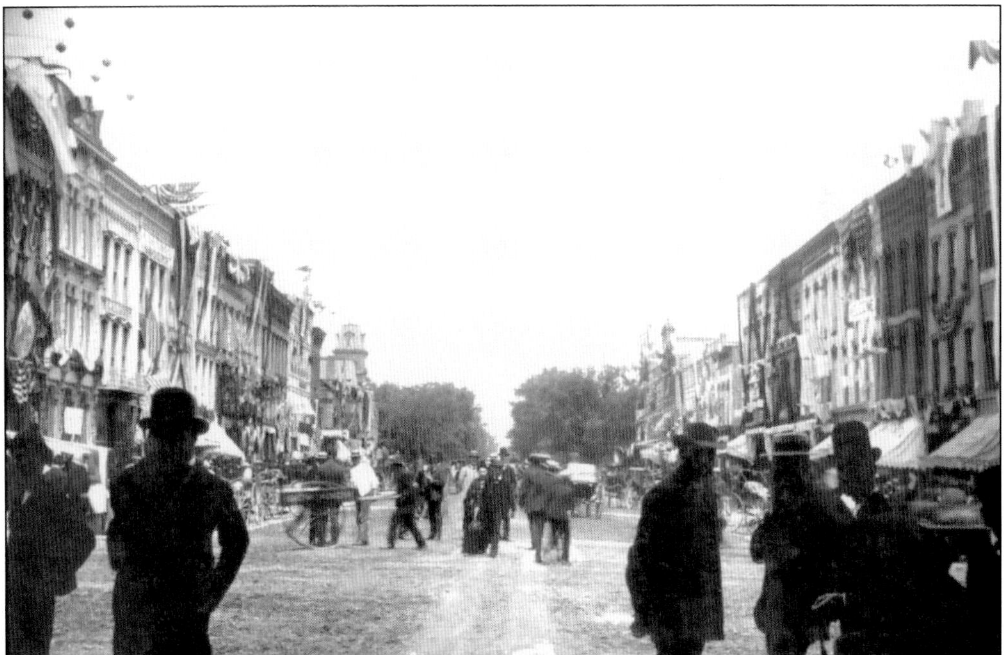

This is likely an Independence Day celebration. By the late 19th century, structures on Liberty Street and Pulteney Square had taken on their still familiar forms. The pushcarts and median strip, however, are only memories.

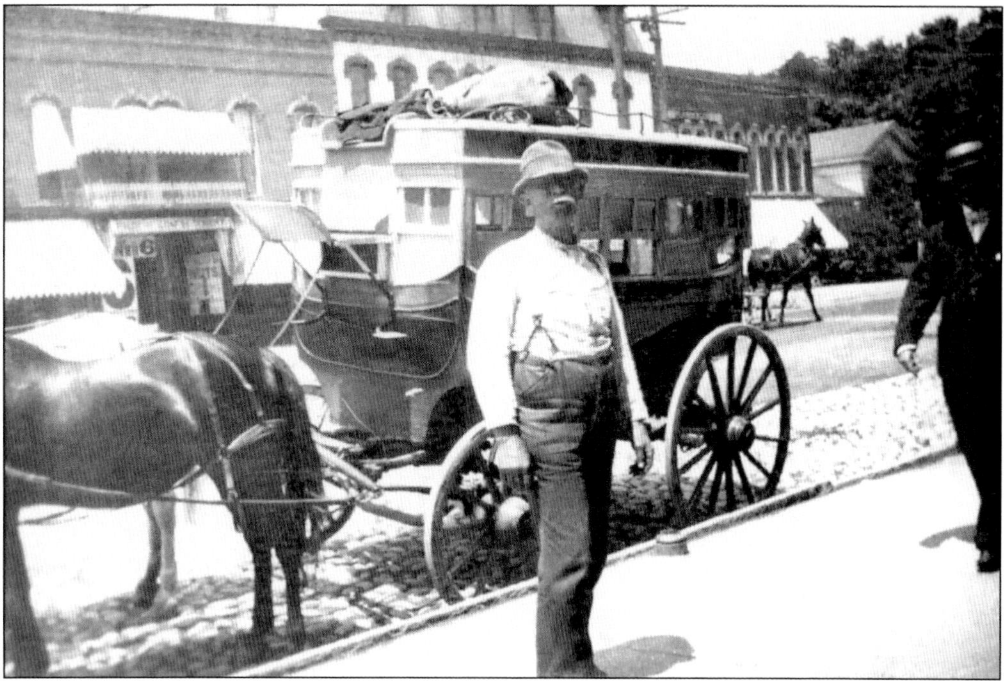

A cobblestone strip lined the space between street and sidewalk. Across the street, a balcony and awning offered protection from sun and rain alike.

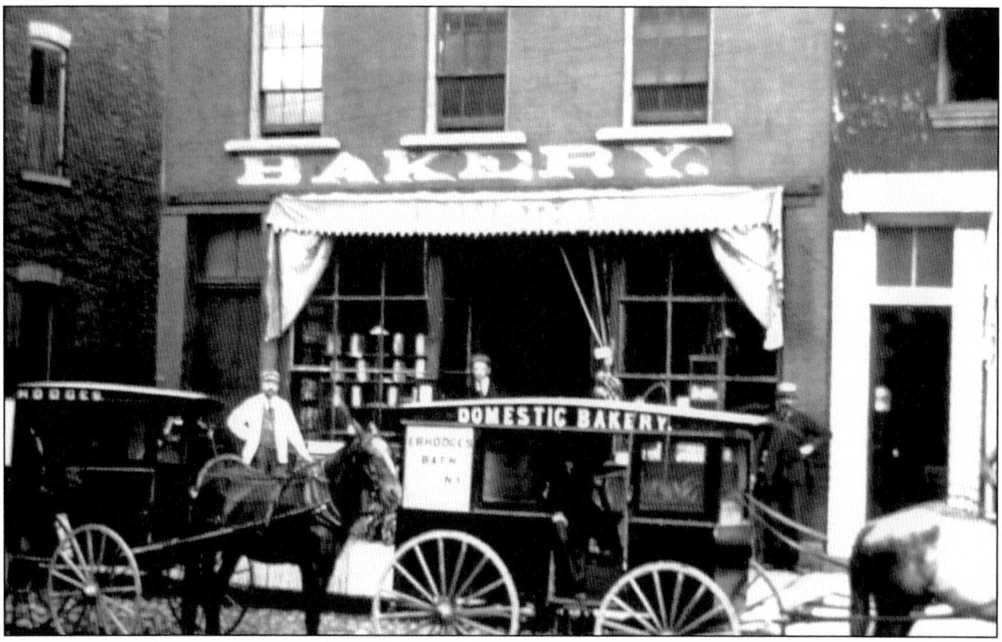

Daily home delivery was vital when few people had transportation or refrigeration. This structure, at 16 Liberty Street, was built c. 1893.

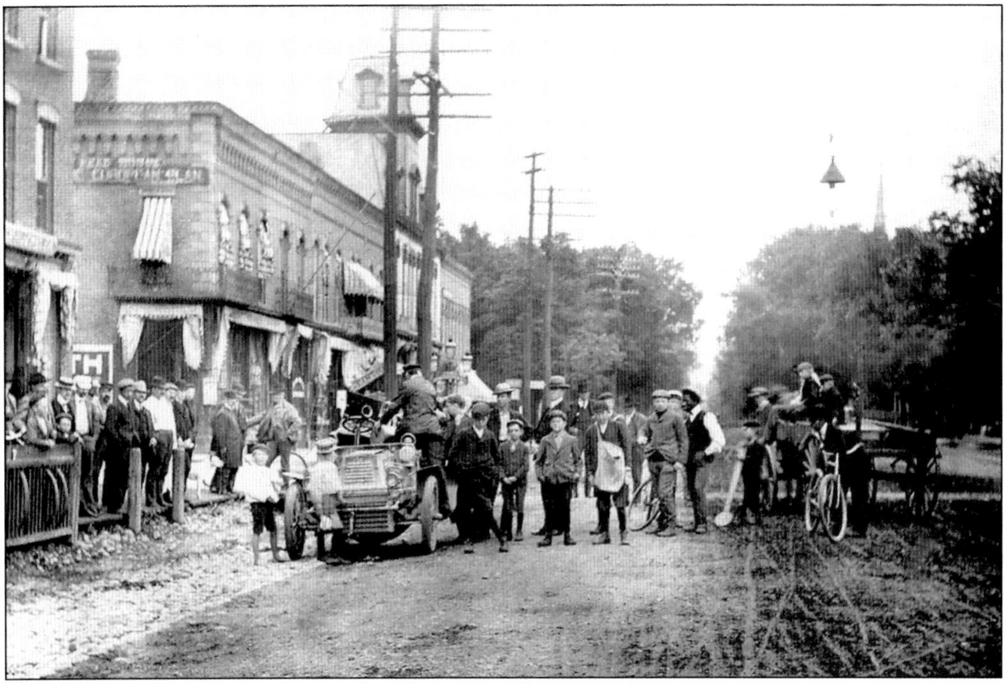

Notice not only the car but also the bicycle rack on the left. A bicycle craze inundated the country between 1890 and 1910. Young Glenn Curtiss operated a seasonal bike shop in Bath for several years.

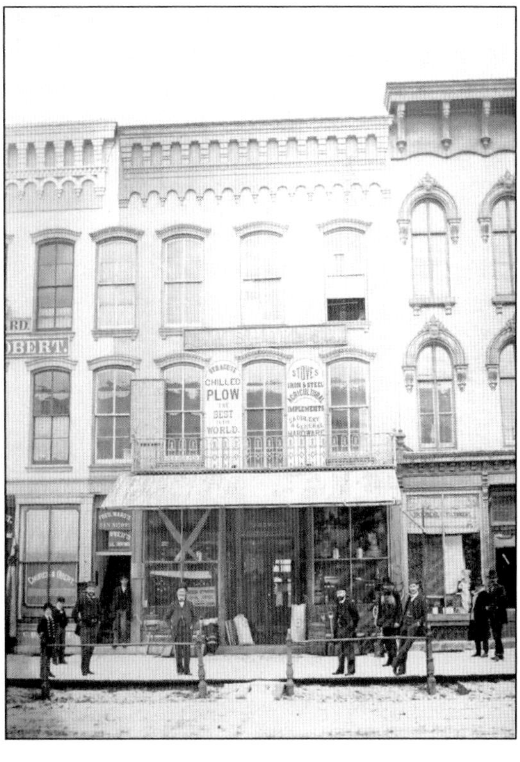

Even back in "the good old days," parking was an issue for merchants. Anyone who wanted customers to come to town offered them places to hitch their teams. The camera seems to have attracted a crowd to the wooden sidewalk.

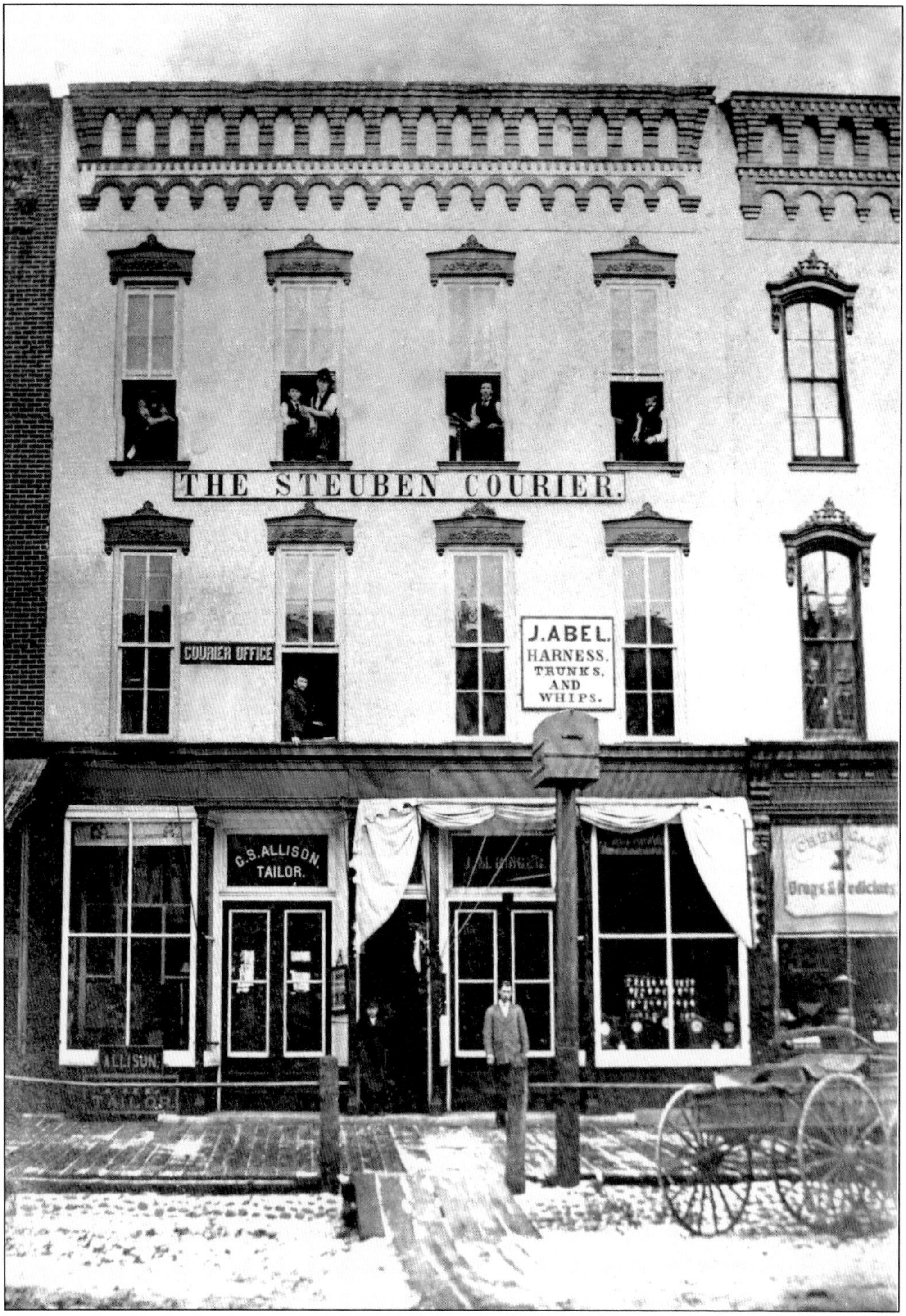

Notice Mr. Abel's trunk atop the pole. That certainly was a unique way of advertising his specialties. It appears he dealt in all things leather except shoes. Note the newspaper office boys in the windows. (Courtesy Steuben County Historian's Office.)

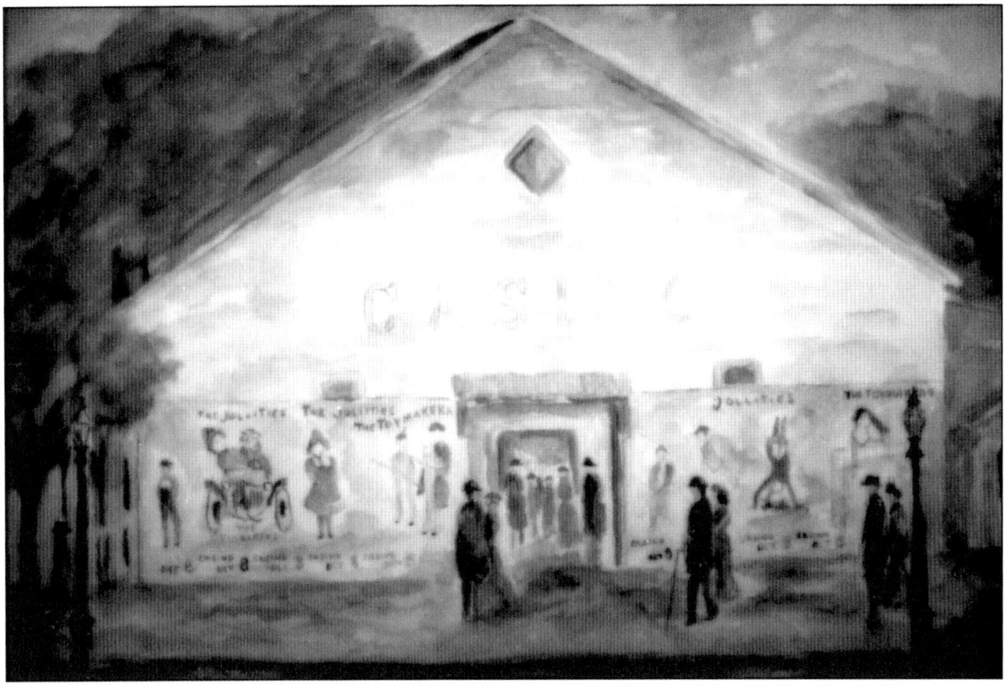

The Casino, where Bath Plumbing and Hardware is now located, packed in avid theatergoers between 1880 and 1910. A portion of the Casino can be seen at the bottom of page 38.

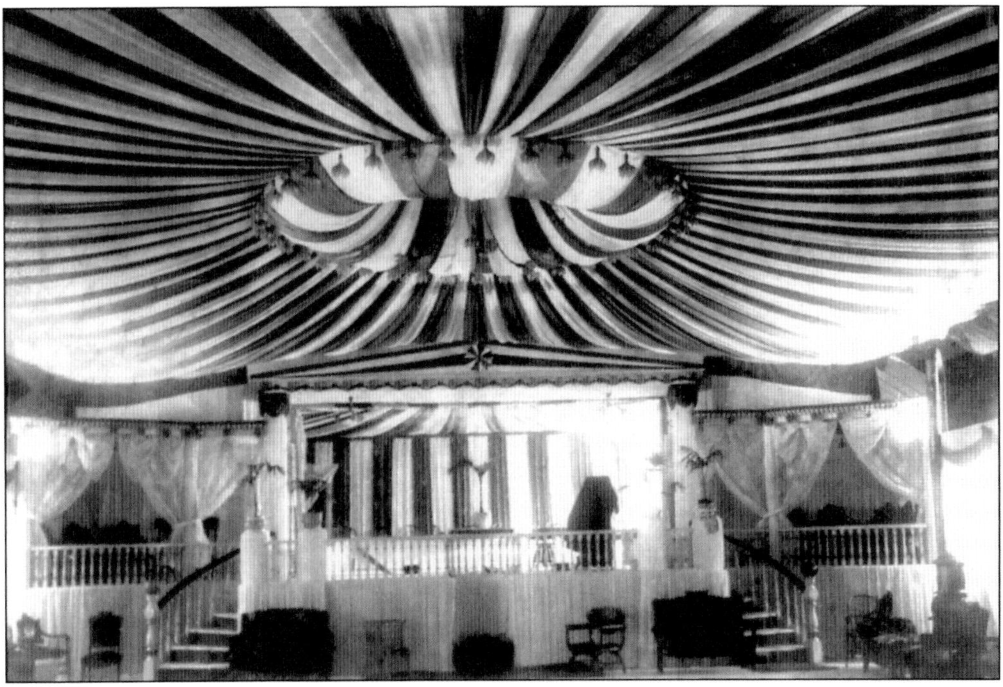

The elaborate draperies of the Casino were cut down and sold as fabric after productions. The chairs and settees are quite ornate—could they have been part of the stage set?

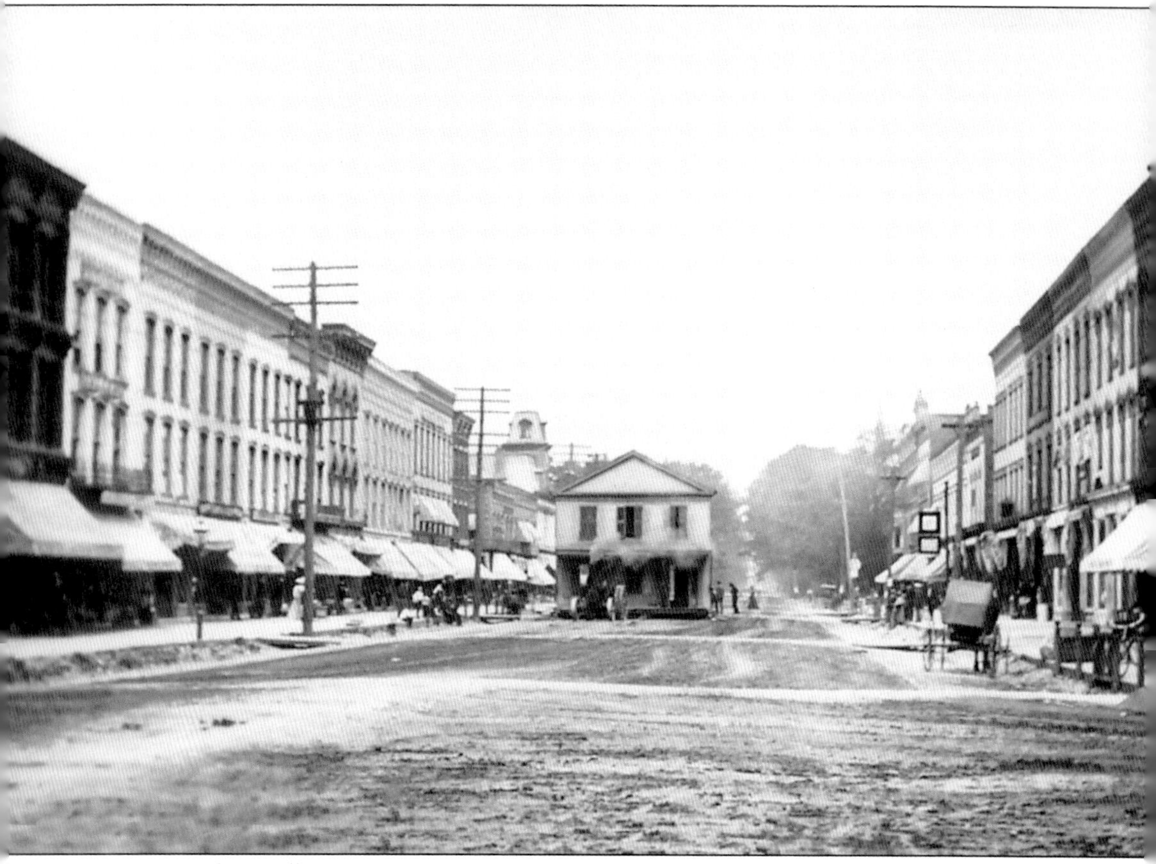

Moving a house (here on its way to 108 West Morris Street) would snarl traffic considerably nowadays, even without the steam tractor. At that time it was not uncommon to move a house, sometimes a distance of many miles. Notice the tower of the Purdy Opera House in the left distance and the St. Thomas steeple in the right distance. Also note the beautiful shade trees.

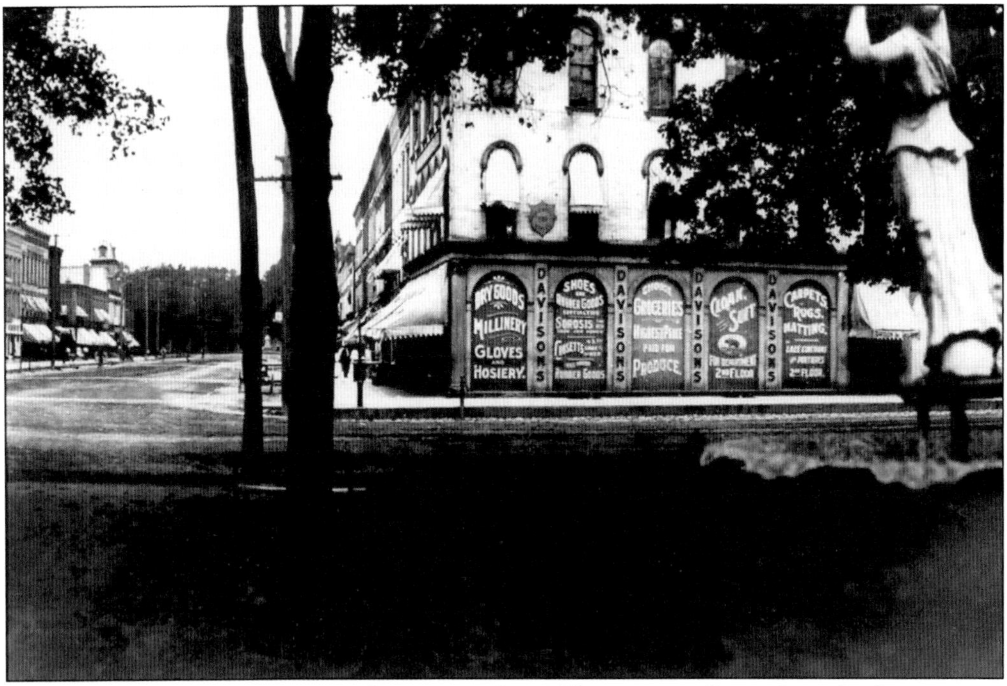

Would Davison's signage pass modern zoning laws? The statue still stands in the fountain . . . but why is the street so empty?

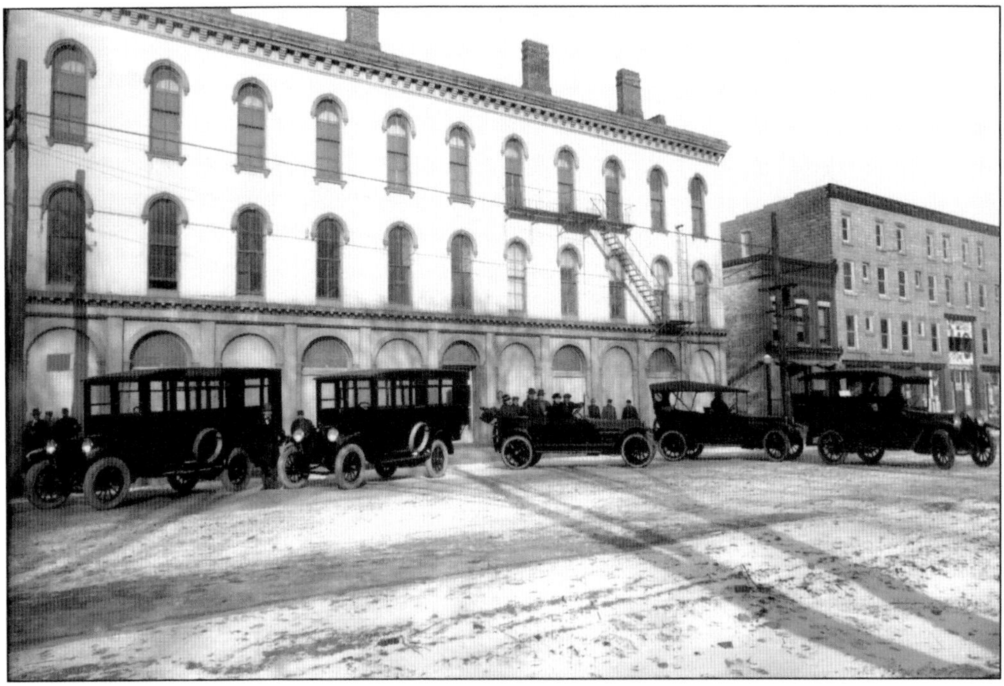
Perine's also held the spot on the northeast corner of Steuben and Liberty Streets. Wouldn't it be fun to ride in one of those buses. (Courtesy Steuben County Historian.)

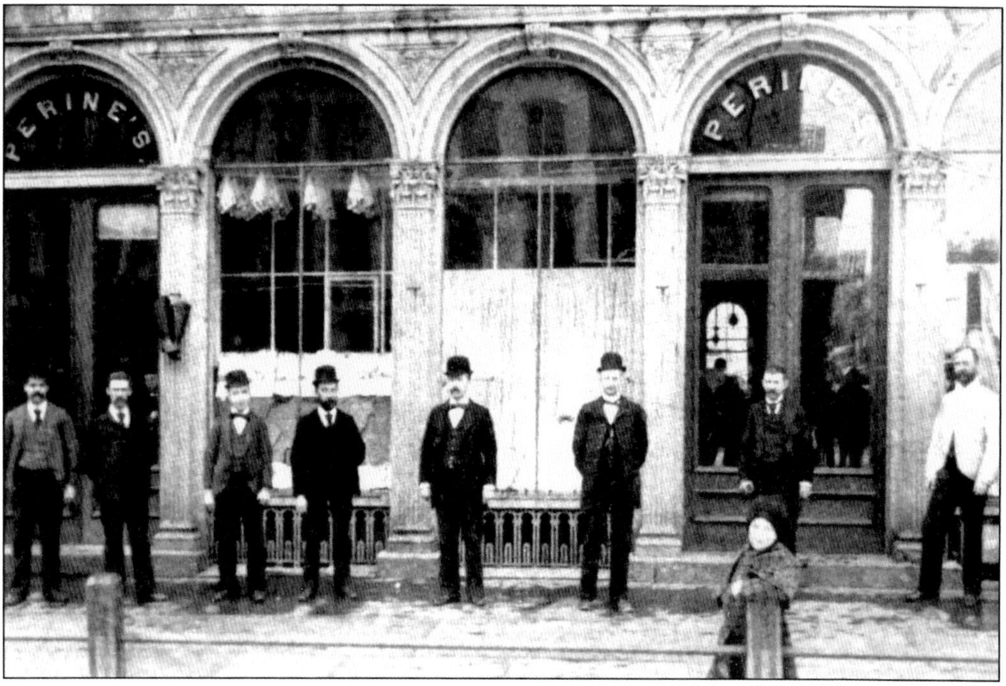

The line of gentlemen in the back looks pretty stodgy, but the child up front is not ashamed to enjoy the experience. Upstairs was the Odd Fellows Hall.

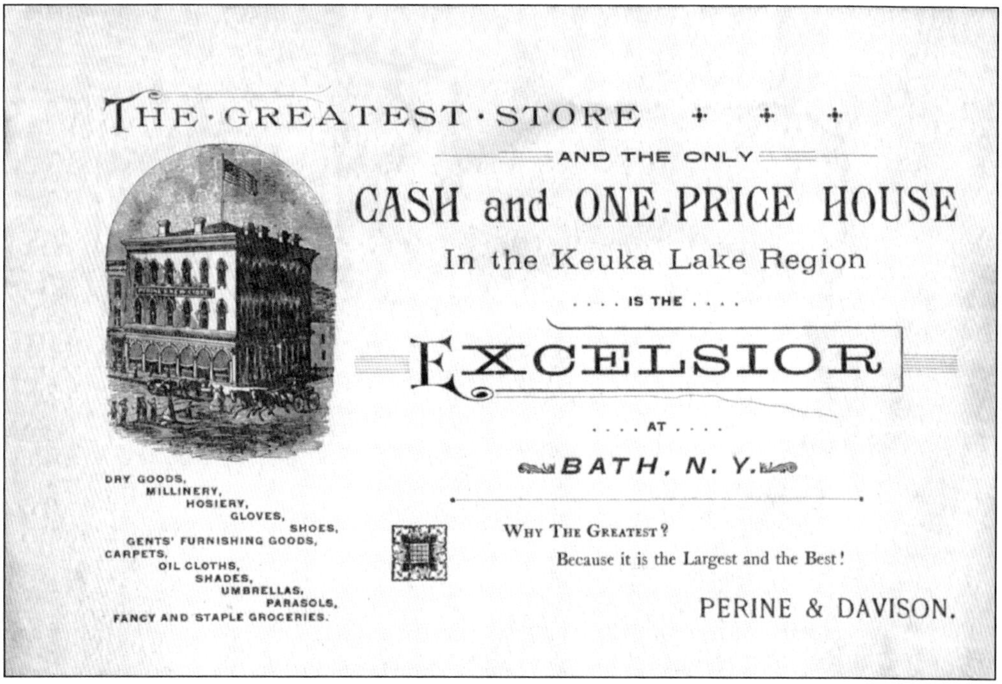

Downtown Bath was a major shopping district in the days before freeways, malls, and megastores. A convenience store—but no grocery shop—stands on Liberty Street now. (Courtesy Steuben County Historian's Office.)

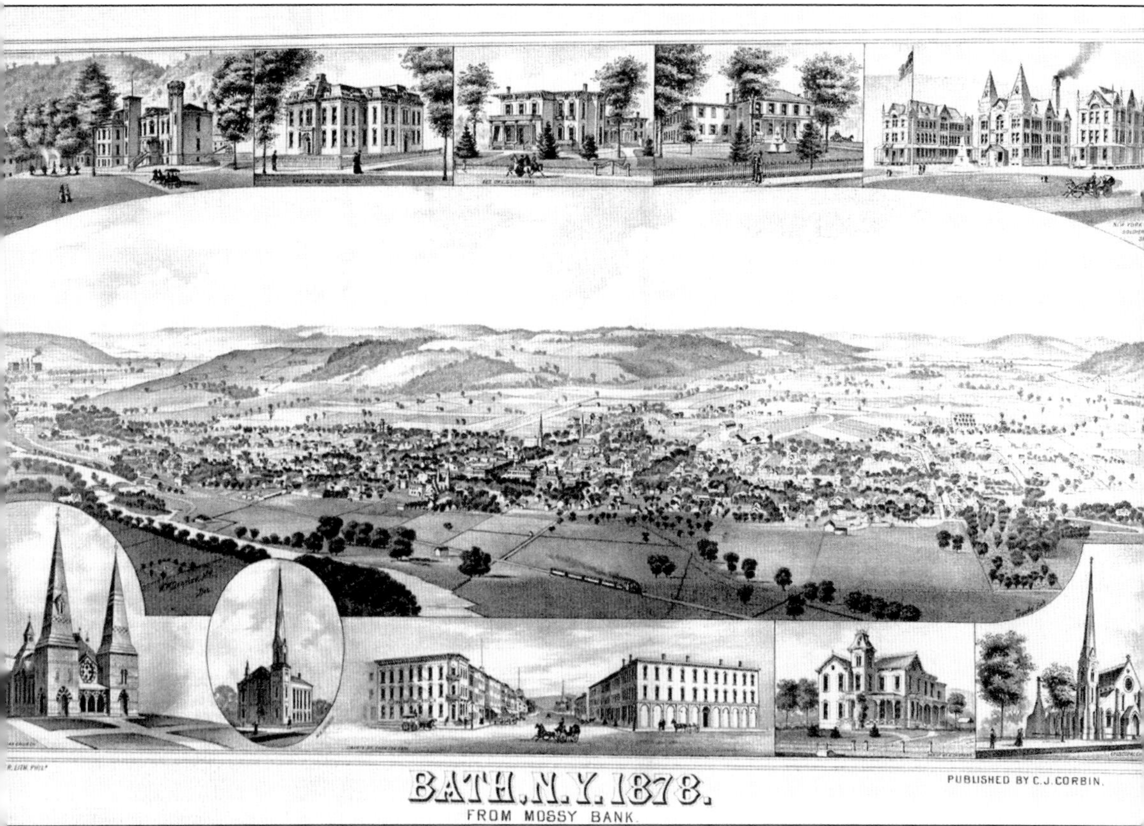

County government, agricultural and retail opportunities, and excellent transportation made Bath a busy, prosperous place. The Davenport estate and the Veterans Home, the subjects of chapter 4, are prominently shown here in the top corners. Churches, homes, and the downtown are all an important part of this promotional print. The Presbyterian church has unaccountably acquired an extra steeple.

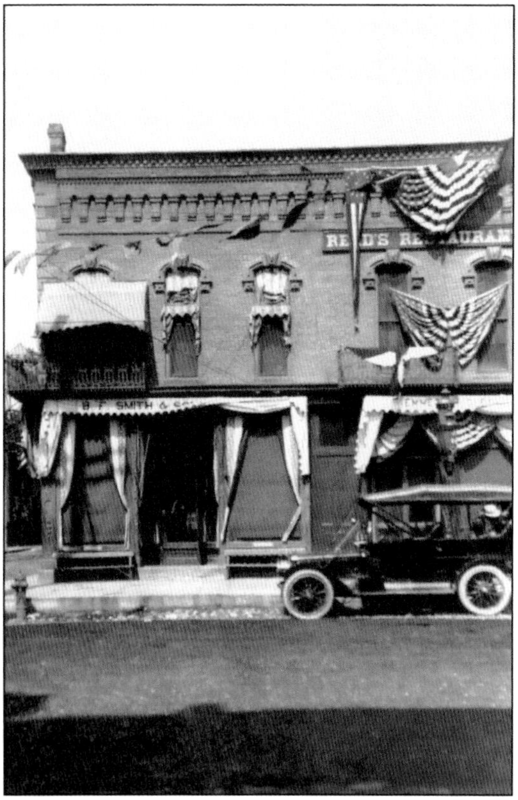

Read's House Hotel and Restaurant—in the 1872 Bushwell block, at Liberty and Buell Streets—operated from c. 1890 to 1912. B. F. Smith and Son Grocers was in business at the Bushwell block from 1899 to 1918. This is obviously a patriotic holiday . . . perhaps the Fourth of July?

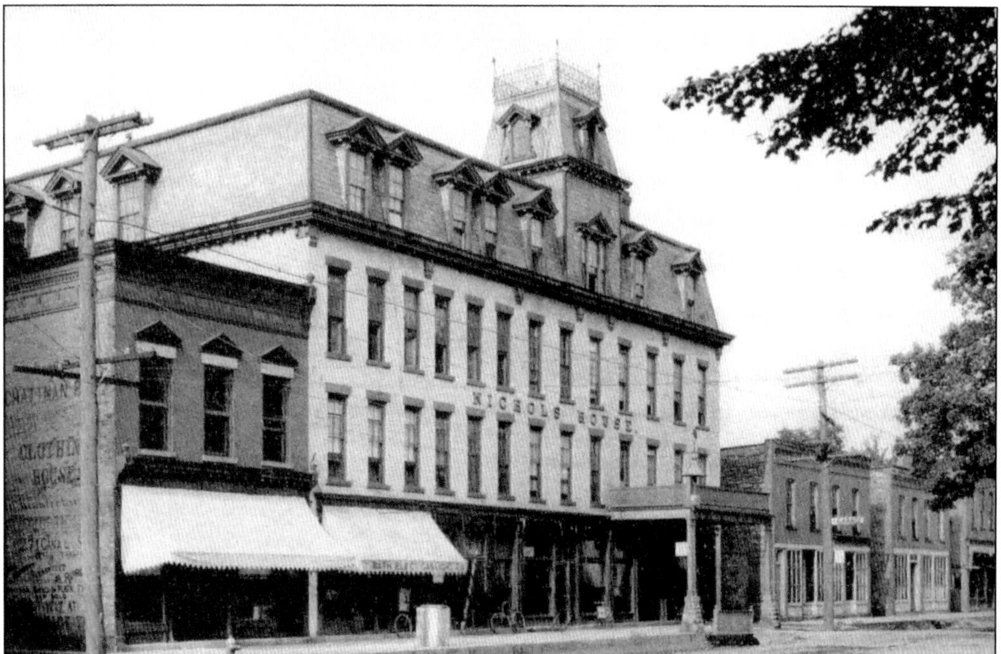

The Nichols House stood on Steuben Street from 1869 until the hotel's loss to fire in 1910. Notice that Bath Electric had its office here. The high curb could accommodate carriages.

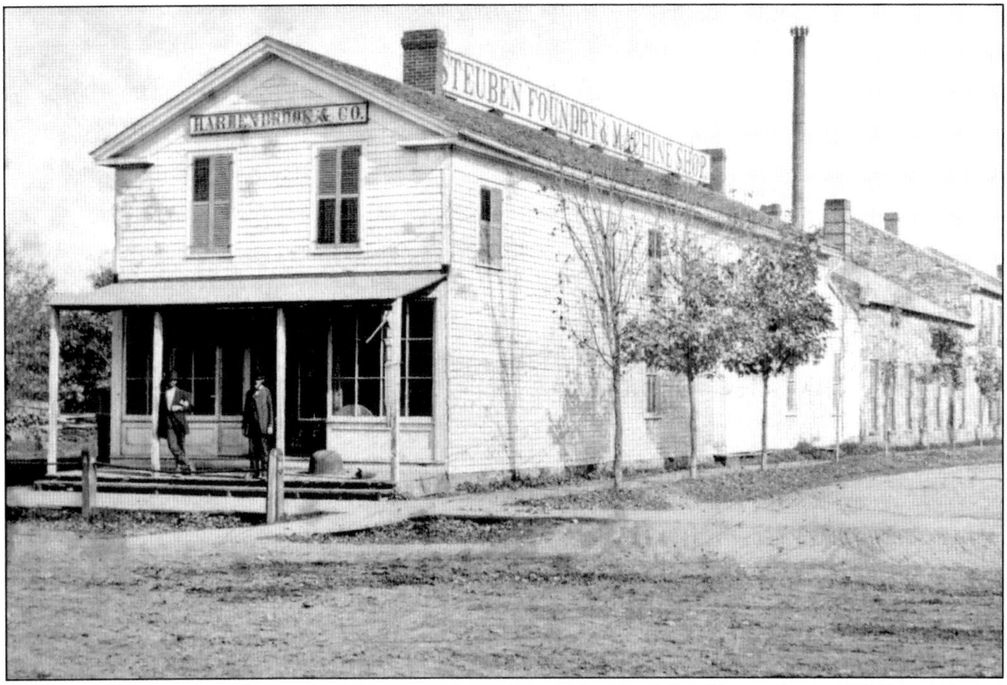

Hardenbrook bought the 1859 Bliss Foundry, adding the back buildings facing William Street in 1872. Those structures remain in use today.

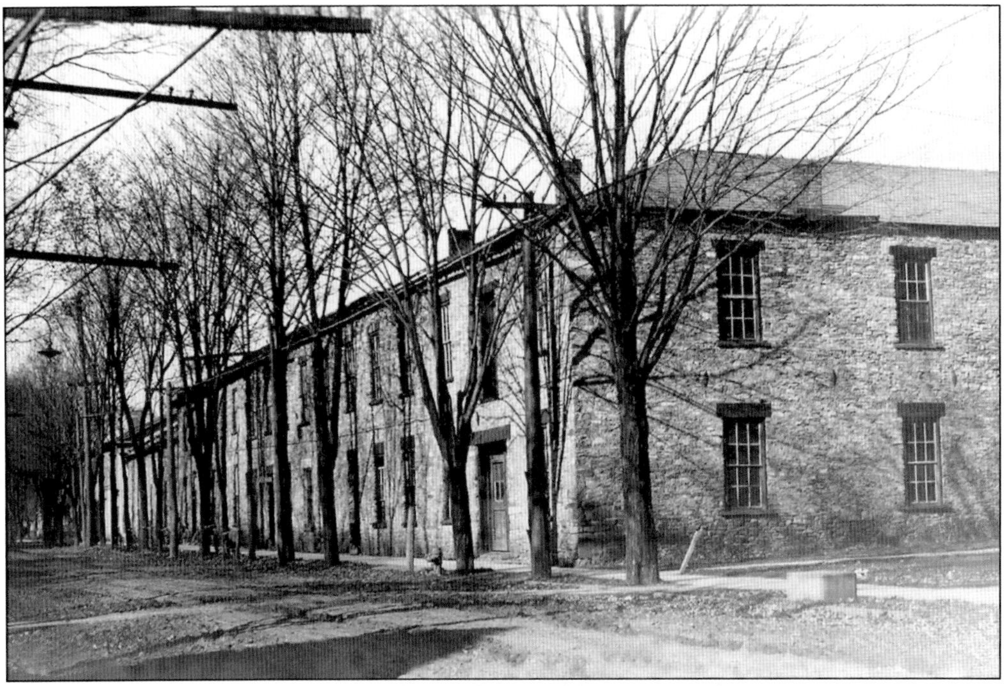

The back buildings supported the Kirkham (later Bath) Motor Works.

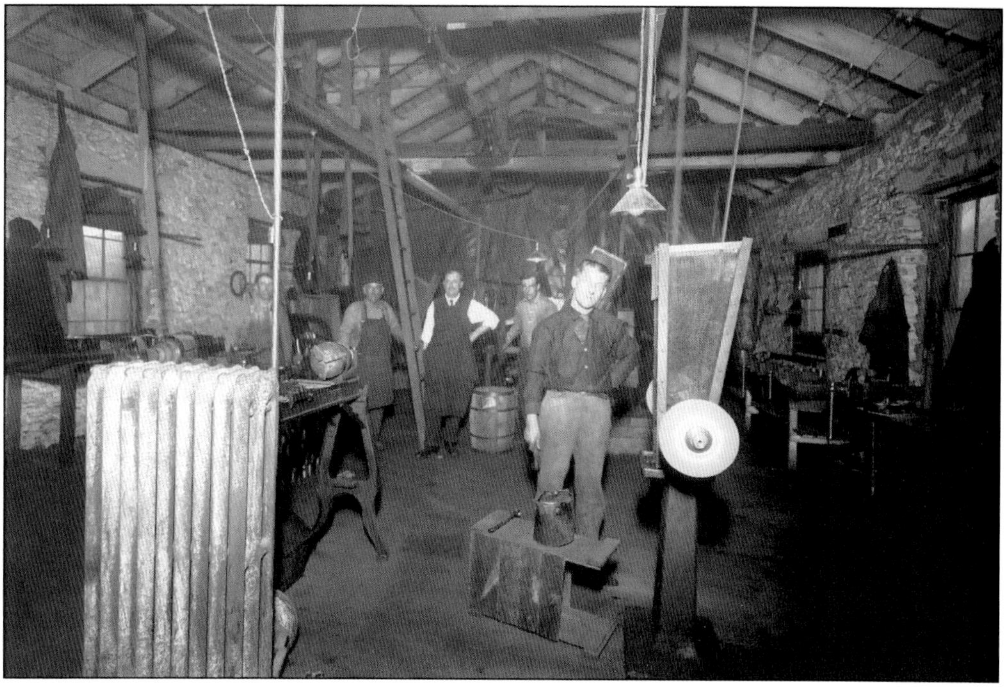

Charles B. Kirkham, a colleague and competitor of Glenn Curtiss, also built aero engines—Alexander Graham Bell used them. Kirkham's regularly supplied its own engines for Pullman automobiles. (Courtesy Curtiss Museum.)

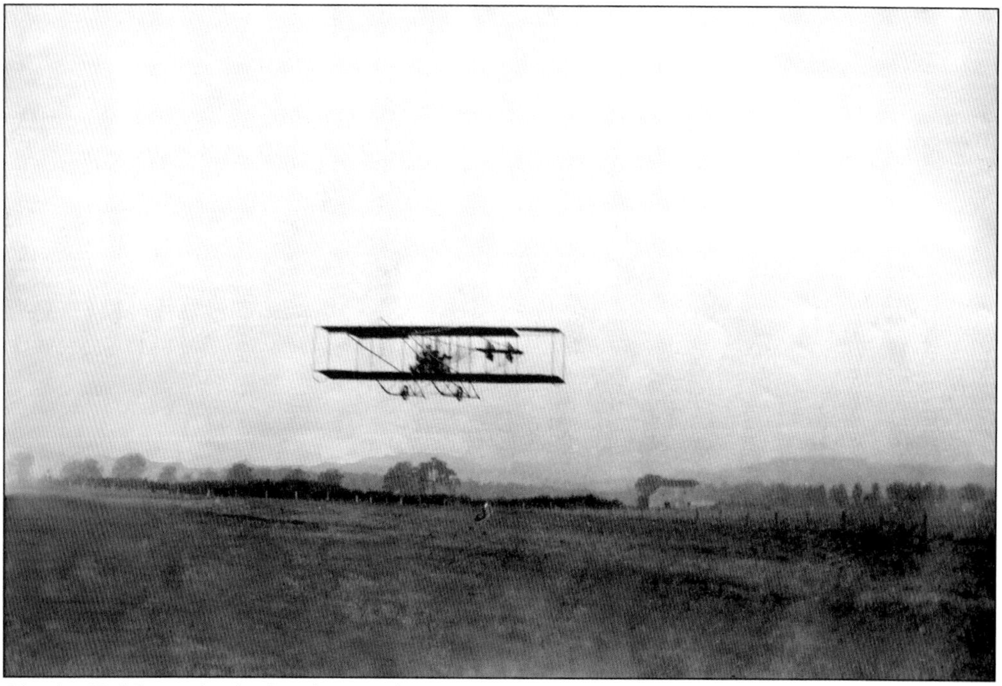

Charles Kirkham also built a few airplanes. His partner Fred Eells was the first man to fly over Bath—not to mention Naples and Rochester. Eells is buried in Nondaga Cemetery. (Courtesy Curtiss Museum.)

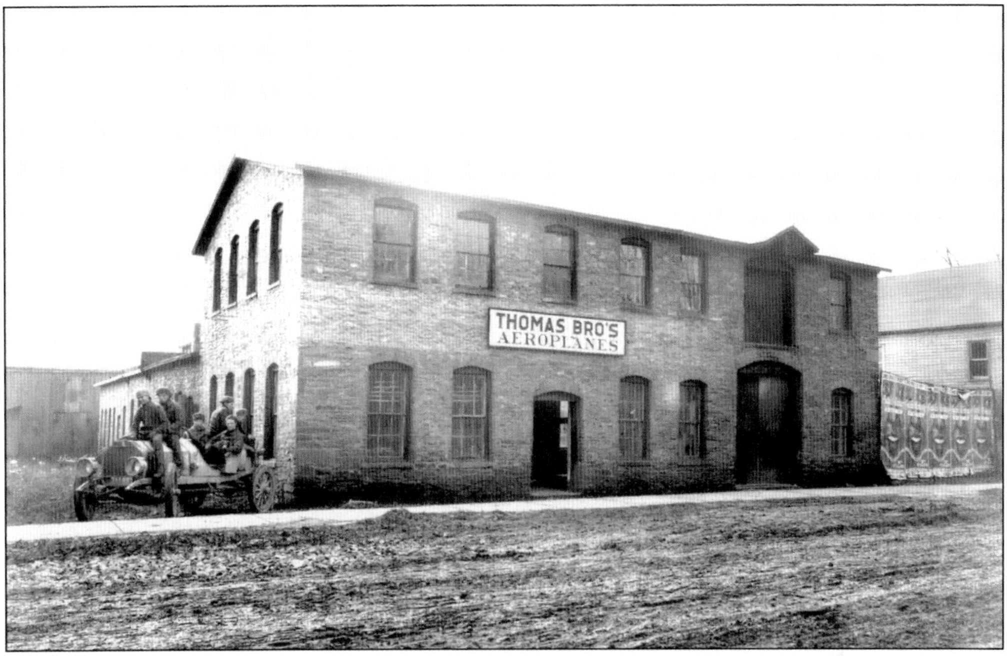

Thomas Brothers was a more successful airplane manufacturer, and its machines set numerous world records. Key Thomas people were also Curtiss veterans. The company later moved to Ithaca, becoming Thomas-Morse. The employees seem a little high-spirited. (Courtesy Curtiss Museum.)

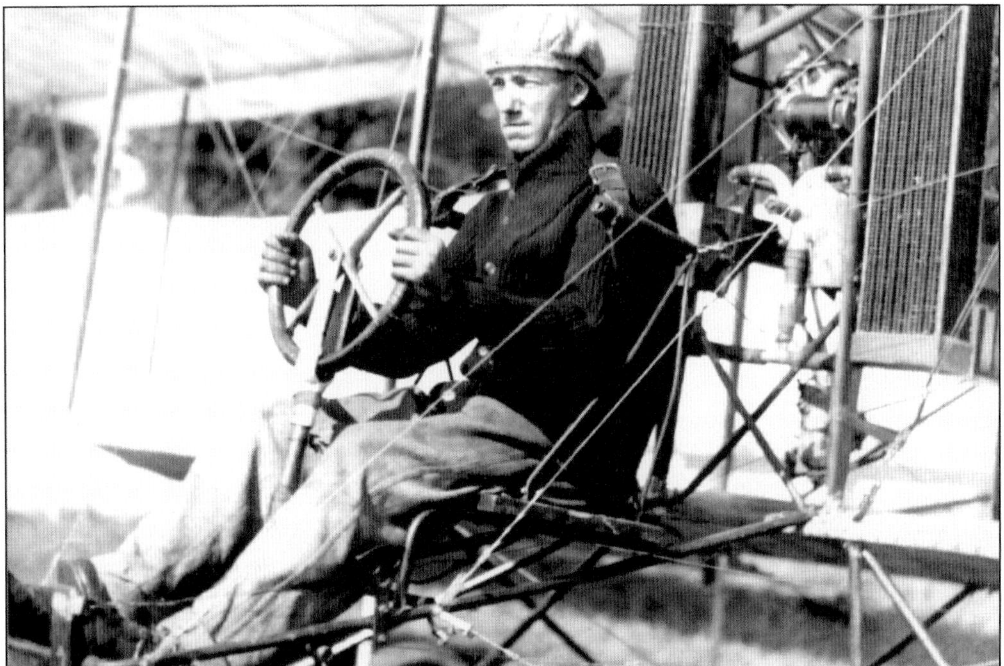

Much of the Thomas Brothers' flying took place near Lake Salubria. The company operated a very successful cut-rate flying school: $250 for full instruction, with the opportunity to work some of that off in the factory. (Courtesy Curtiss Museum.)

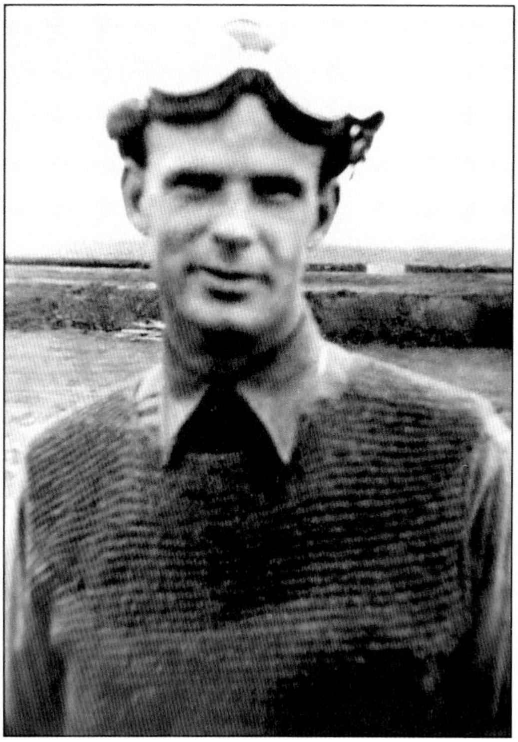

Thomas Brothers aviator Walter Johnson took Florence Scraffard for a short hop off frozen Lake Salubria. After her father recovered his temper, he allowed Johnson to come calling. Exhausted from work, Johnson would often put his head in Florence's lap and fall asleep instantly. Once he woke up, they were married, under an arch of electric lights in the Presbyterian church, and lived happily ever after. (Courtesy Curtiss Museum.)

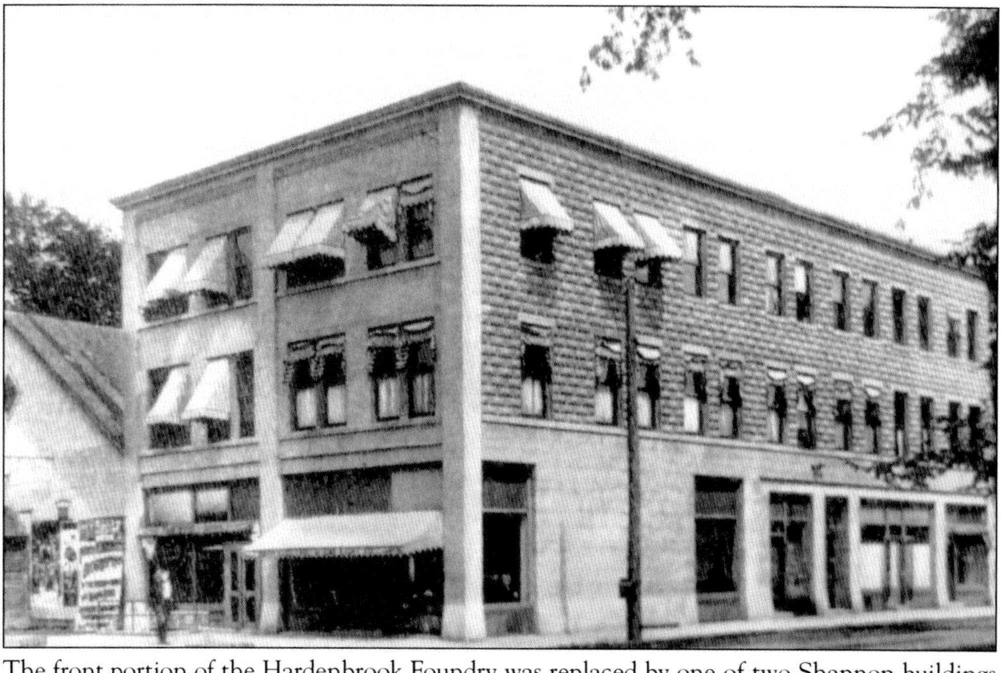

The front portion of the Hardenbrook Foundry was replaced by one of two Shannon buildings on Liberty Street. The old post office, in the left foreground, was a sort of club and gossip center for village gentlemen. The Bath Electric office (moved from the Nichols building), later Western Union, is now the Liberty Street Café. A small basement bowling alley even existed once upon a time.

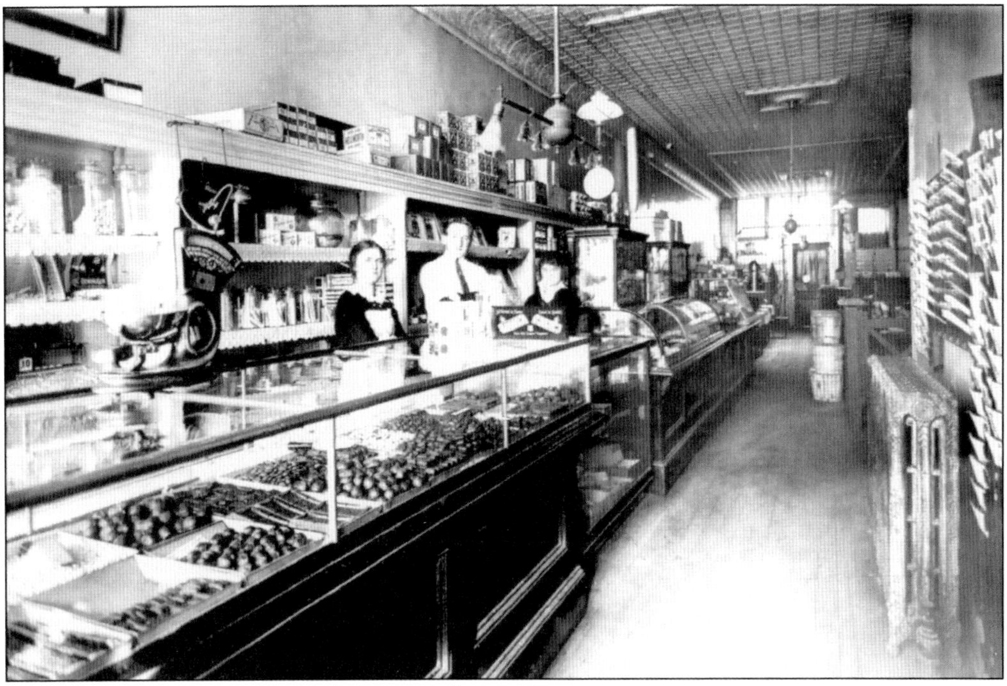

Castrilli's, at 56 Liberty Street, was a popular candy store.

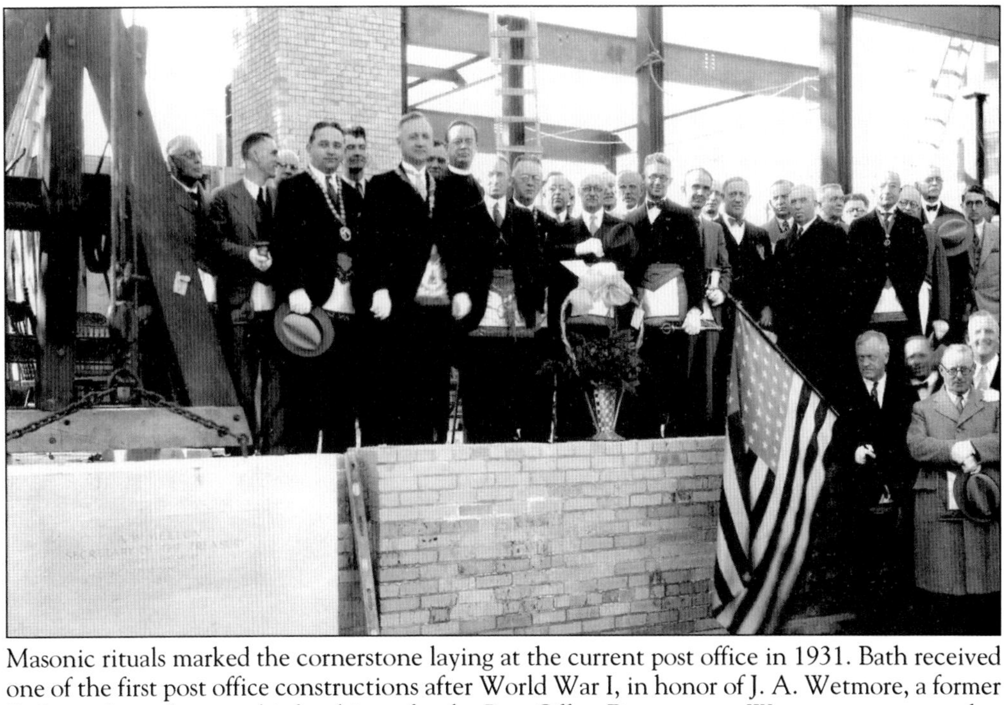

Masonic rituals marked the cornerstone laying at the current post office in 1931. Bath received one of the first post office constructions after World War I, in honor of J. A. Wetmore, a former Bath resident who was chief architect for the Post Office Department. Wetmore once served as acting treasury secretary for two months during the secretary's convalescence.

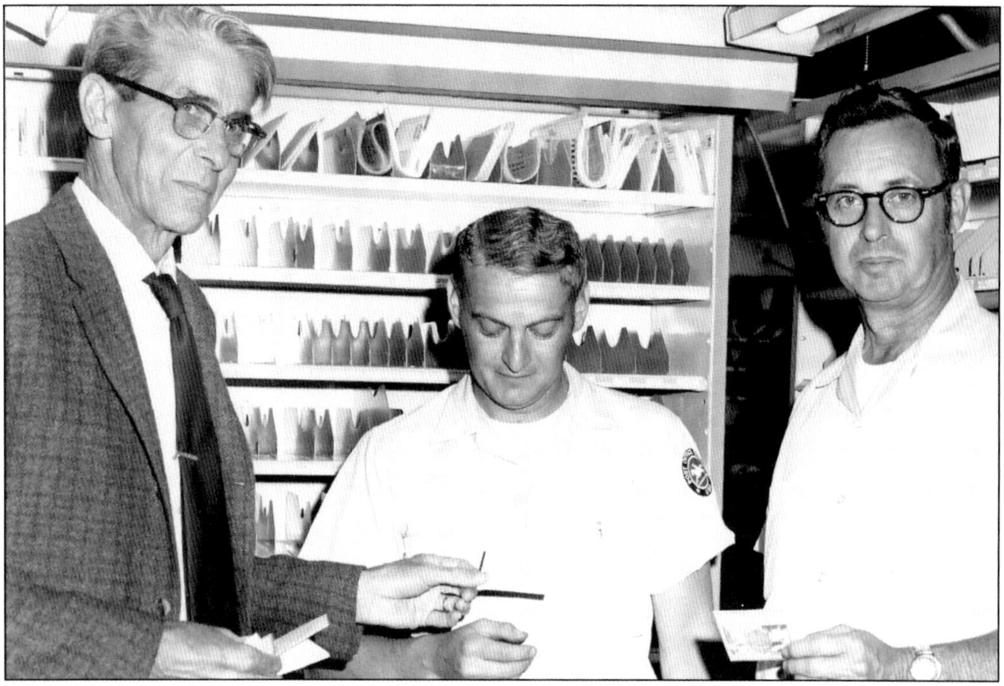

Paul Newth, Herman "Jack" Clark, and Jim Hope (left to right) served the public in the new post office. Hope eventually became the official Bath historian.

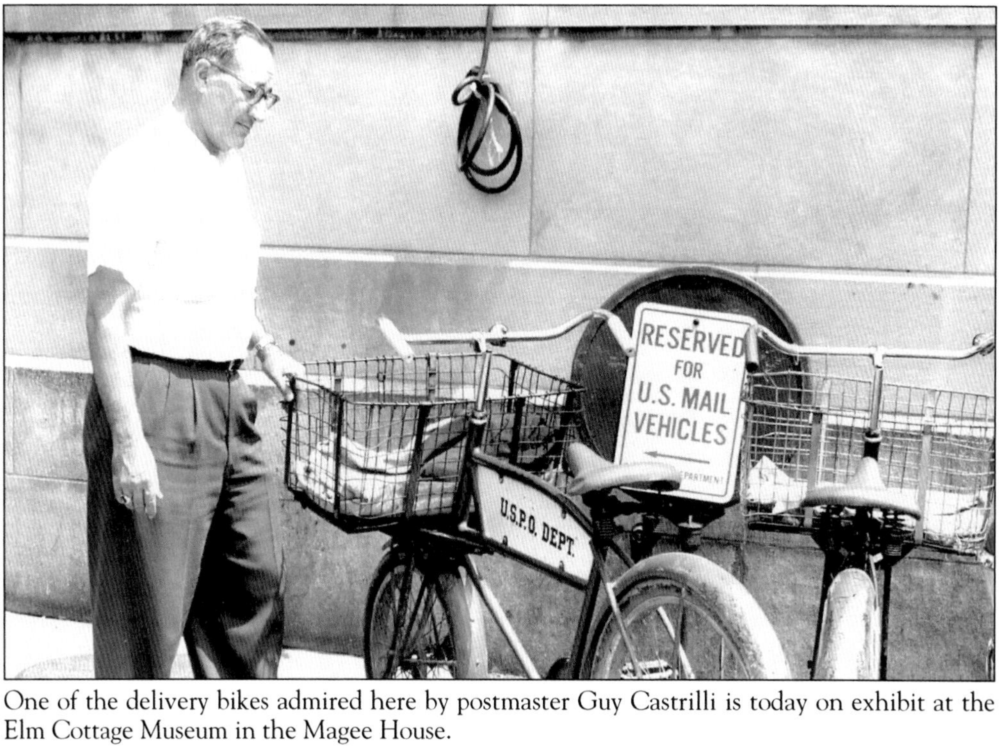

One of the delivery bikes admired here by postmaster Guy Castrilli is today on exhibit at the Elm Cottage Museum in the Magee House.

Anchoring South Liberty Street at the corner of St. Patrick Square (or Washington Square) is the stone St. Thomas Episcopal Church, with doors painted red to represent the blood of Christ. The cornerstone was laid in 1869. A $20,000 gift from Constant Cook helped finance the construction.

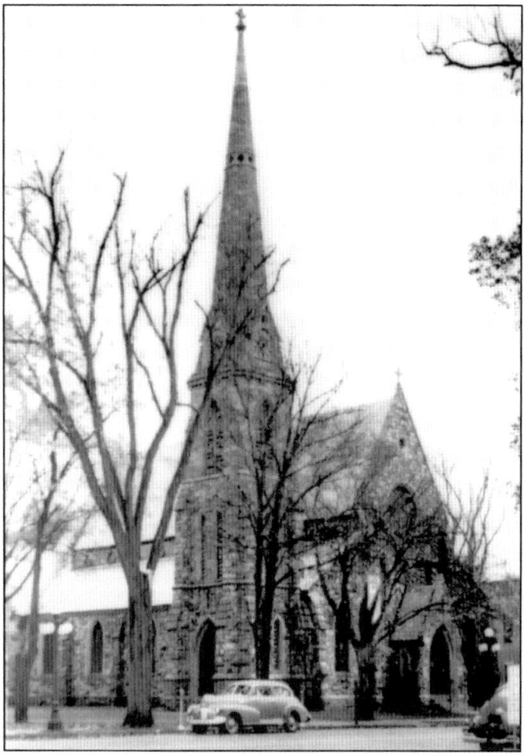

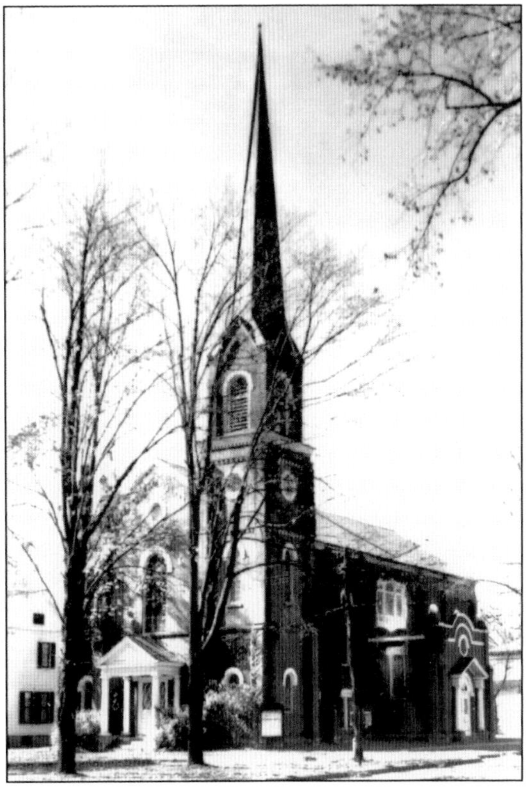

The old Centenary Methodist Church, replaced after 1963 by a newer structure, faced St. Thomas across Liberty Street. The old church, dedicated in 1867, honored 100 years of Methodism in America.

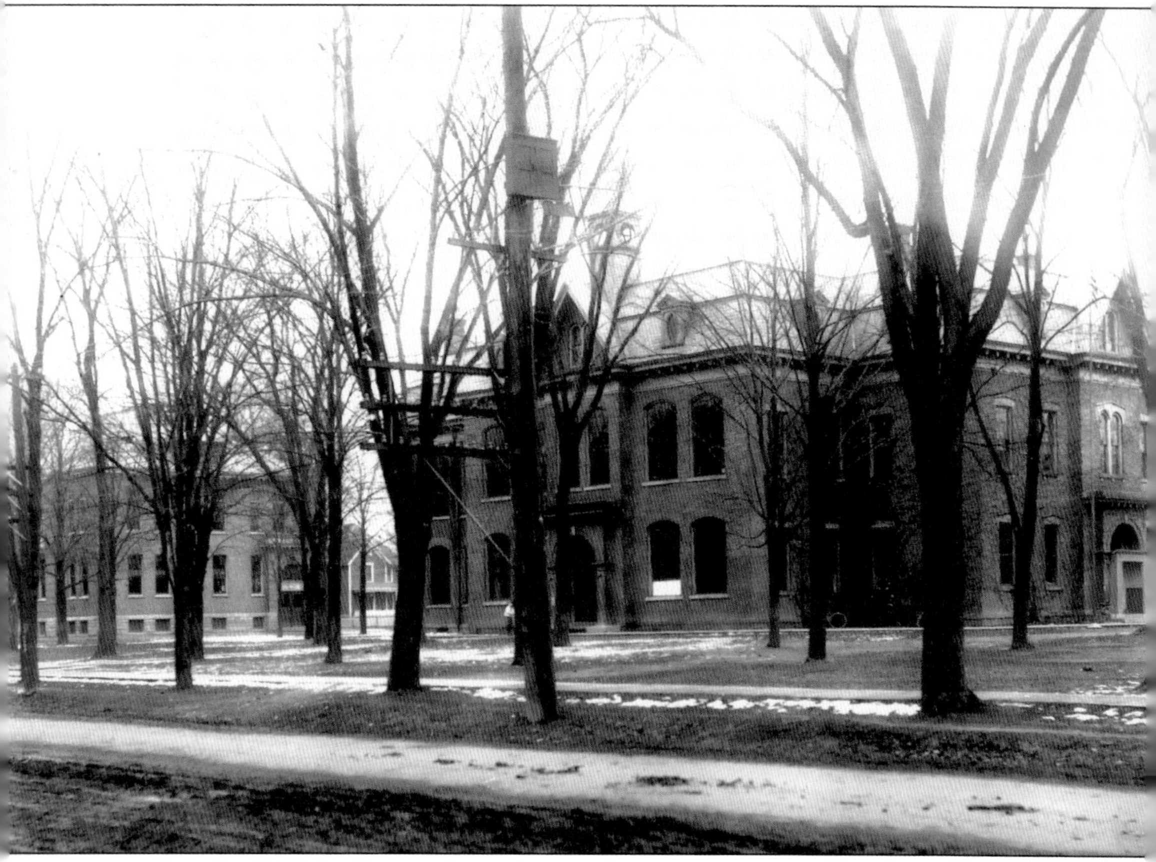

Fronting St. Patrick Square from the northeast corner was Haverling High School. This is the second structure on the site, standing from 1868 to 1923. The image was printed from an 8- by 10-inch glass negative, as were most others from this historian. The Primary Annex (left) remained in use until the complex closed for good in 2002. (Courtesy Steuben County Historian's Office.)

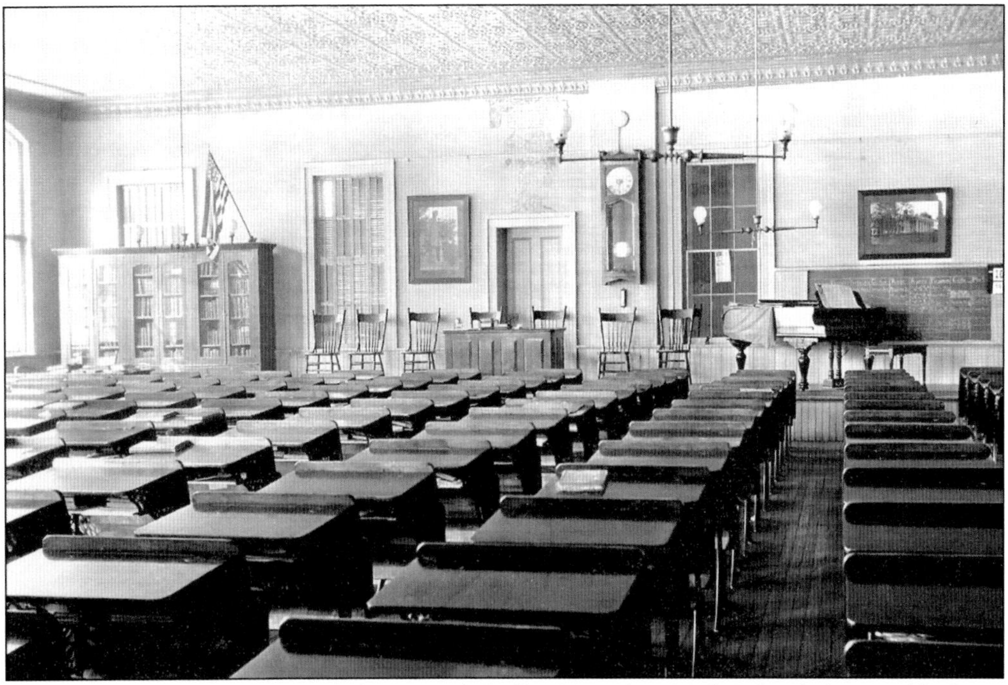

If students completed their work during study hall at Haverling High School, they could admire the rich wood finishings or the picture of Mount Vernon, above the piano.

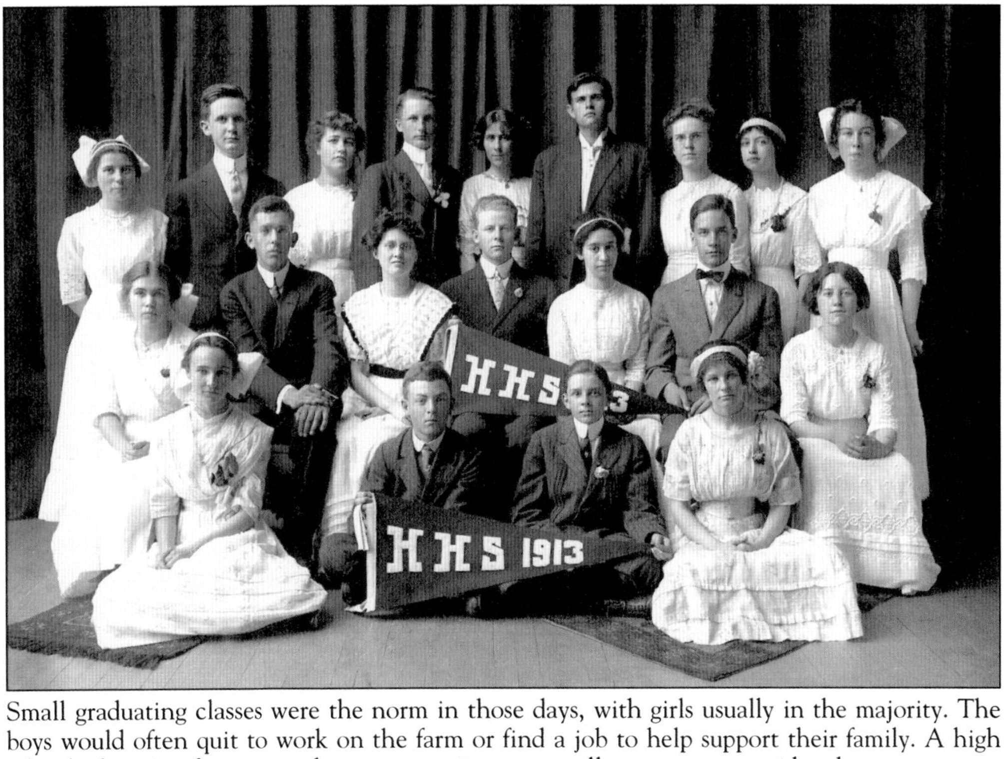

Small graduating classes were the norm in those days, with girls usually in the majority. The boys would often quit to work on the farm or find a job to help support their family. A high school education for a man who was not going on to college was not considered necessary.

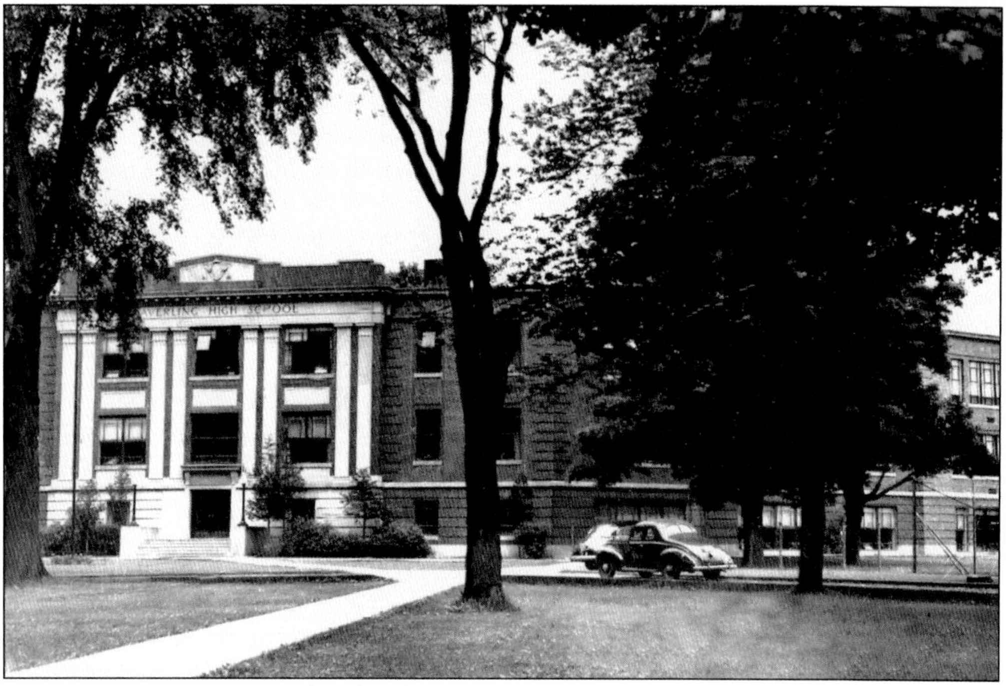

New construction in 1923 dwarfed the 1901 Primary Annex, just out of view to the left. Haverling High School continued here until a new building arose on Robie Street in 1954. This old complex, later the Dana Lyon Elementary School, remained in use until 2002.

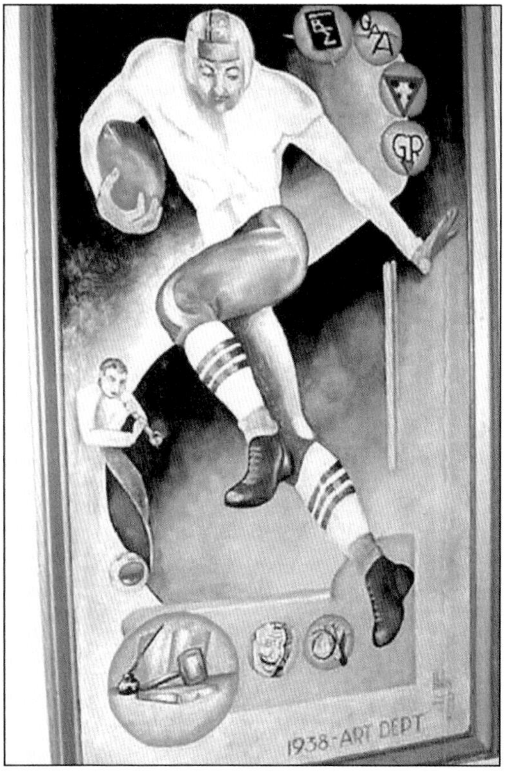

George Johnson Haley painted the school's football fresco before graduating as class valedictorian in 1939. Studying at Syracuse University when World War II broke out, he joined the segregated Tuskegee Airmen. Re-upping for Korea, fighter pilot Haley stayed in as a career man, completing 140 combat missions, the last of them in Vietnam. Retiring as a lieutenant colonel, he died in 1996.

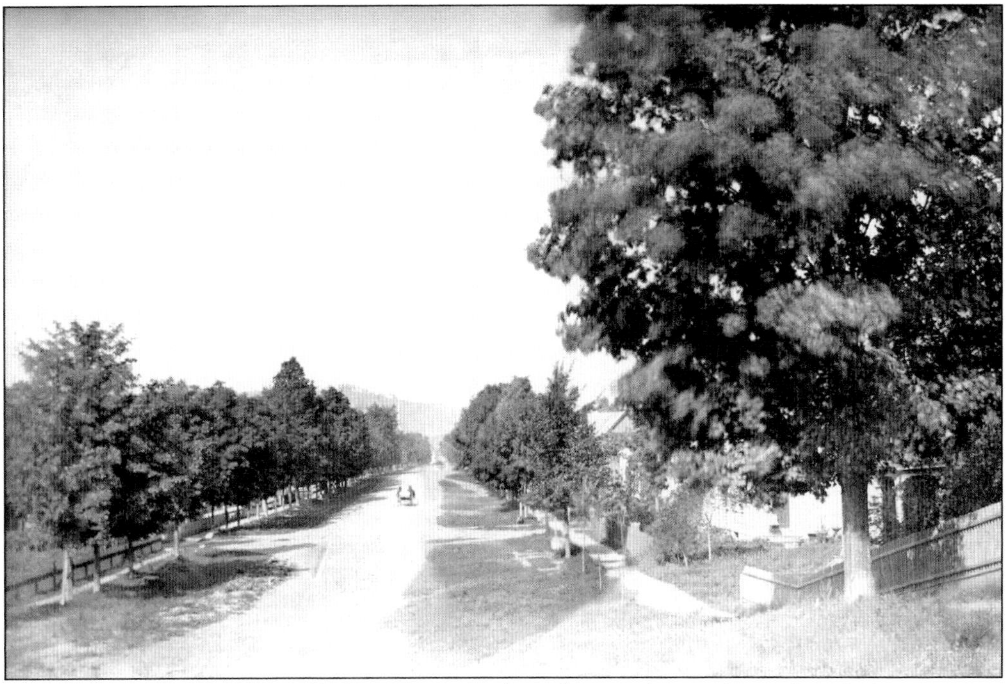

East Washington Street is still almost as quiet these days, and every bit as dignified.

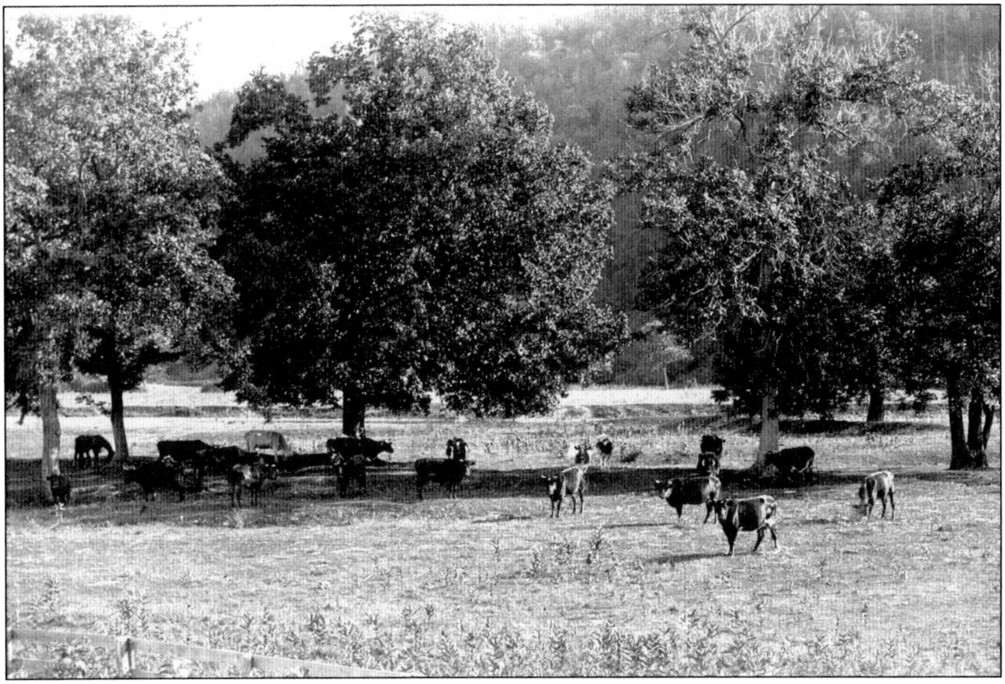

Cattle no longer graze within the village limits, although Bath town and its environs are still dairy country.

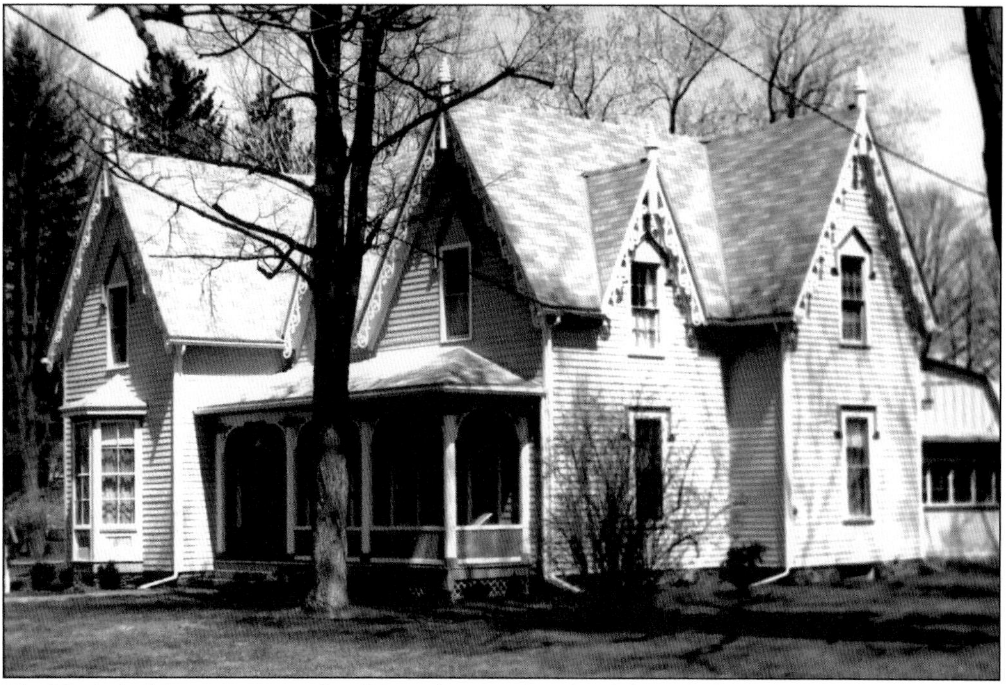

The Underhill house, just north of Haverling High School, later belonged to Henry "I fix him" Kleckler, a pioneer aviation colleague of Glenn Curtiss. Kleckler operated a mechanic and refrigeration business for years.

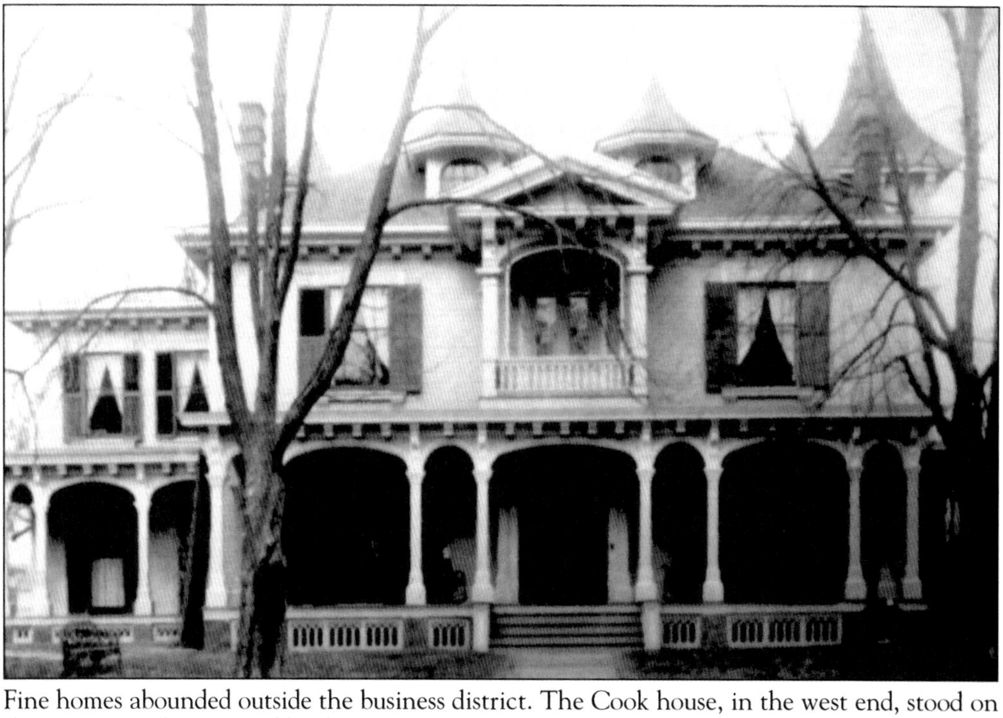

Fine homes abounded outside the business district. The Cook house, in the west end, stood on the site currently occupied by the Days Inn.

This house could not be identified, but its occupants must have had a fine Christmas.

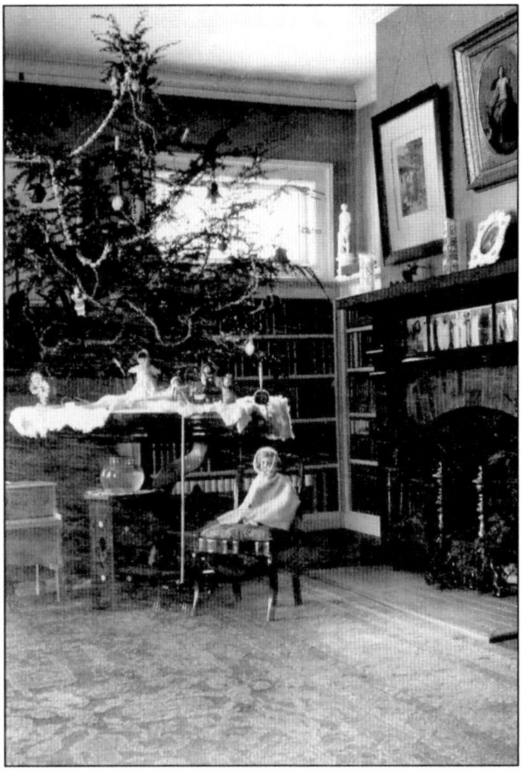

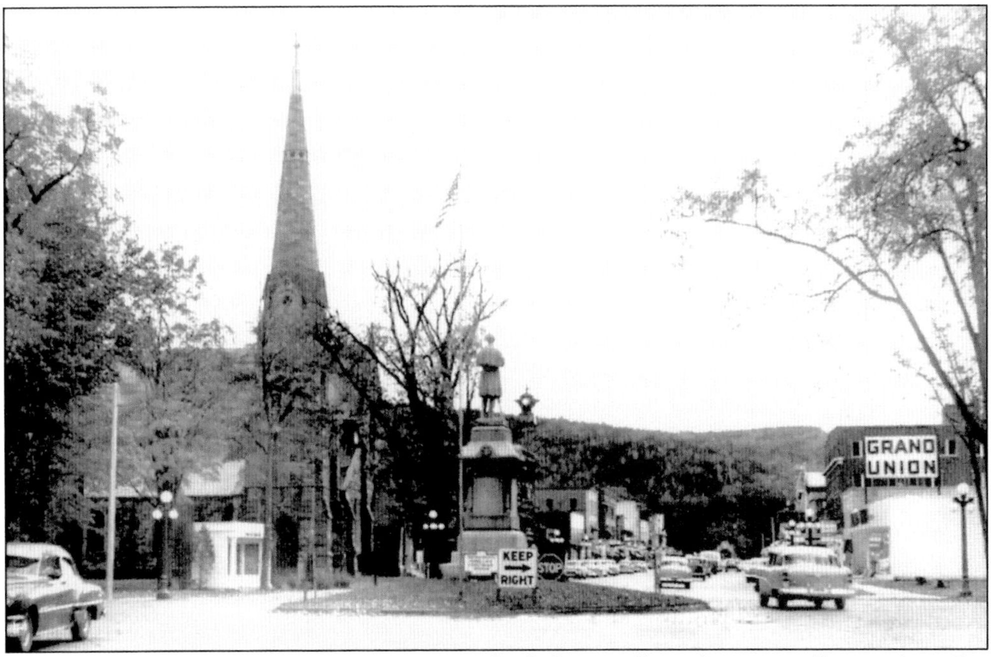

Most communities made heavy investments—both financially and emotionally—in their Civil War monuments. Eventually, automobile traffic forced the monument's relocation from the center of Washington and Liberty Streets to tiny Davenport Park, near the fork of Liberty, Geneva, and Haverling Streets.

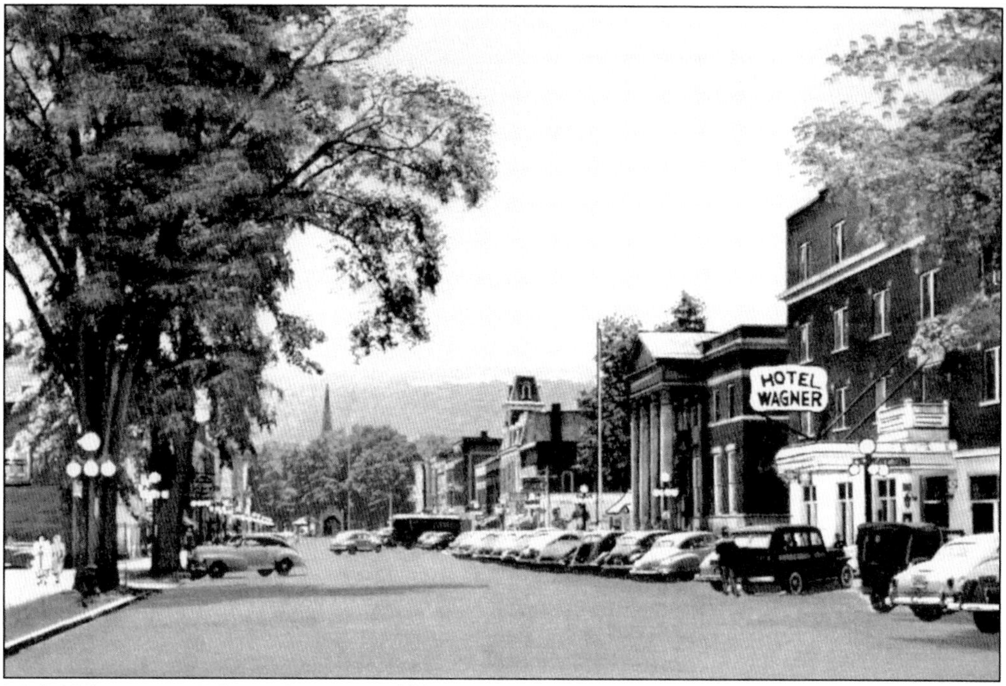

Mid-20th-century Liberty Street would have seemed quite familiar to residents from the 19th century. Even today, it is still a busy place.

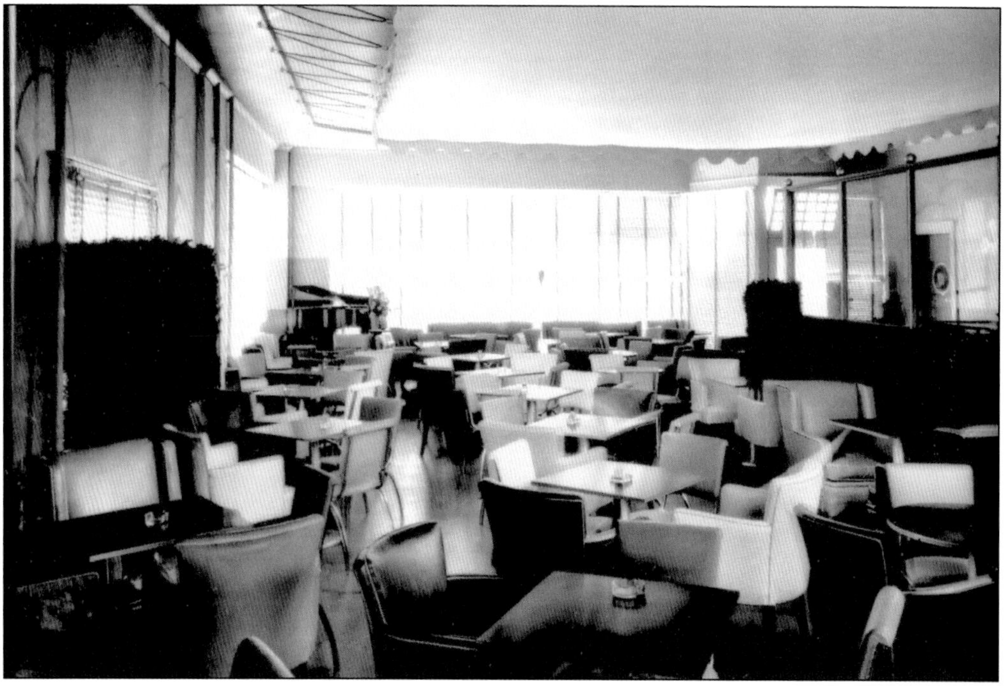

The Hotel Wagner, later an automobile dealership, is now home to the county's mental health services.

The Farmers and Mechanics Bank (F & M) became Security Trust, Norstar, Fleet, and now, in newer quarters, Community Bank.

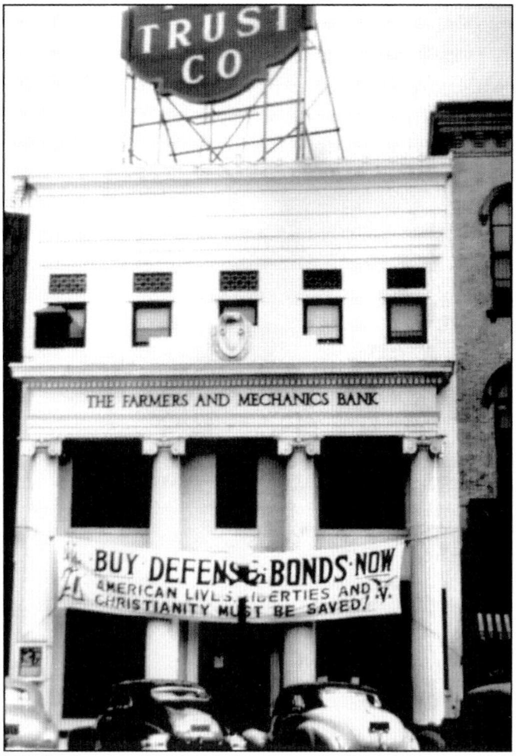

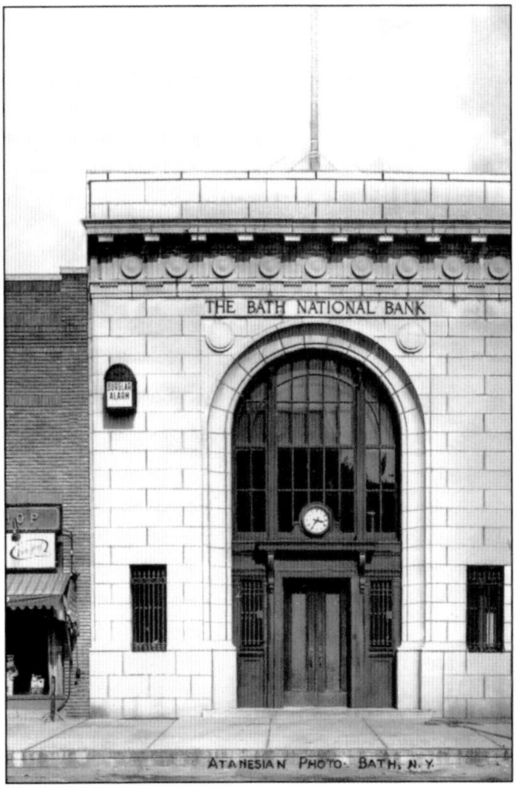

Bath National Bank, founded in 1912, still keeps its main branch in the 1917 Liberty Street building.

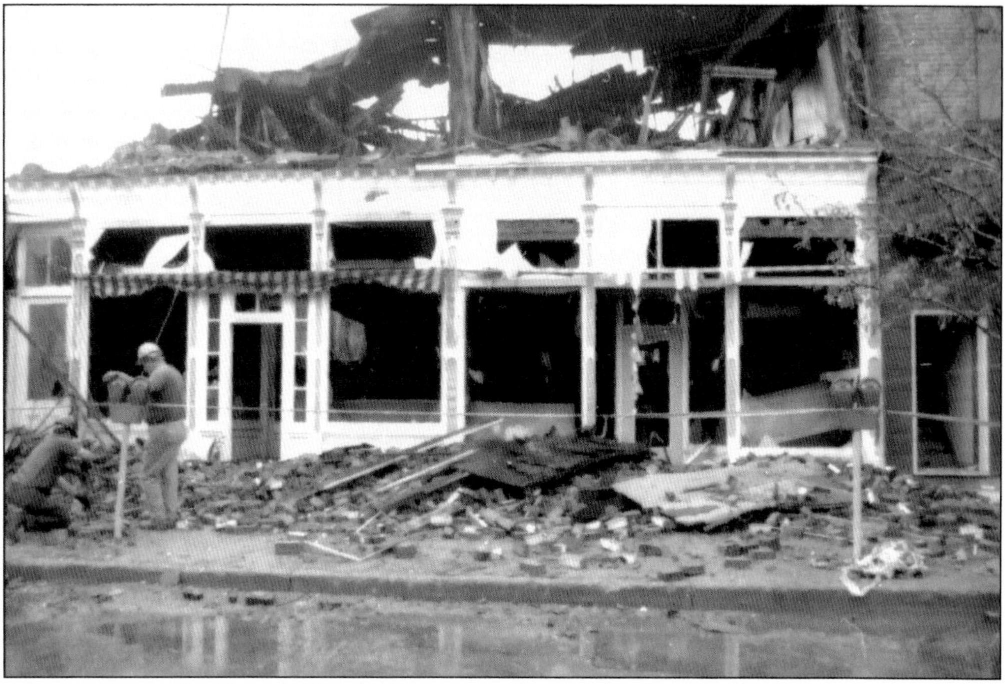

A fire at the nearby Chat-A-Whyle Restaurant changed the face of Liberty Street in the 1990s. However, the Chat rebuilt and reopened, much to the relief of local diners.

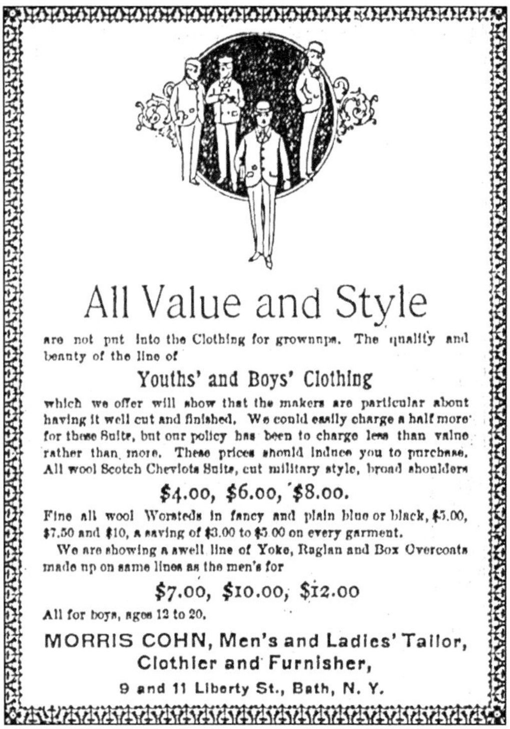

Immigrant Morris Cohn, after working Steuben County for years as a peddler, opened a department store in Addison in 1881. He opened a Bath store 14 years later; this advertisement graced the *Hammondsport Herald* during the 1900 Christmas season. (Courtesy Steuben County Historian's Office.)

The Bath store stayed in business until the death of Morris Cohn's grandson Bill Cohn, who is pictured with daughter Sarah Marcotte in 1996.

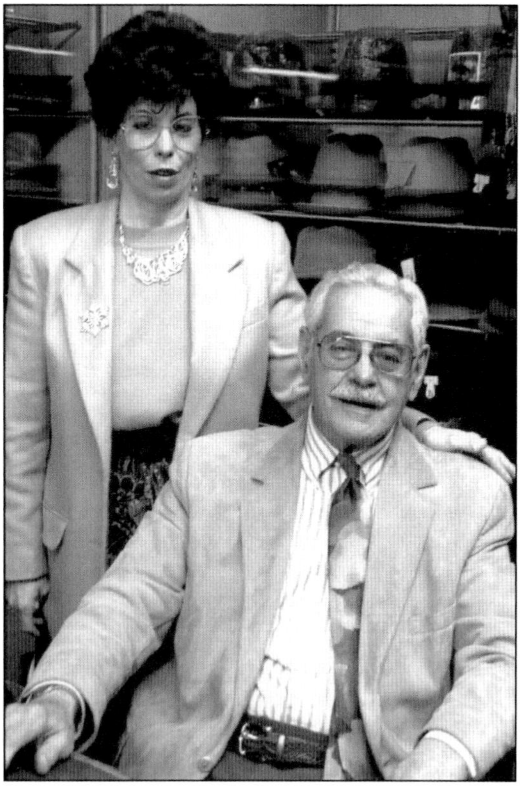

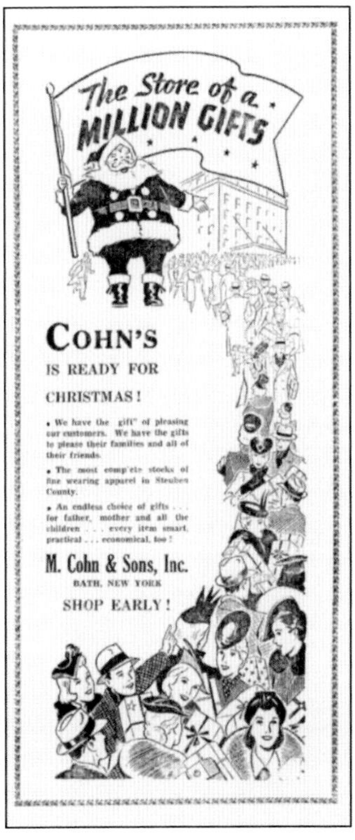

For more than a century, Cohn's and Christmas just went together.

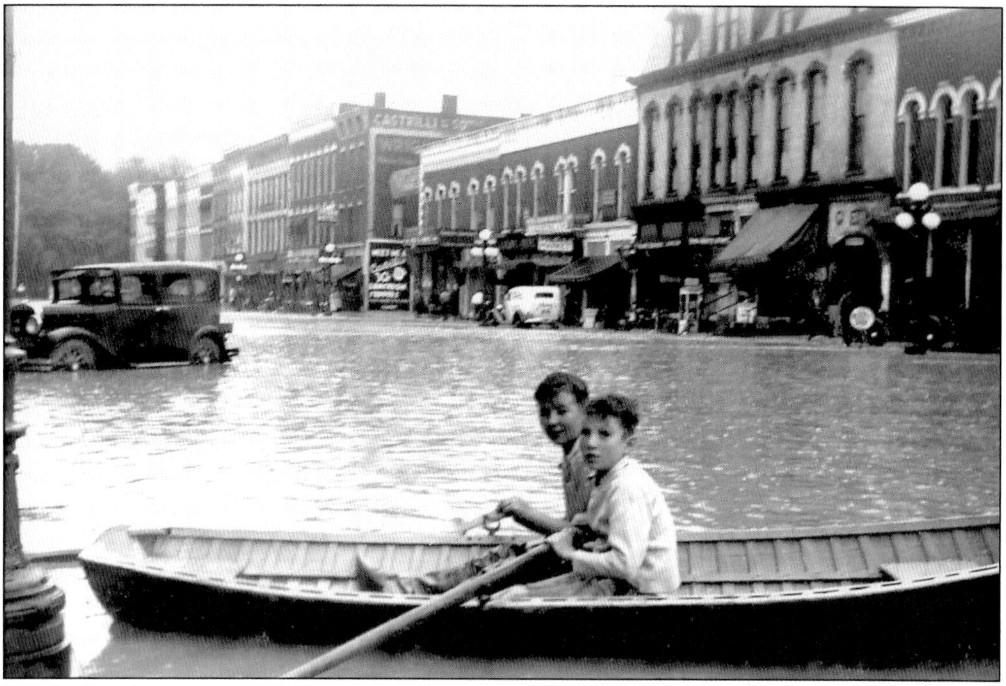

While the disastrous 1972 Hurricane Agnes is still vivid in memory, an even greater flood submerged Bath in 1935. Repeated days of heavy rain were followed by a day of nonstop torrents, and on July 6, the Conhocton River vaulted from its banks. Lesser streams did the same. Modern flood-control measures make further disasters on that same scale far less likely.

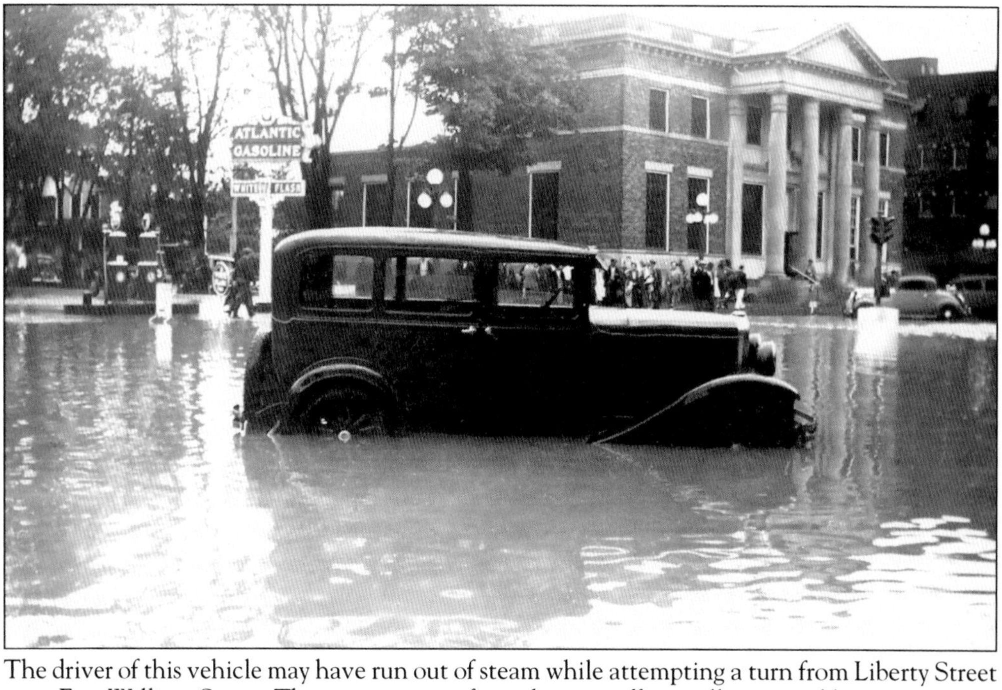

The driver of this vehicle may have run out of steam while attempting a turn from Liberty Street onto East William Street. The corner across from the post office, still occupied by a gas station, is now Misba Mart instead of Atlantic Gasoline.

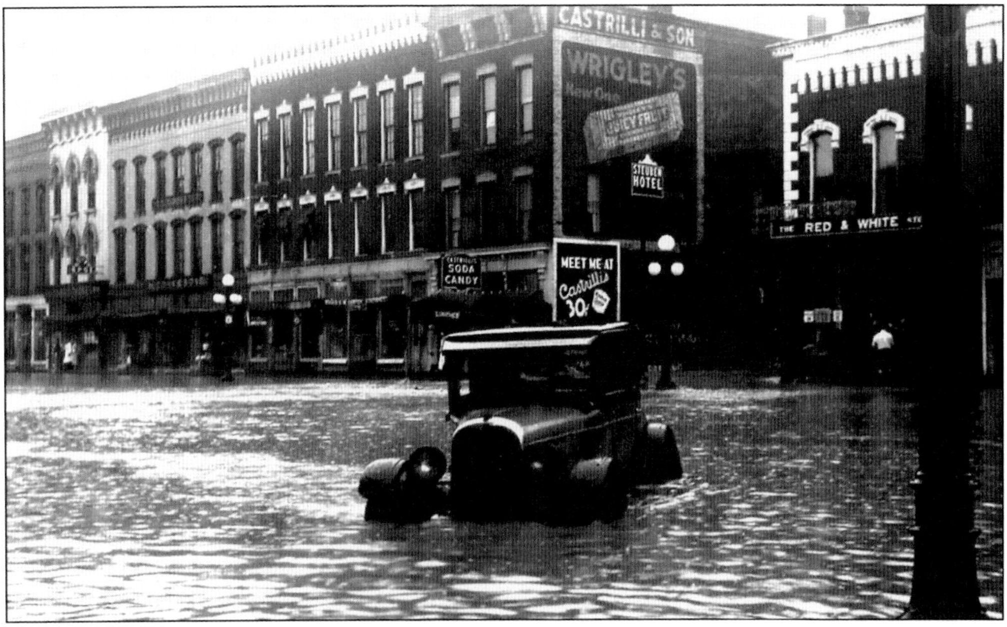

The Wrigley's and Castrilli wall art is still legible on Buell Street. A few Red and White Stores remain in the area, although none are in Bath.

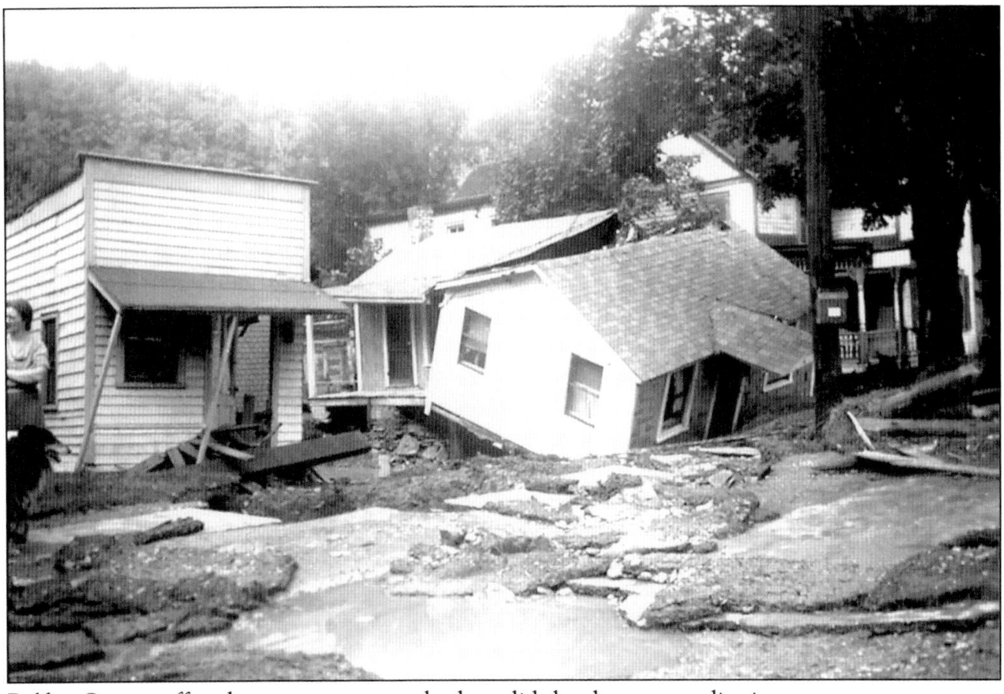

Belfast Street suffered even more severely than did the downtown district.

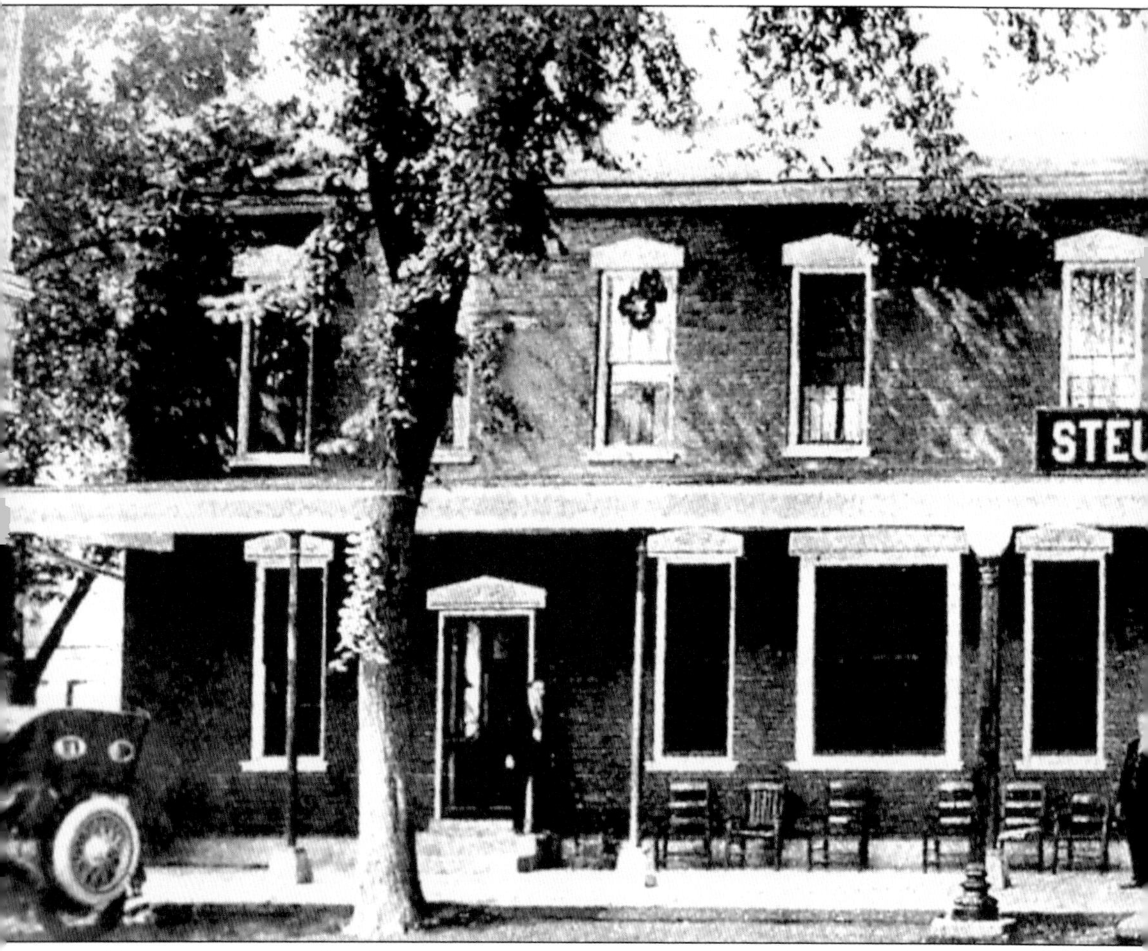

This fine hotel on Buell Street is now home to Off-Track Betting and to the office of

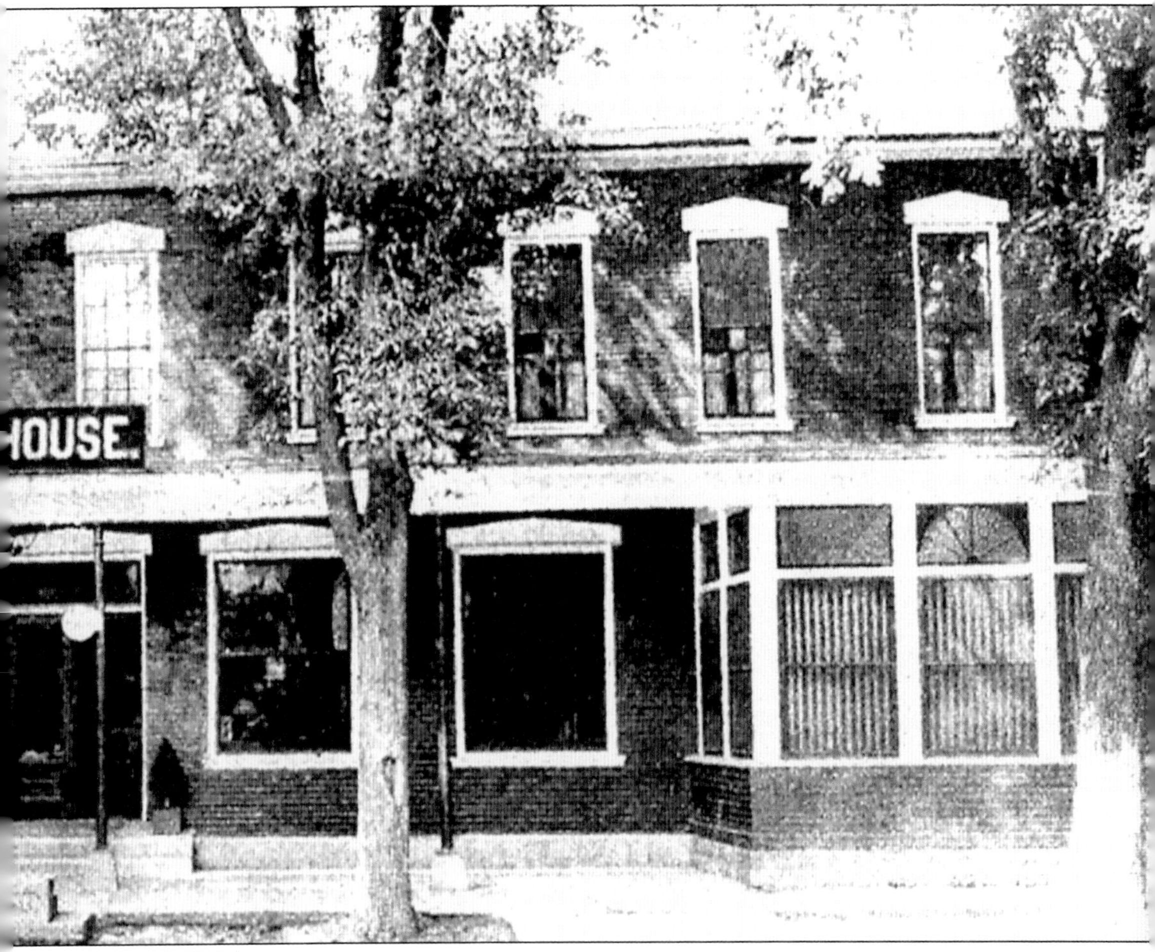

Sen. Randy Kuhl.

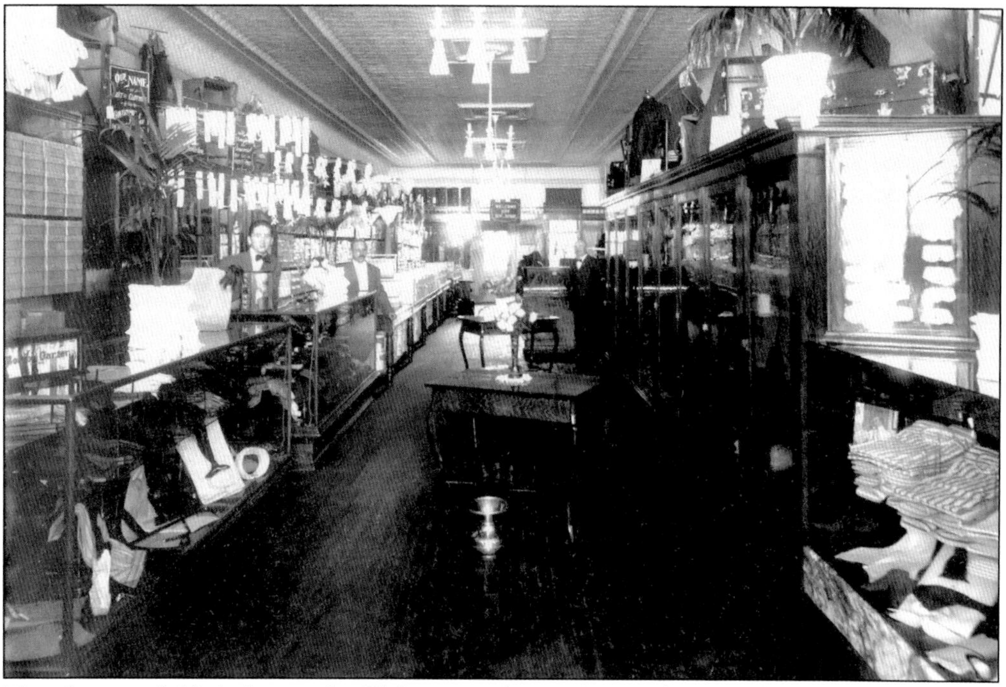

This photograph likely depicts the Globe, a popular men's wear shop on Liberty Street. (Courtesy Steuben County Historian's Office.)

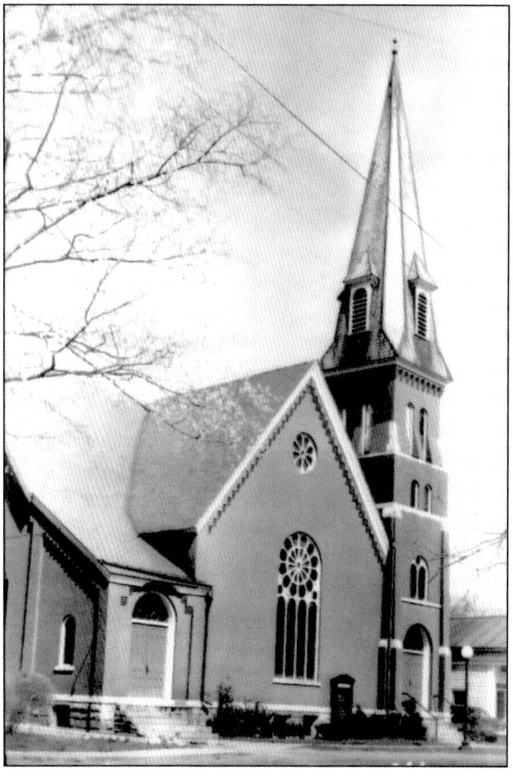

The Baptist church on Howell Street was dedicated in 1888.

Mr. Hughes repaired harnesses next door to the Steuben House.

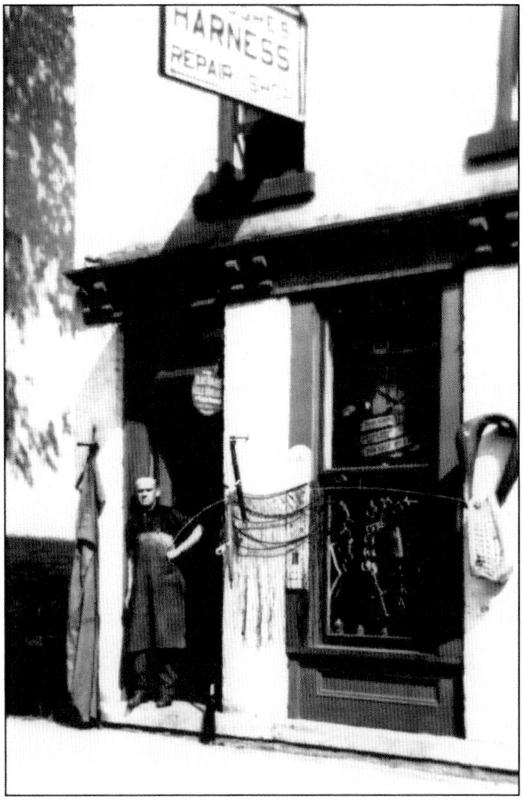

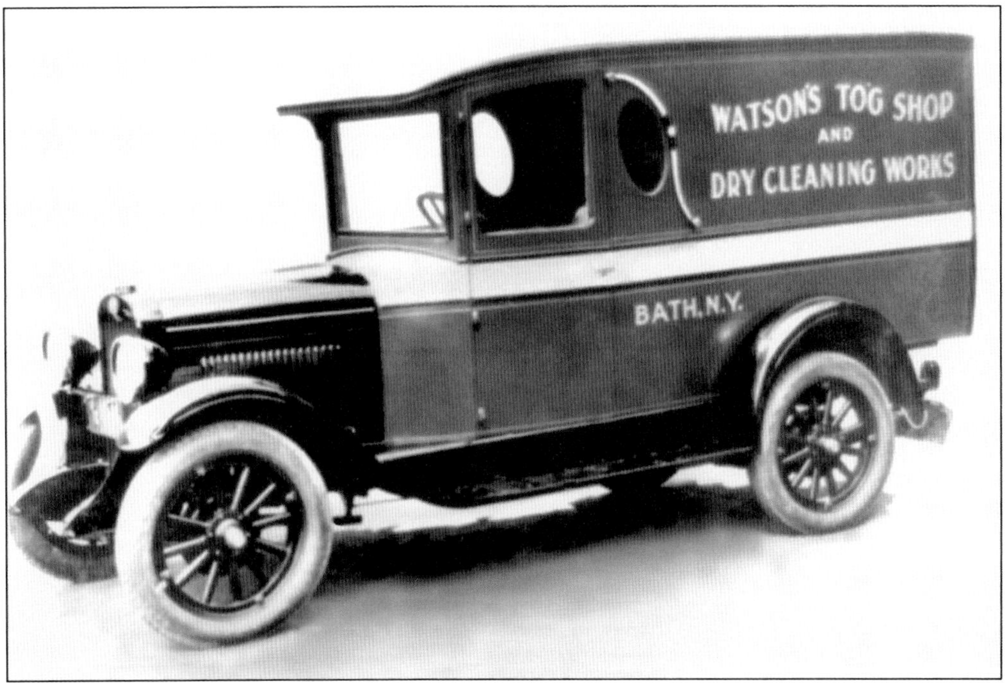

Watson's Tog Shop, operator of this early "SUV," was in business from 1923 to 1929.

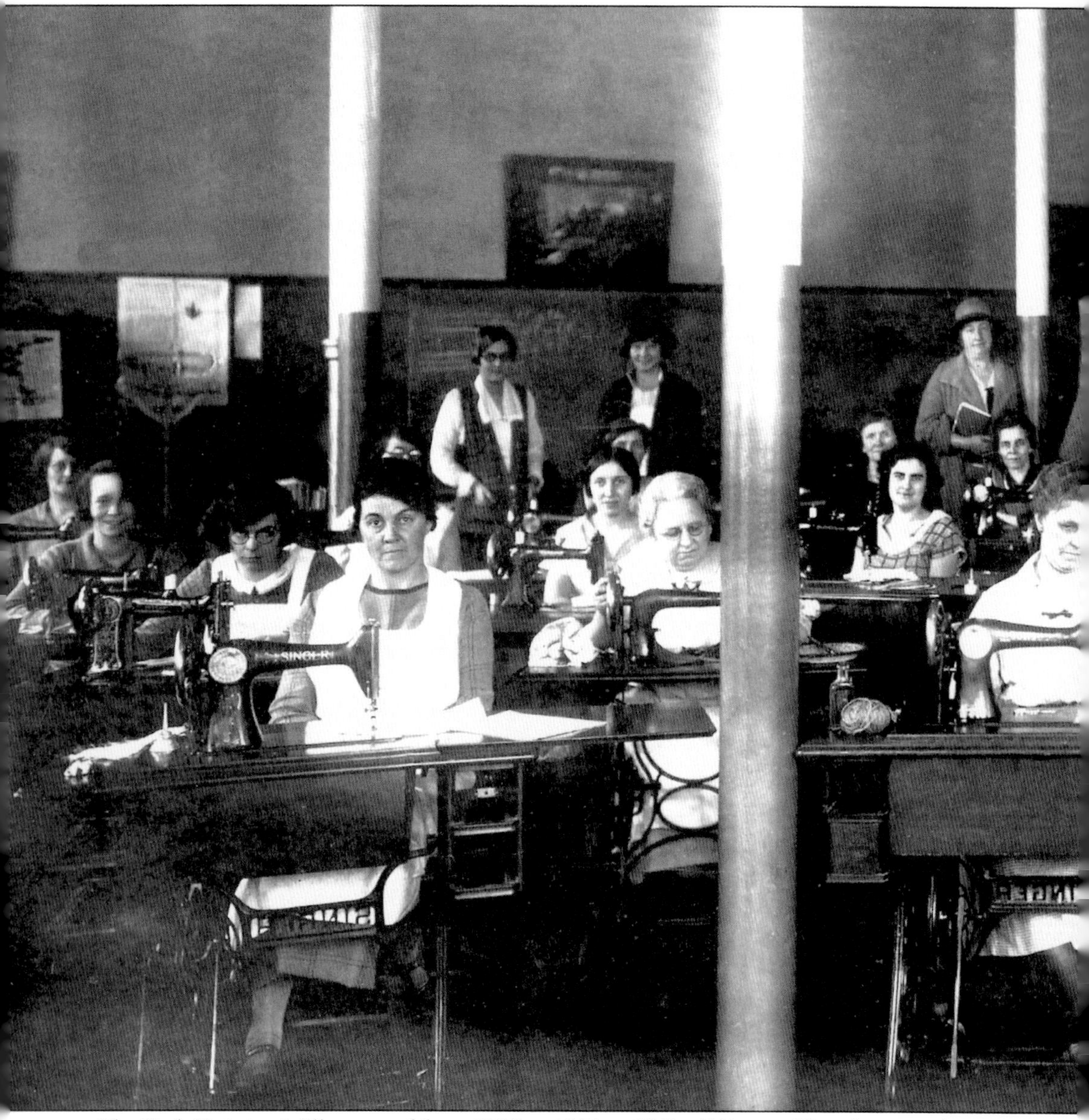

The Bath Knitting Mill operated from 1906 to 1911 at 13 Buell Street. This photograph appears to have been taken in a classroom where seamstresses were being trained. The supervisors in the

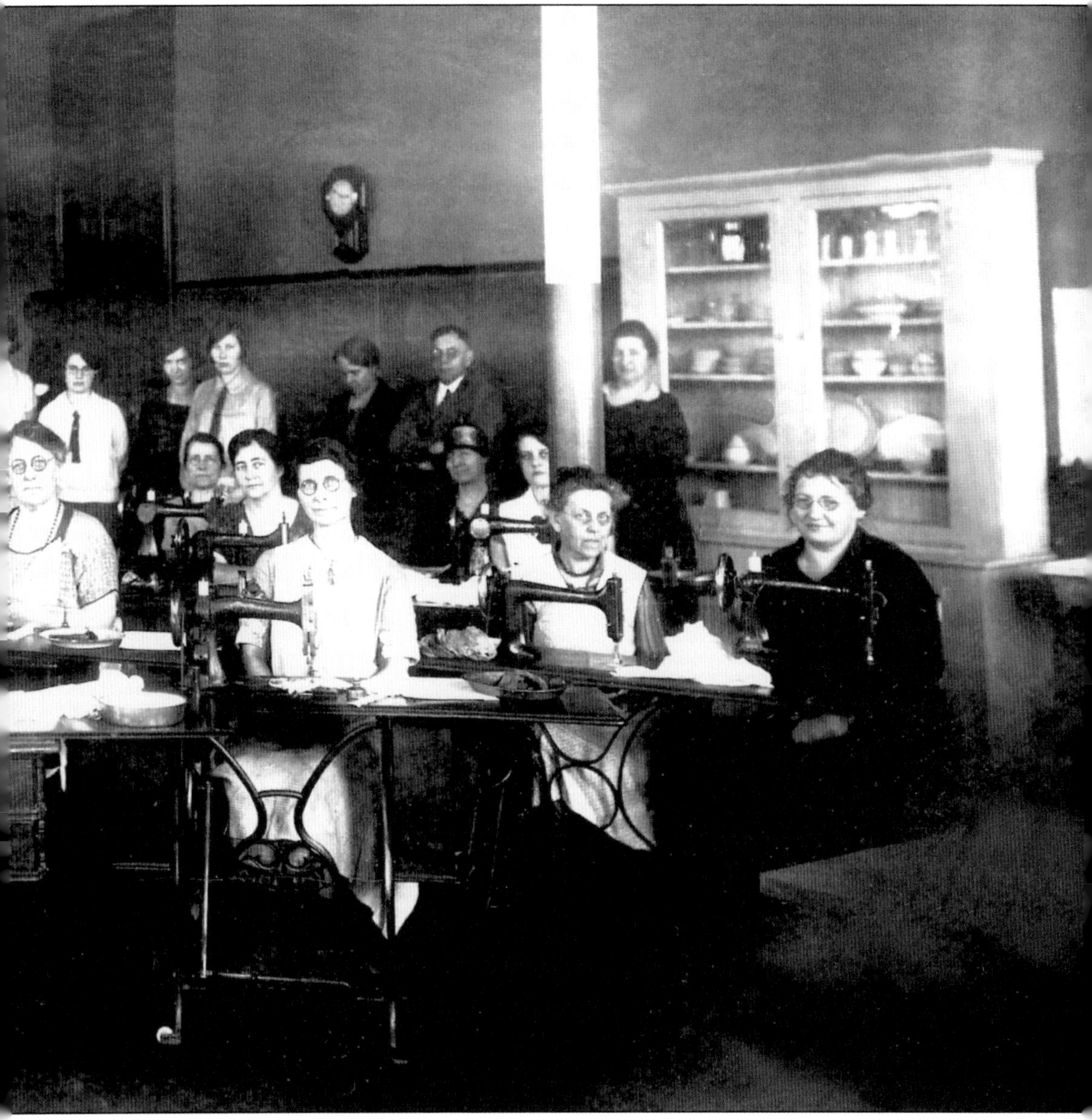

background come close to outnumbering the women working.

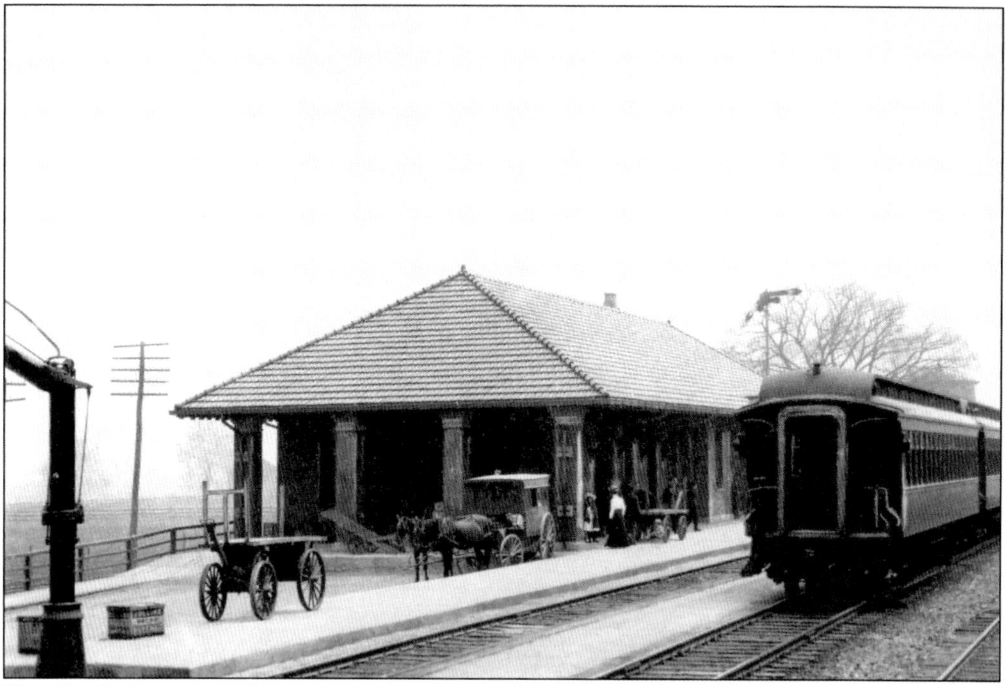

The *Phoebe Snow* visited Bath every day. The Delaware, Lackawanna, & Western Railroad was one of three lines serving the village.

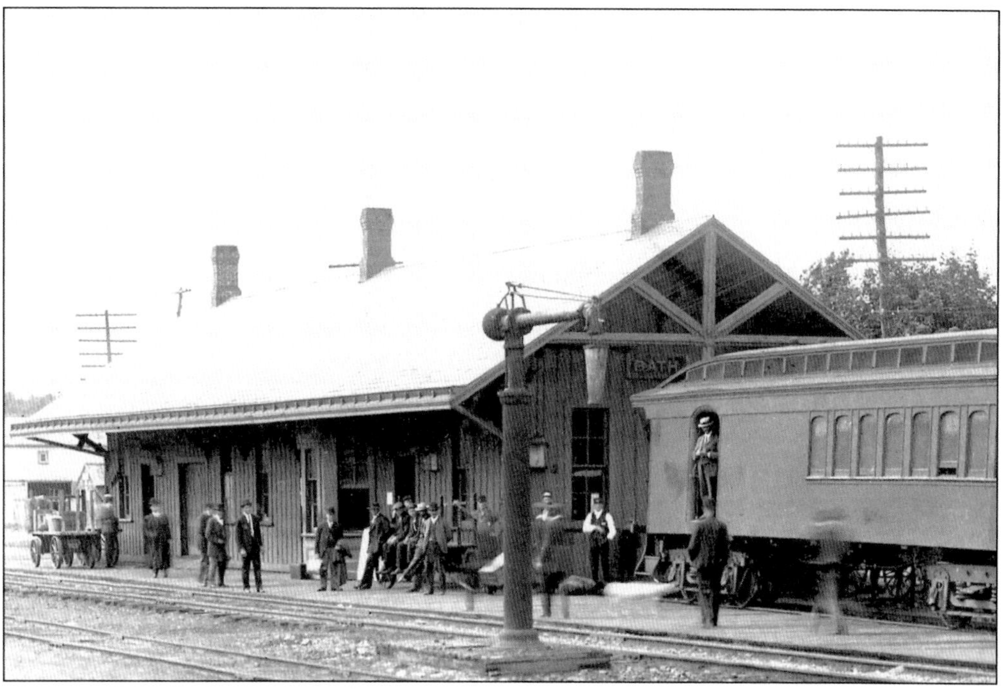

Erie Avenue commemorates another great line: the Erie Railroad.

BATH & HAMMONDSPORT RAILROAD

Time-table No. 69, Taking Effect Monday, Sept. 10th, 1900

The company reserves the right to vary therefrom as circumstances may require.

North—First-Class.				STATIONS.	South—First-Class.			
No 8	No. 6	No.	No. 2		No. 1	No.	No. 5	No. 7
P. M.	P. M.	P. M.	A. M.	Depart. Arrive	A. M.	A. M.	P. M.	P. M.
7 50	3 10	......	8 45	...Erie Depot, Bath...	7 50	......	1 35	6 30
7 52	3 12	......	8 47	..D., L. & W., Bath..	7 49	......	1 33	6 28
†7 55	†3 16	......	†8 51	.Washington Street.	†7 47	......	†1 29	†6 24
†7 58	†3 19	......	†8 54	....County House....	†7 44	......	†1 26	†6 21
†8 01	†3 23	......	†8 58	N.Y.S. Fish Hatchery	†7 39	......	†1 22	†6 17
†8 03	†3 25	......	†9 00	.....Cold Springs.....	†7 36	......	†1 20	†6 15
†8 05	†3 27	......	†9 02	......Hermitage......	†7 33	......	†1 18	†6 13
†8 08	†3 31	......	†9 05	...Pleasant Valley...	†7 30	......	†1 14	†6 09
†8 10	†3 33	......	†9 08	.........Rheims........	†7 27	......	†1 07	†6 07
†8 13	†3 36	......	†9 13	....Thorp Avenue....	†7 22	......	†1 02	†6 02
8 15	3 40	......	9 15	...Hammondsport...	7 20	......	1 00	6 00
P. M.	P. M.	P. M.	A. M.	Arrive. Depart.	A. M.	A. M.	P. M.	P. M.

A Dagger (†) indicates that trains stop only on signal.

Connecting with trains on the Erie Railroad at their station, and with the Delaware, Lackawanna & Western Railroad at their station at Bath, and with Steamers on Lake Keuka at Hammondsport.

The 10-mile-long, one-track Bath & Hammondsport short line connected with the Erie Railroad. In Hammondsport, passengers could pick up lake steamers. The Bath & Hammondsport successor, now owned by the Steuben County Industrial Development Agency, is currently operated by the Livonia, Avon, & Lakeville Railroad. (Courtesy Steuben County Historian's Office.)

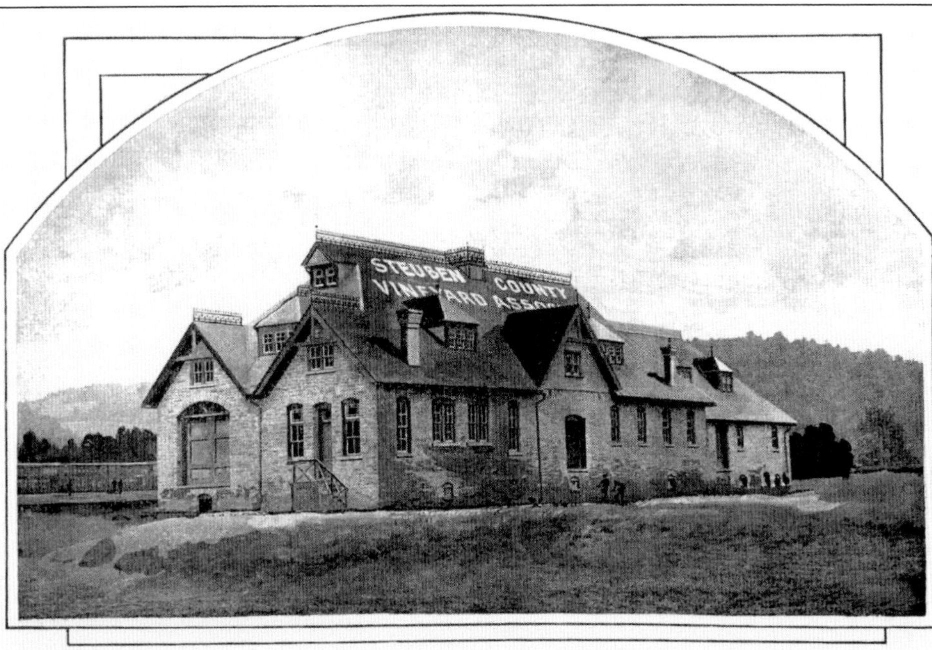

STEUBEN COUNTY VINEYARD ASSOCIATION, BATH, N. Y.

Napa Auto Parts is often mistaken for an old depot, but its stone building was in fact once part of a winery.

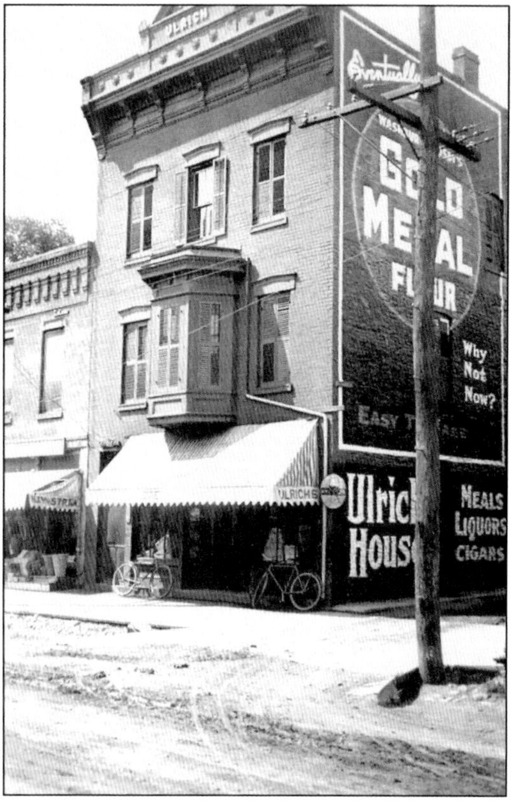

The former Ulrich Hotel, somewhat modified, still stands at West Steuben and Exchange Streets.

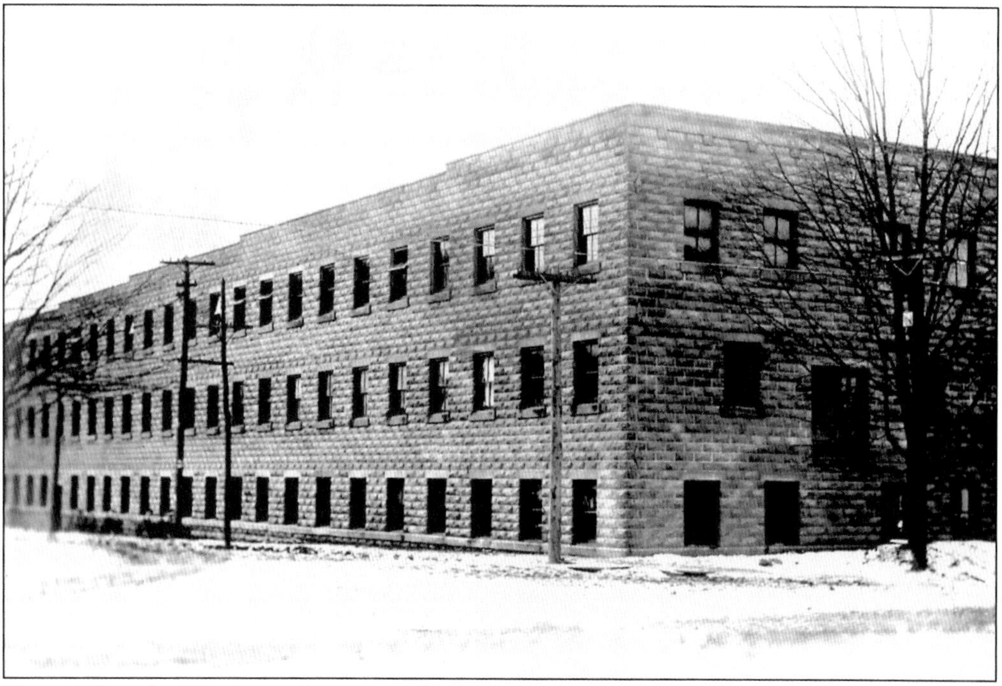

Elmira's Board of Trade tried to pirate the Bath Harness Factory, which spurned its advances and built a new plant on Railroad Street in 1905. The building is now Bath Packing.

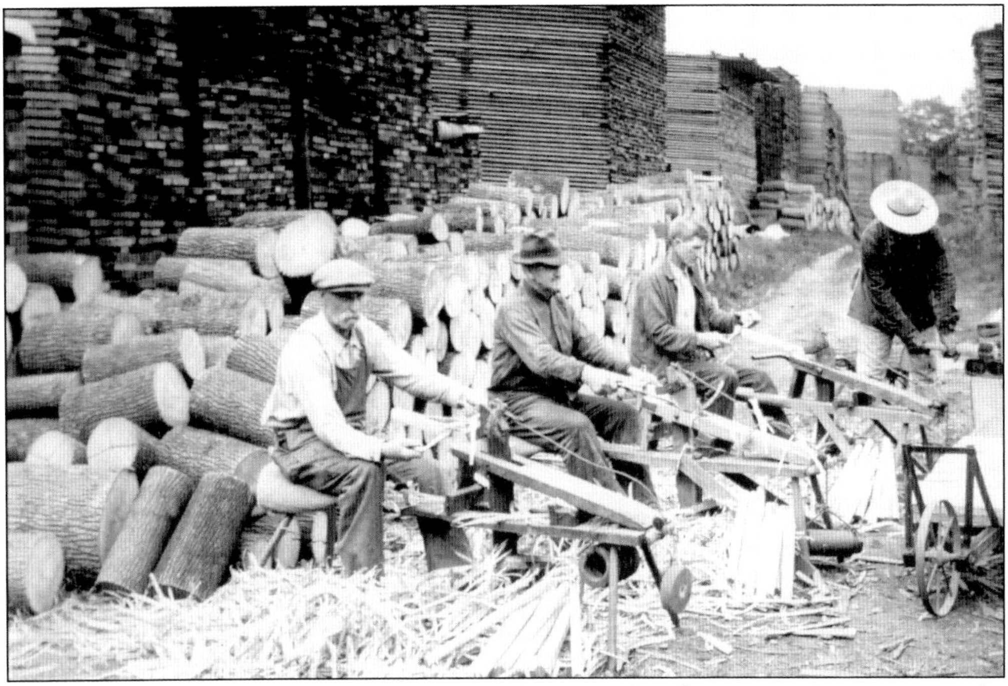

The W. W. Babcock Company, or Babcock Ladder, opened its doors in 1905. Proximity to the railroad must have been a real advantage.

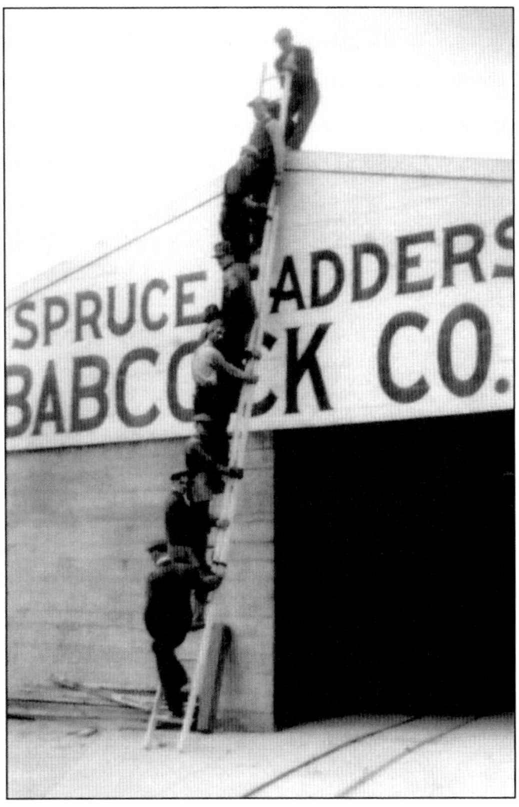

Babcock still lives up to its motto: "Standing on quality."

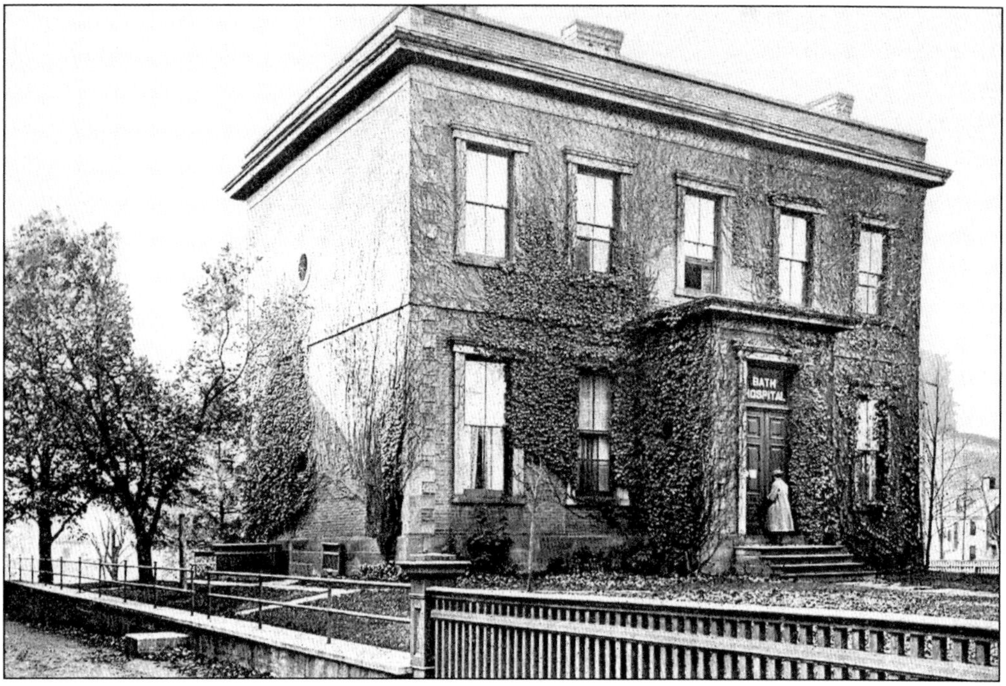

Built for the Land Office in 1867, the handsome brick structure on Pulteney Square housed Bath Hospital from 1910 to 1916. The first baby born within its walls was future department store owner Bill Cohn. When the building was razed in 1920, materials were used to make what is now the Bath Plumbing and Hardware building.

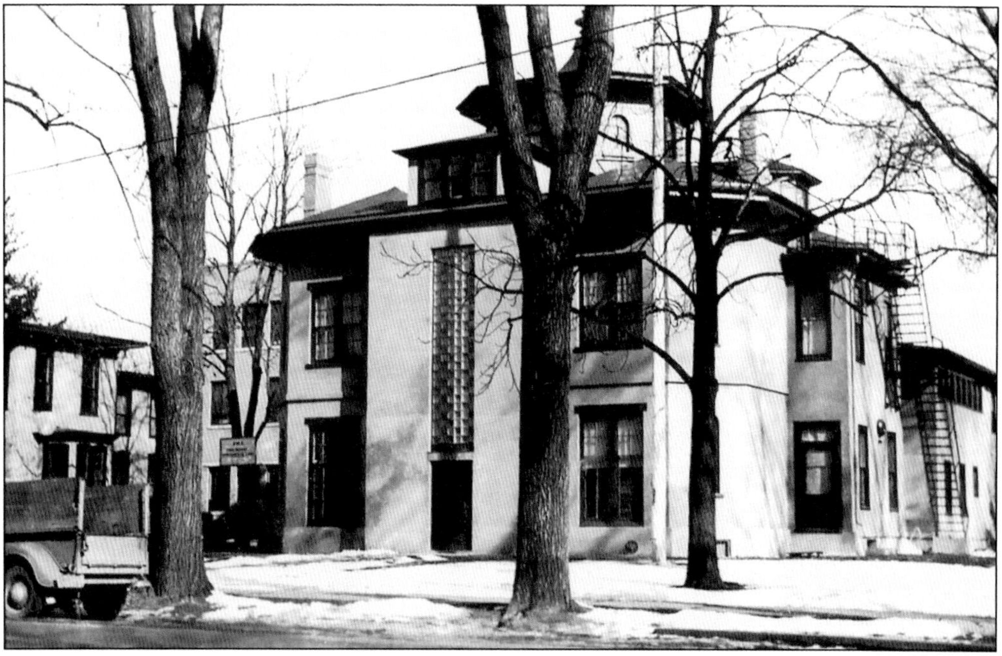

The 1916–1960 Bath Hospital on Steuben Street is now home to Pro-Action.

The current stone Presbyterian church was dedicated in 1877.

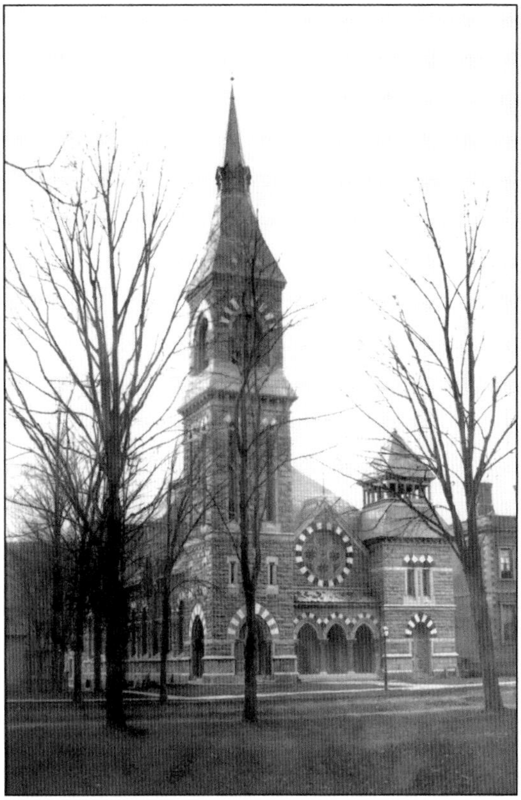

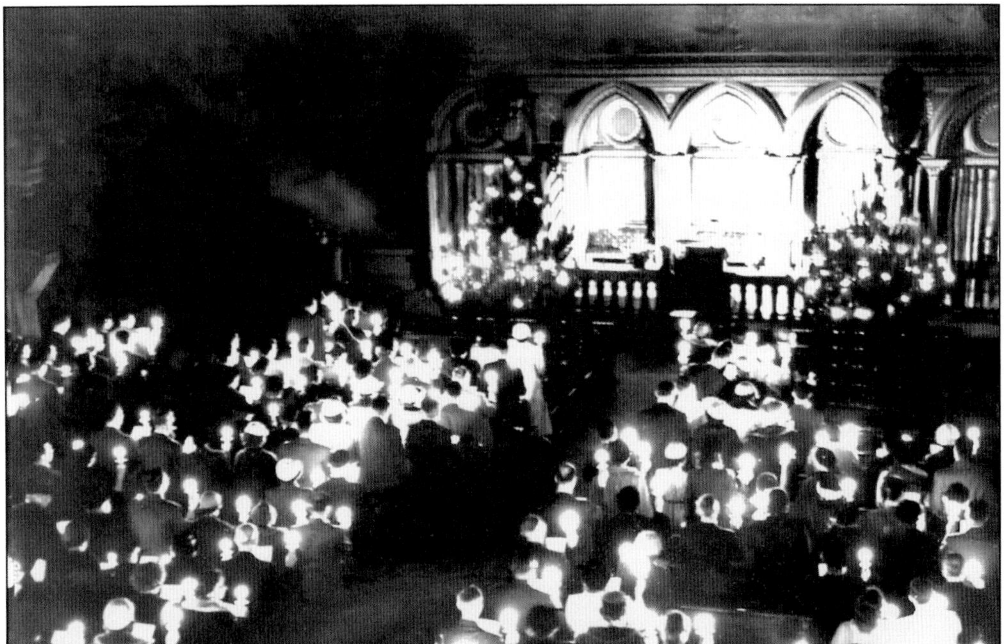

The Presbyterian church makes a memorable setting for candlelight services.

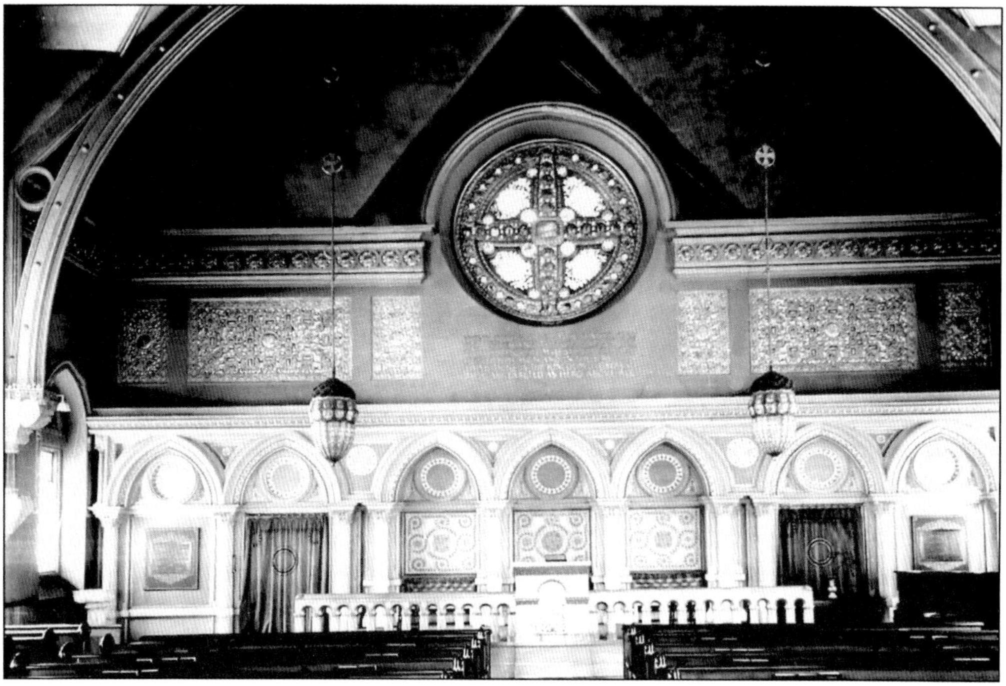

Ira Davenport Jr. commissioned a rare Tiffany interior to honor his brother John Davenport 20 years after the Presbyterian church was built.

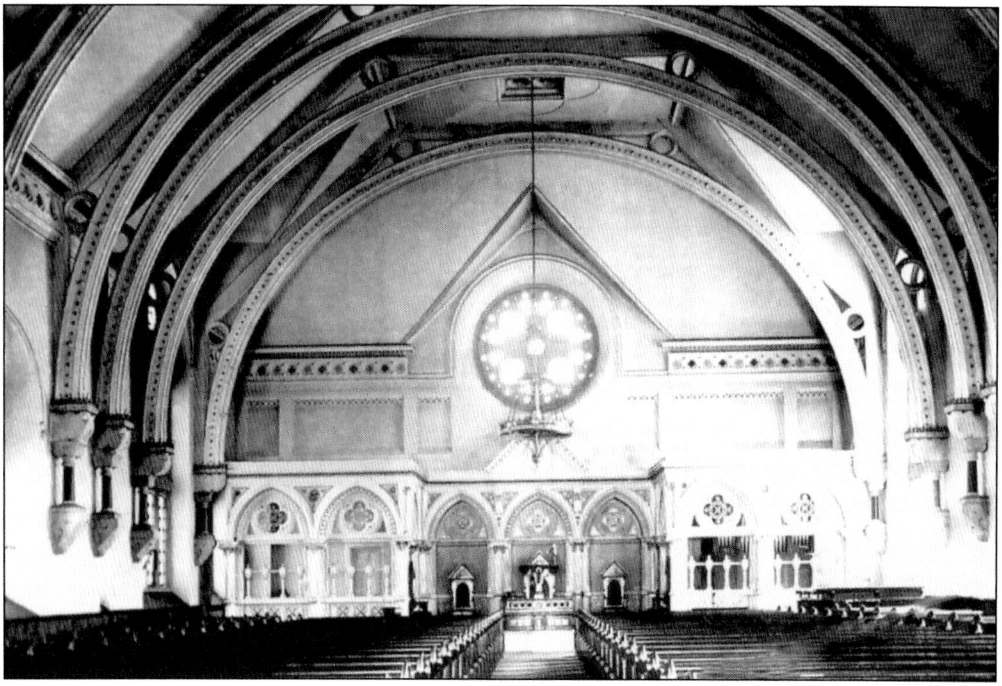

This longer view shows off the church's interior vaulting.

Bath Presbyterian's Bessie Hille traveled to China as a missionary in 1913. Thirty years later, she was released from Japanese captivity to sail home in the only World War II repatriation of Americans.

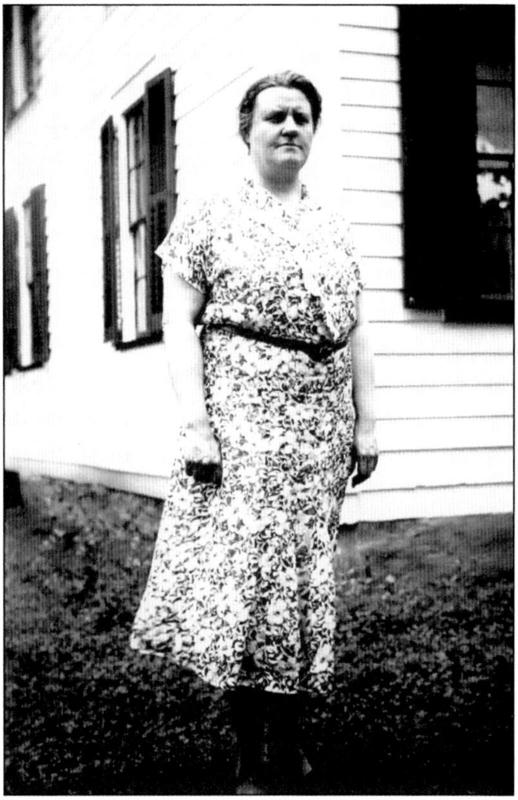

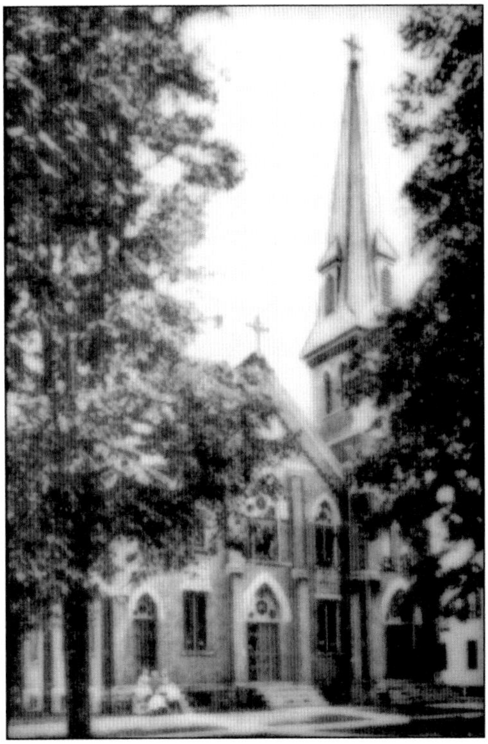

St. Mary's Catholic Church broke ground for its new building in 1891. Parishioners celebrated the centennial of that event by raising a new steeple. St. Mary's operated its own school in the 19th century and again from 1960 to 1987.

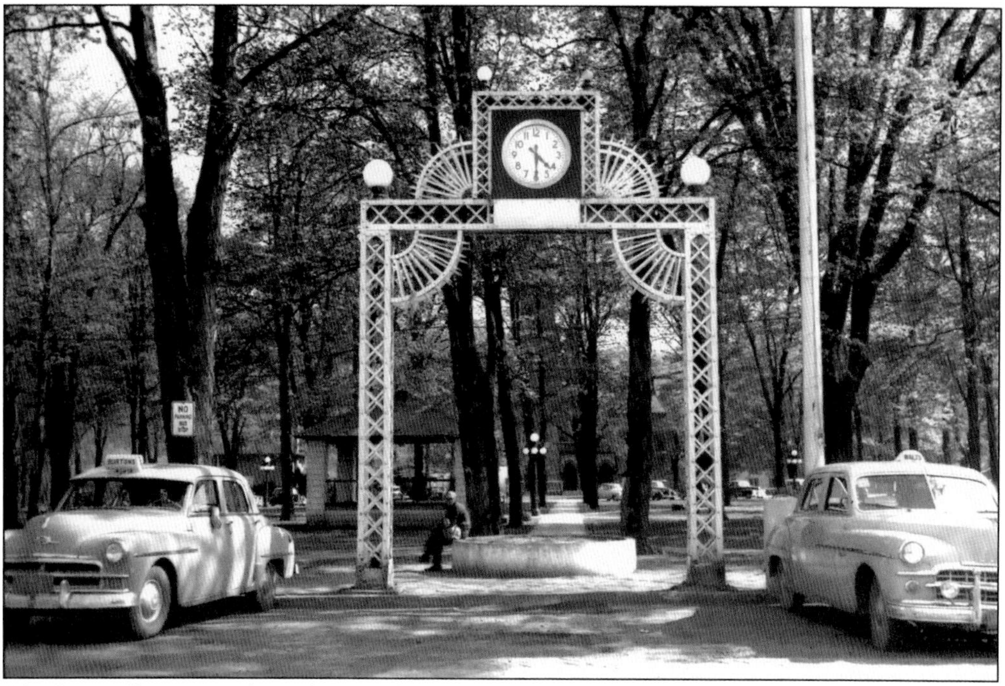

Charles Williamson's first clearing has become Pulteney Park, in Pulteney Square. Local businesspeople donated the arch and clock in 1905.

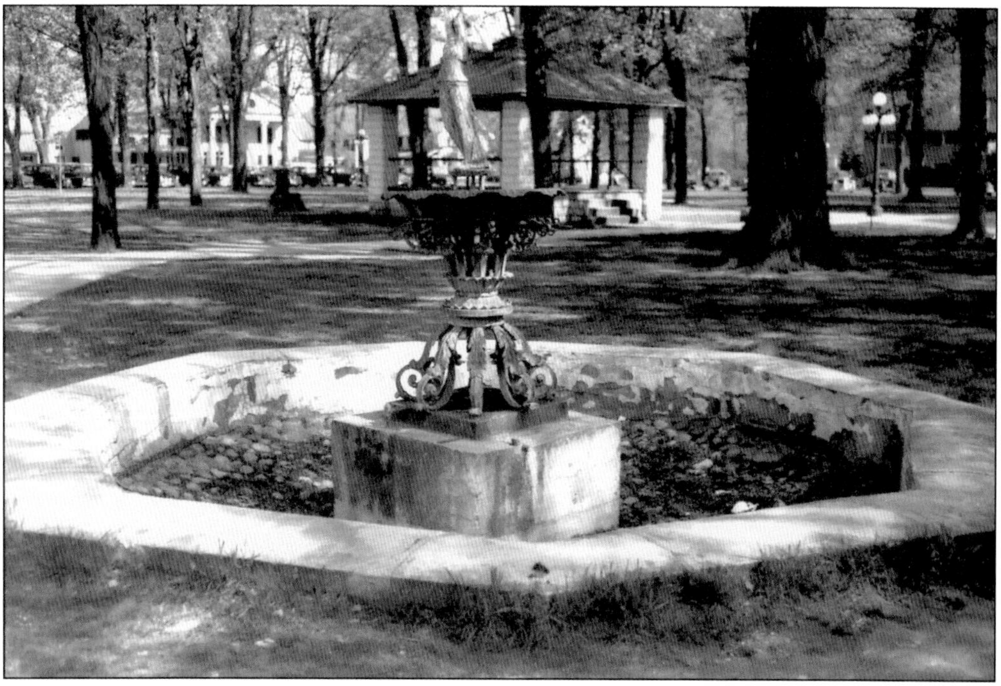

The Pulteney Park fountain—although somewhat improved—remains, but the stone bandstand has been replaced by a wooden model.

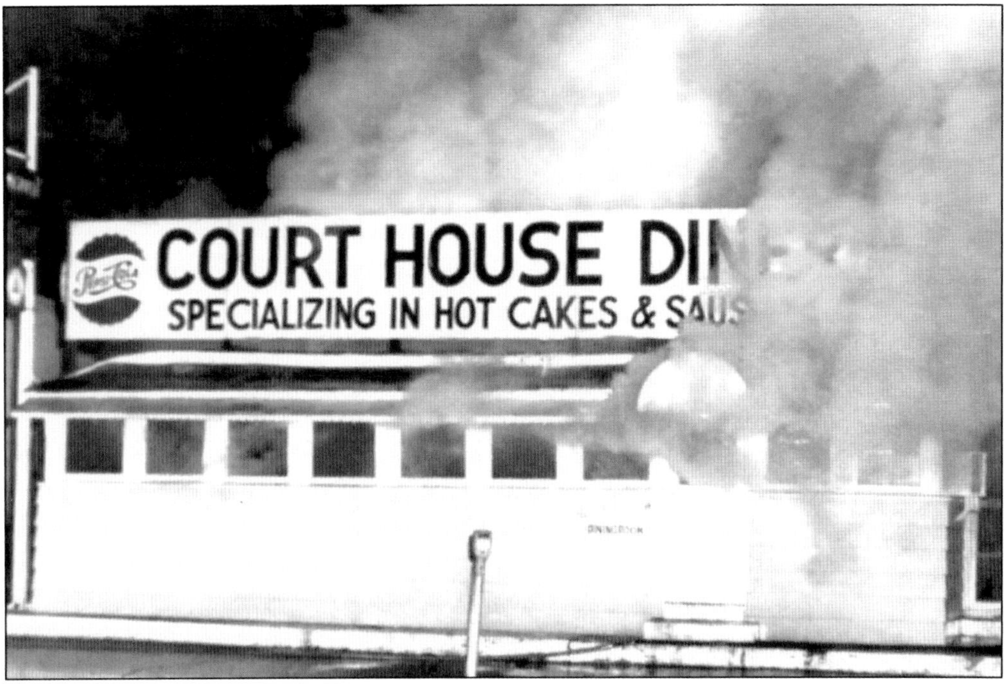

Just off Pulteney Square, a much-loved diner burned in 1973. The Four Seasons Market is now at that location.

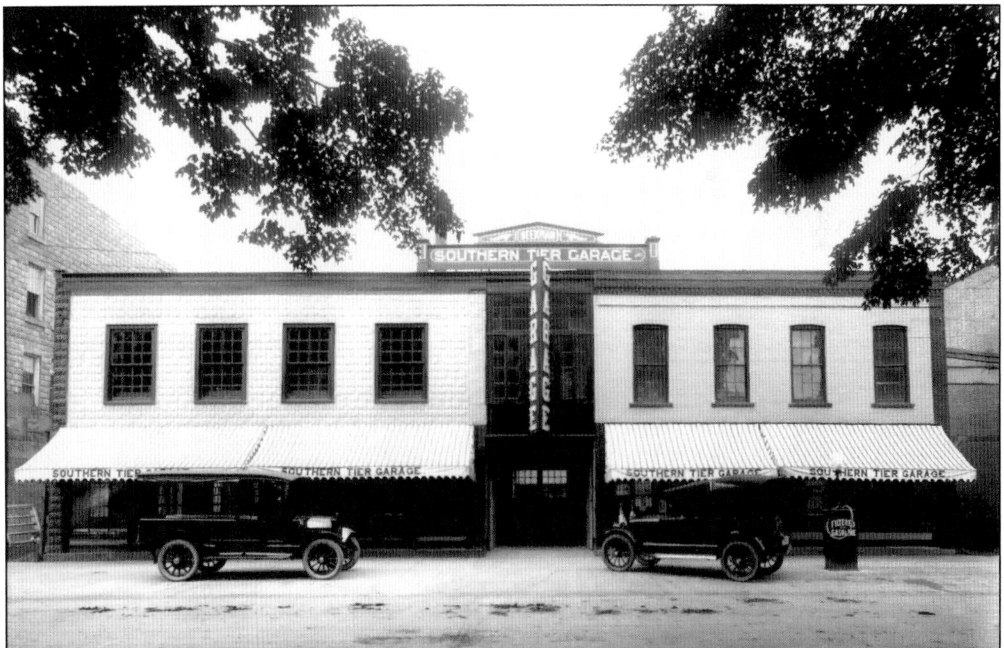

Near the Four Seasons Market, the Steuben Bowling Academy has replaced the garage that replaced the livery stable that replaced the sash works. The livery stable, garage, and bowling alley have all shared parts of the same structure. (Courtesy Steuben County Historian's Office.)

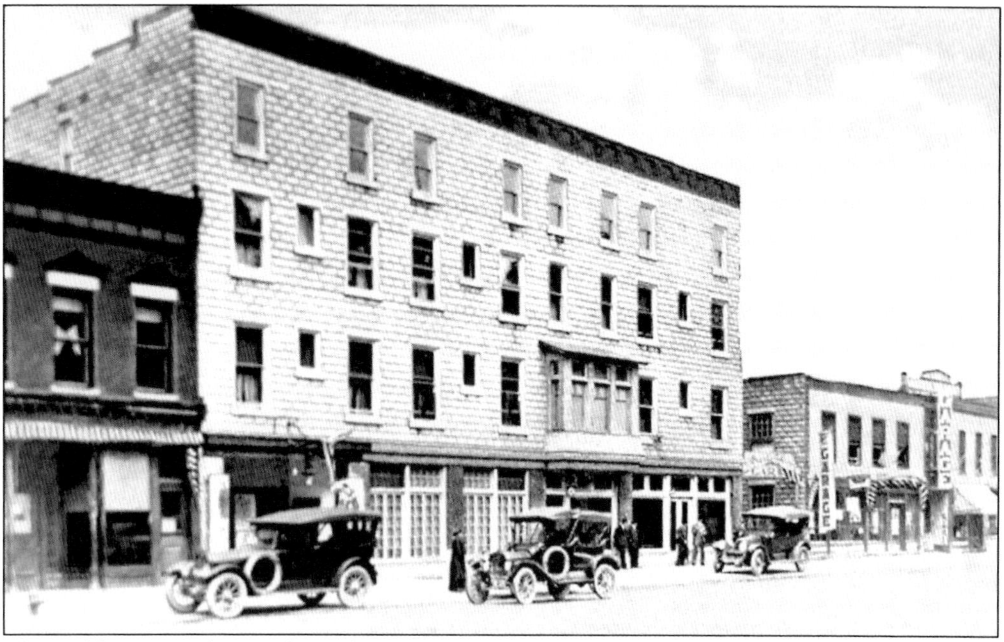

The Old National Hotel, with its elegant old-fashioned interior, remains a popular accommodation and dining spot. The brick building on the left now houses law offices.

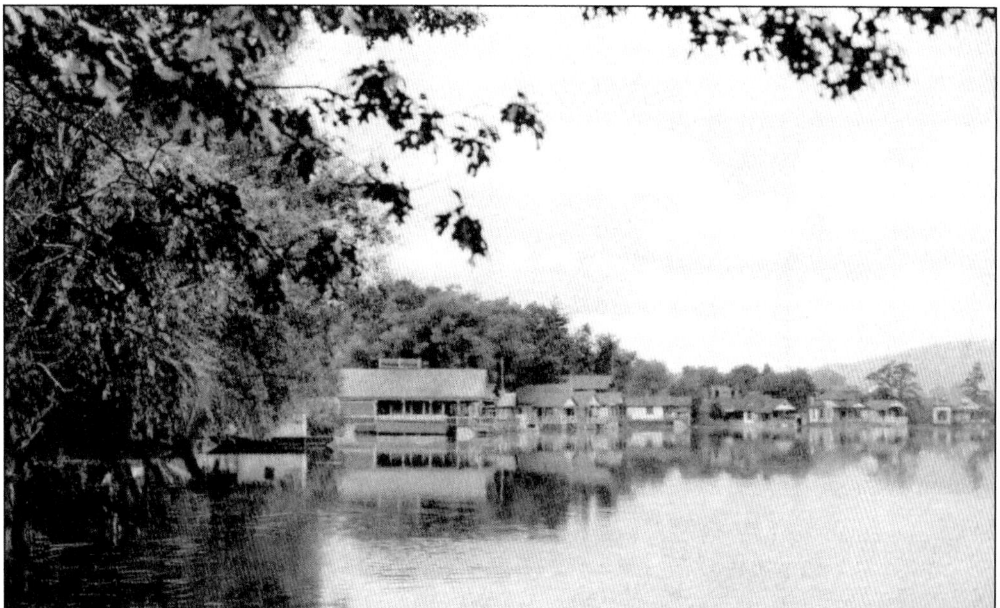

Local folks described Lake Salubria as "a mile across and a mile around"—topologically unlikely, to say the least.

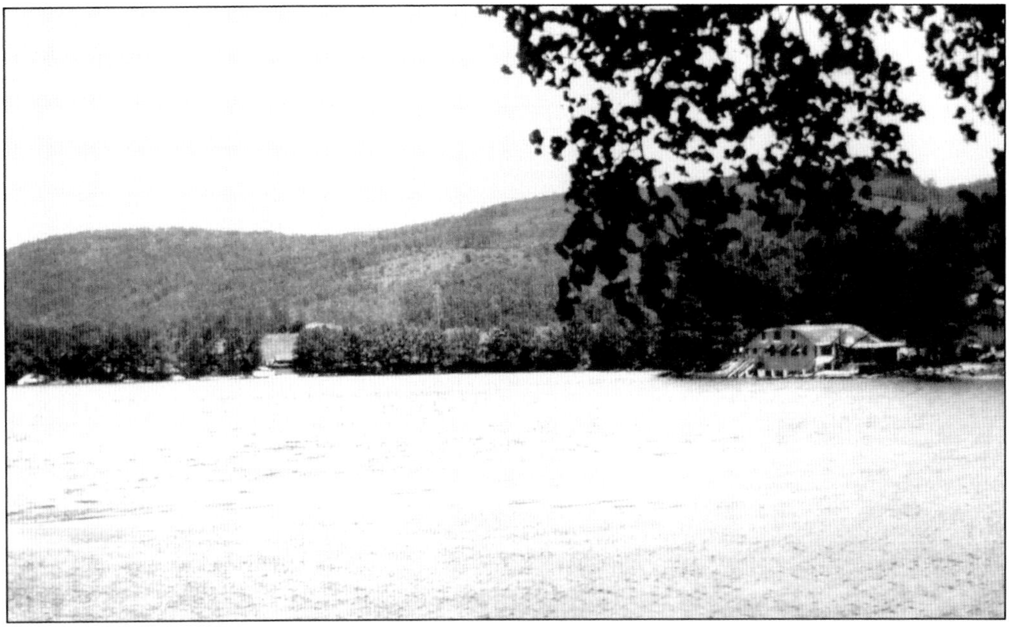

The Moonlit Rendezvous (right), which replaced an earlier dance pavilion, burned in 1969. The site has since become Tyrtle Beach, home of WVIN's annual fund-raiser for youth services. Various dignitaries and popular figures take turns jumping in the lake.

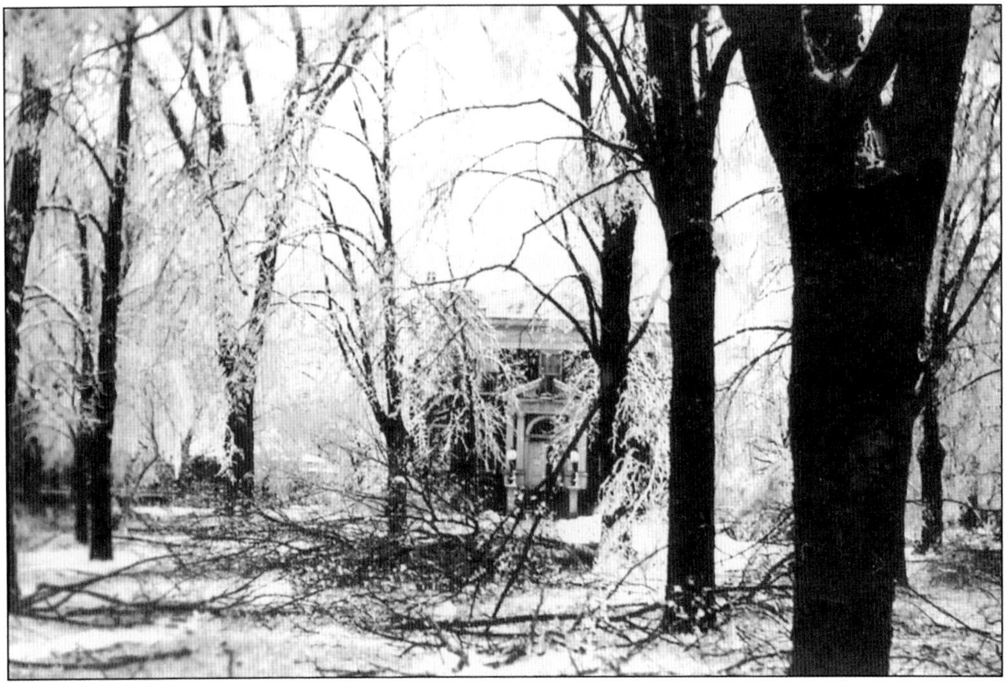

As if the flood, Mussolini's invasion of Abyssinia, and the Great Depression were not enough, 1935 was also the year of the great ice storm, adding insult to injury. John Magee's 1831 home, at Morris and Cameron Streets, was for years the Davenport Library. Magee House is now home to the Steuben County Historical Society, the Steuben County Historian's Office, and the Elm Cottage Museum.

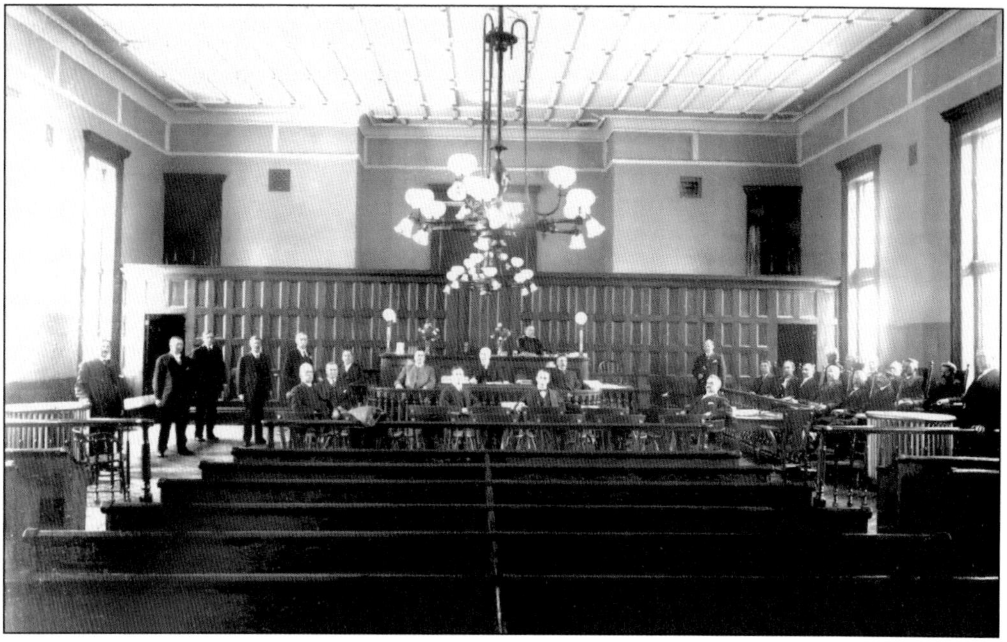

While court was once a major social event, what went on inside was serious business. (Courtesy Steuben County Historian.)

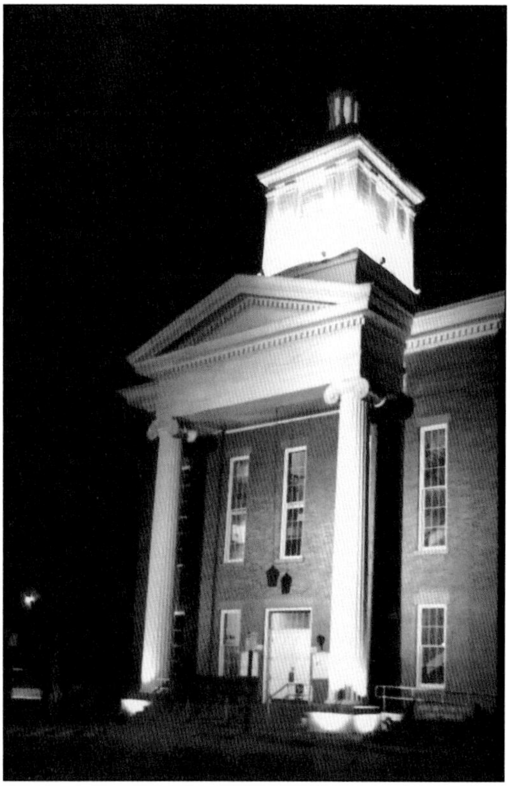

The courthouse remains an enduring symbol of Bath.

Three

FUN AT THE FAIR (AND ELSEWHERE)

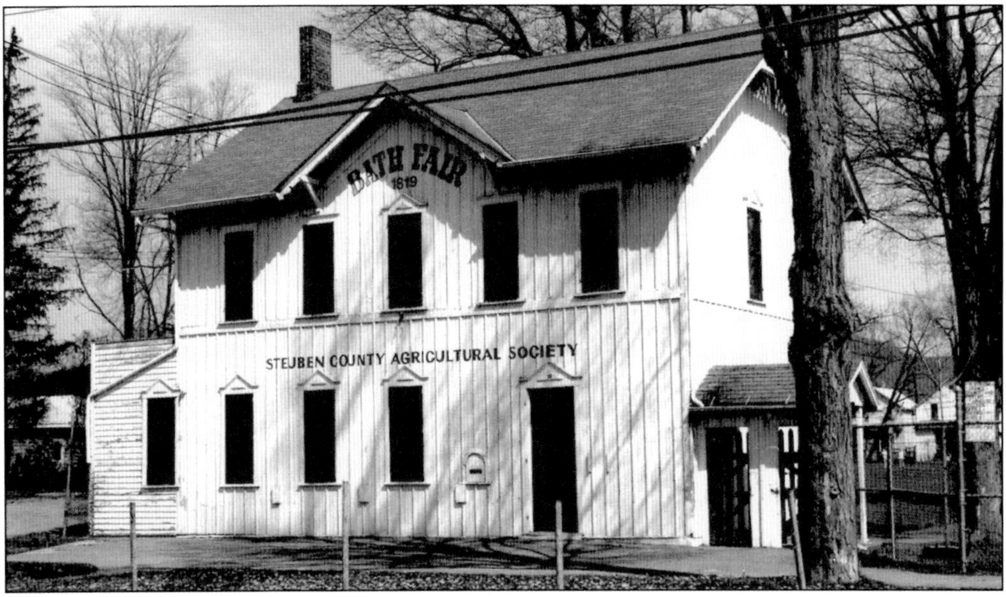

Charles Williamson's 1796 World's Fair brought in visitors from as far away as Maryland, Virginia, Massachusetts, and Canada. Highlighted by a flat race in which Silk Stockings beat Virginia Nell, Williamson's fair was a booming success, attracting 1,500 participants and stimulating land sales in the Pulteney Purchase. The Steuben County Fair, which first took place in 1819, was an on-again, off-again proposition until 1853, when the state legislature encouraged fairs. The new Steuben County Agricultural Society has sponsored the fair every year, beginning in 1853. Since 1854, the fair has been held on the same Washington Street site. By some reckonings, it is the oldest county fair in the United States. Besides their entertainment and social advantages, fairs through the first half of the 20th century were vital to the rural farm family. They provided important opportunities for education in addition to chances for studying the latest equipment, tools, and household products. Local towns closed their schools, emptied their streets, and ran special trains when the Bath Fair was on. Needs are different in the 21st century, but the Bath Fair is still a big deal. The fairgrounds themselves also host the Dairy Festival, 4-H activities, the Western New York Mule Show, the Home Show, the Lumberjack and Jill Festival, the Mennonite Southern Tier Relief Sale, and even high school graduation.

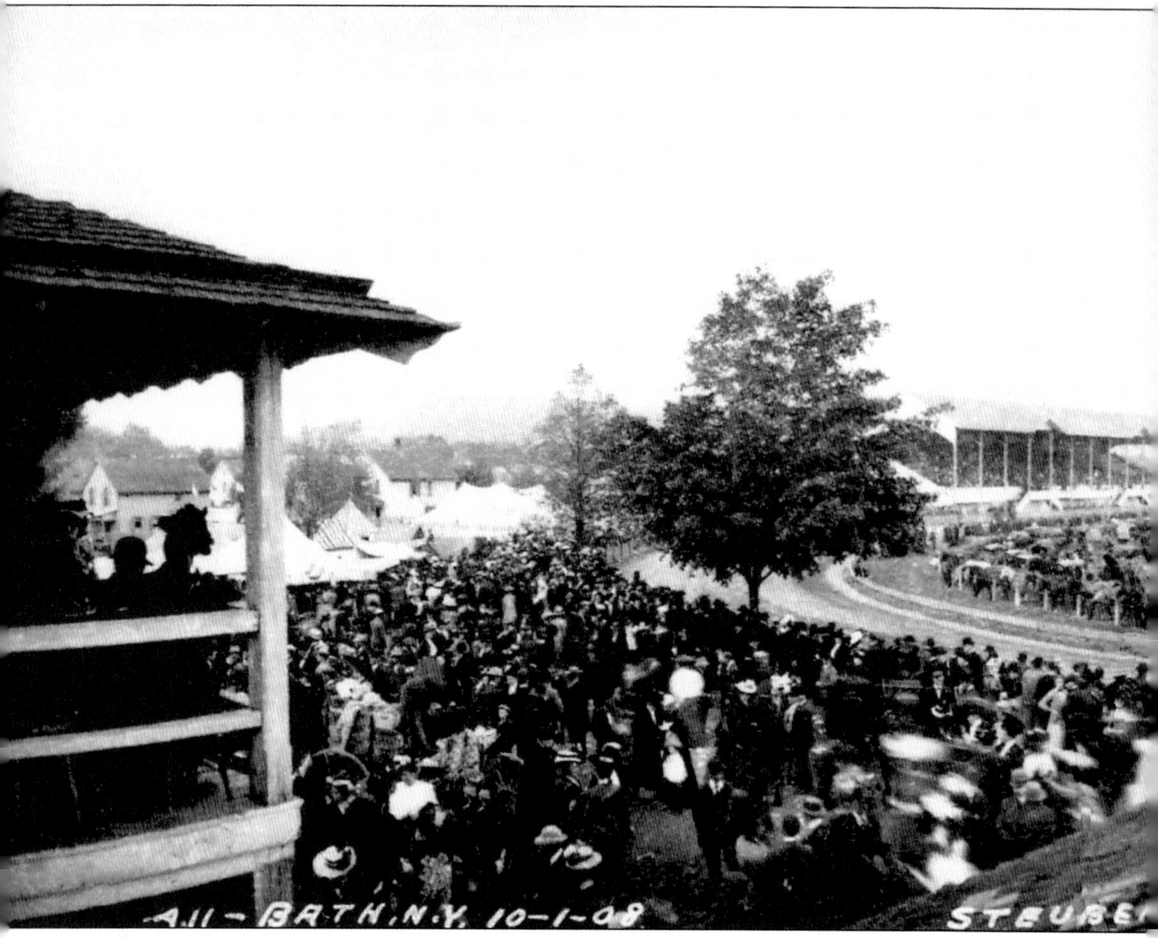

The grandstand, track, and many fair buildings are well over 100 years old. The balcony at the left, on the pre-1870 exhibition hall, was only closed in 2003 due to a lack of handicap access, and the infield now parks mostly cars, although local Mennonite and Amish families

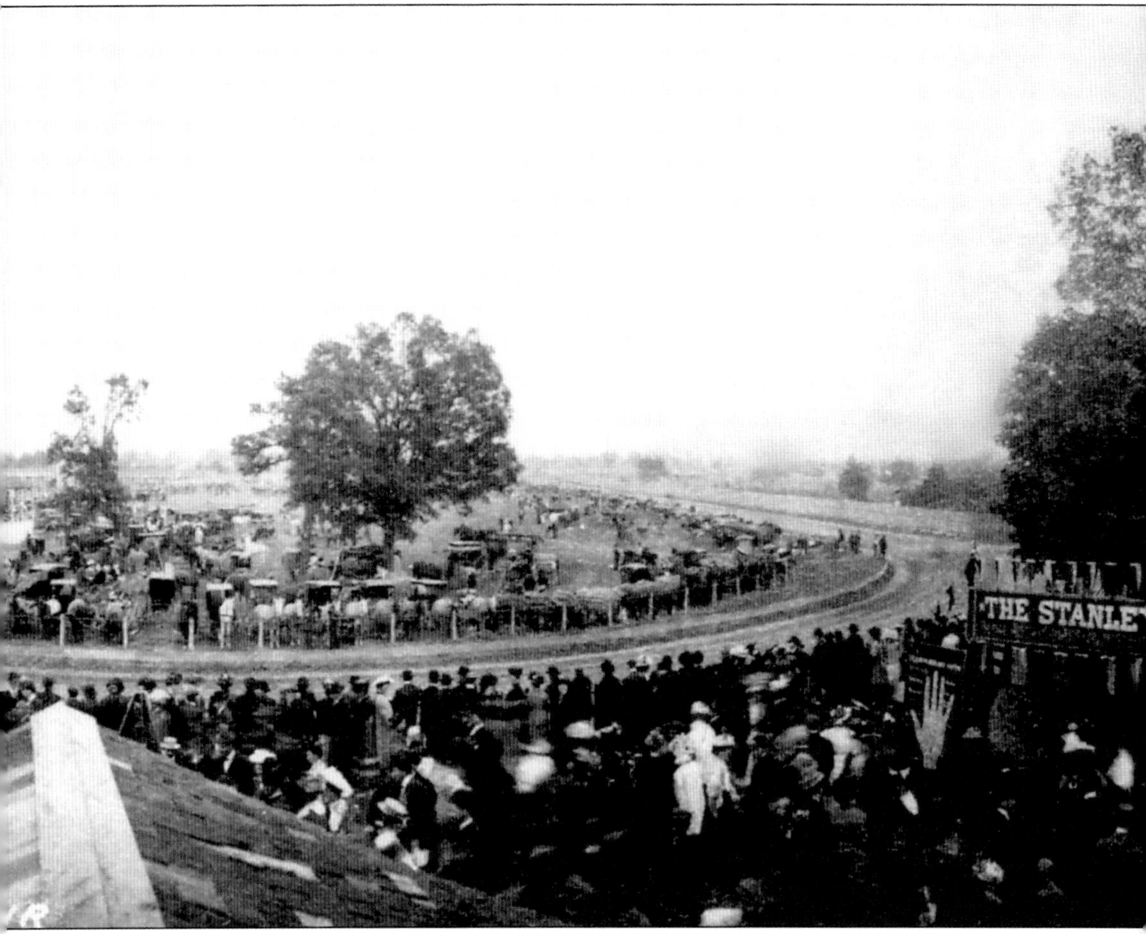

still come in by buggy. Teenaged Glenn Curtiss raced bicycles on the track, probably never dreaming that one day it would host demolition derbies. This panoramic image was captured on October 1, 1908.

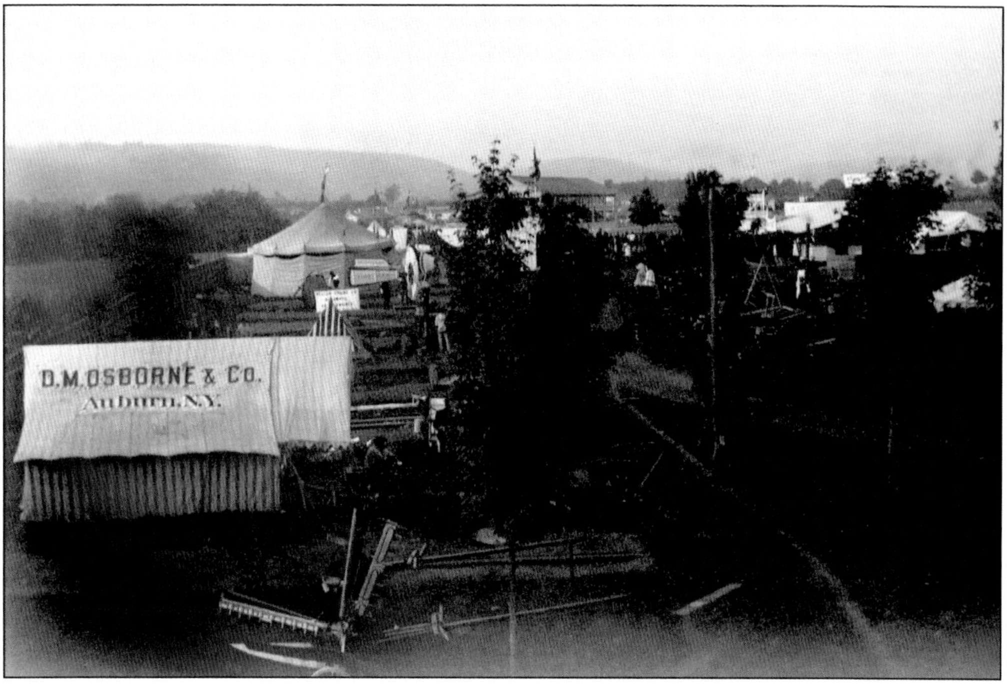

Fairs through 1950 served the same purpose they had in medieval days: gathering wares, like the windmill in the background, into one spot so that the farm folks could inspect them.

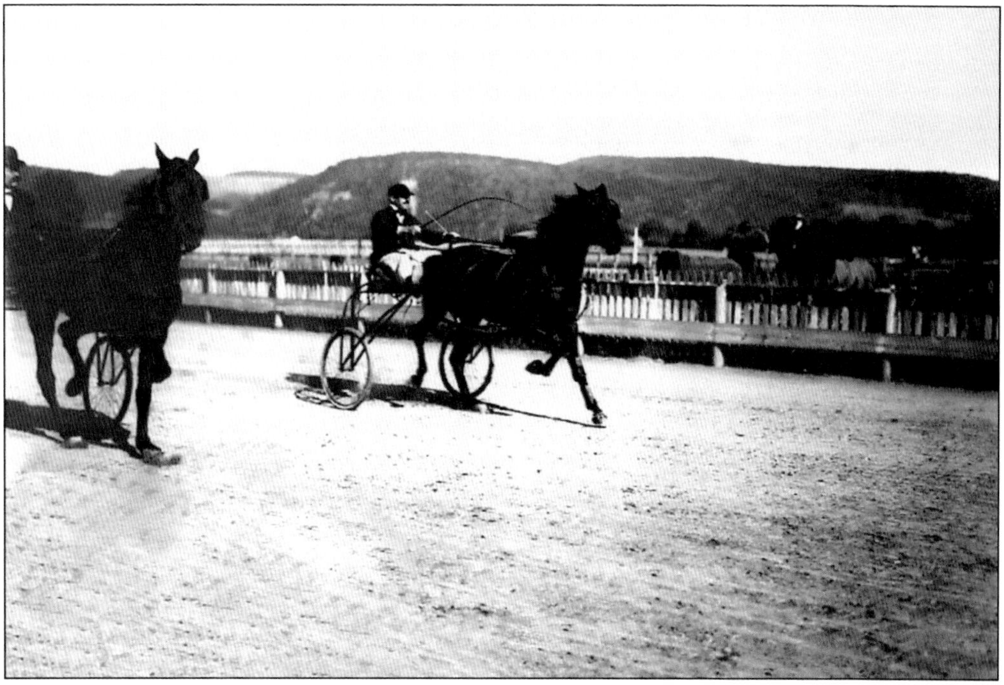

Standardbred racing is a regular feature of the Bath Fair. Pacers and trotters work out year-round with their sulkies.

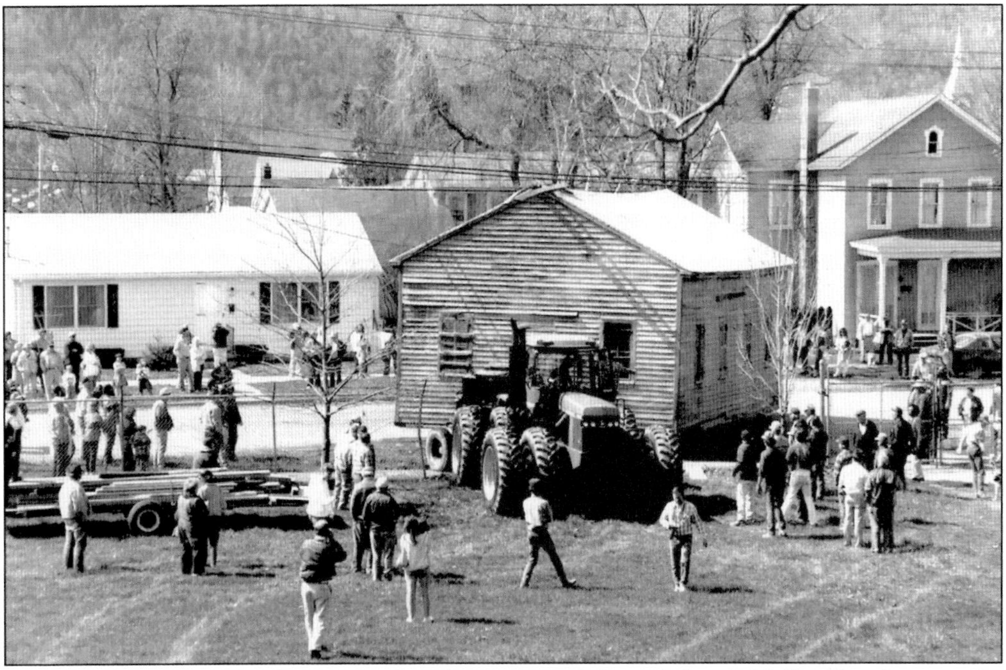

The old District 11 School was moved to the fairgrounds from Babcock Hollow Road in time for the 1993 Bath bicentennial. The Steuben County Historical Society operates the schoolhouse and the Pioneer Log Cabin as museums. Note the Presbyterian steeple on the right.

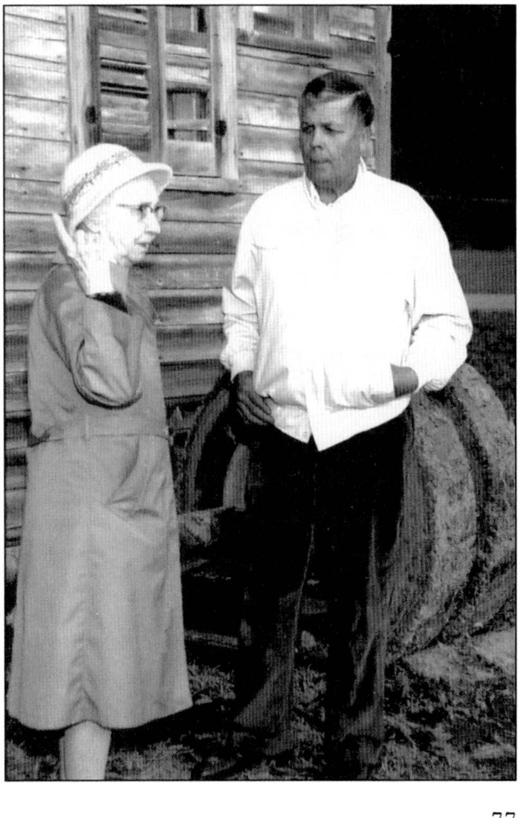

Don Chatfield donated the District 11 Schoolhouse to the Steuben County Historical Society. Catherine Walker had been a teacher at the school.

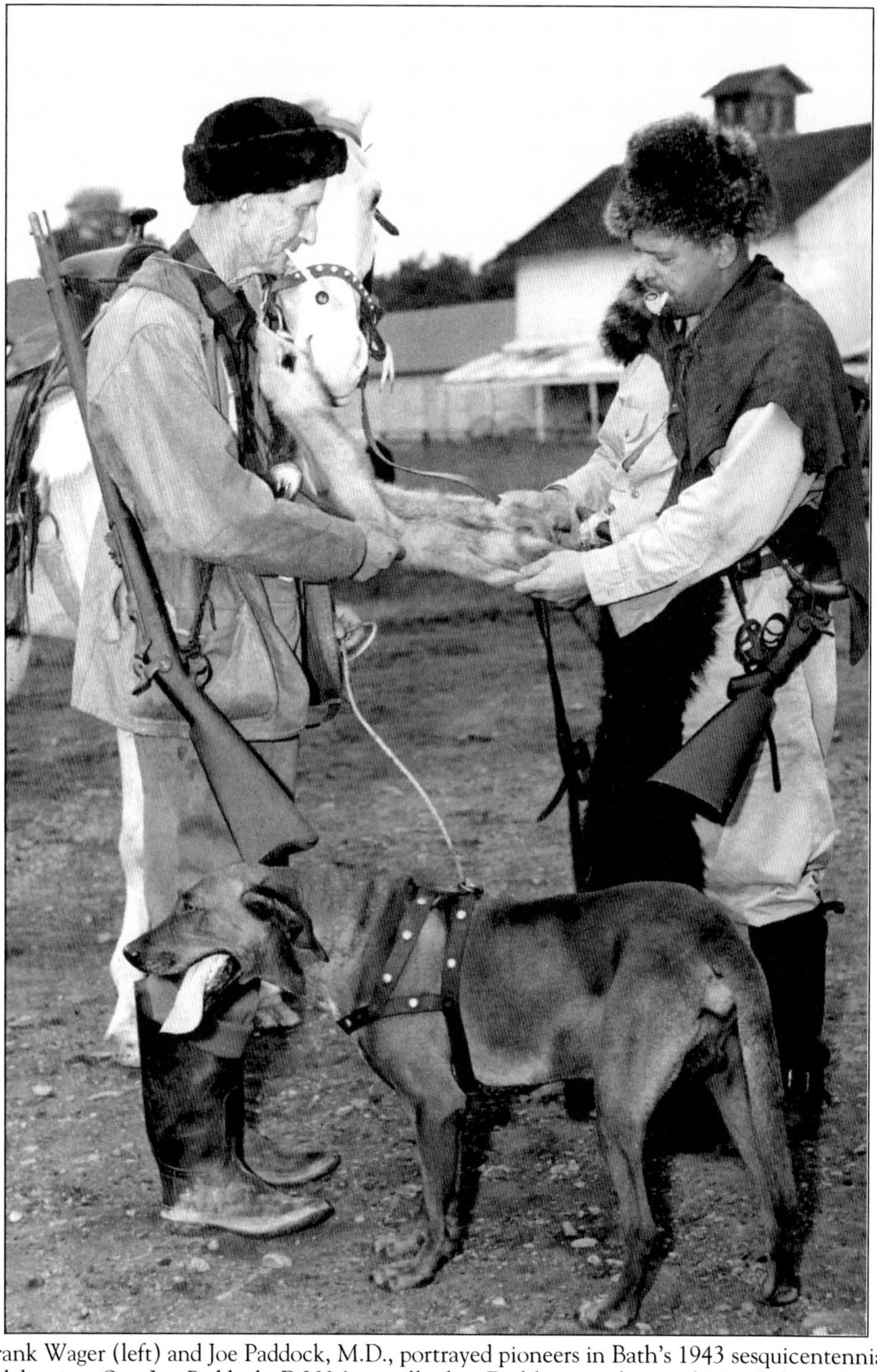

Frank Wager (left) and Joe Paddock, M.D., portrayed pioneers in Bath's 1943 sesquicentennial celebration. Son Joe Paddock, D.V.M., recalls that Dad borrowed one of Mom's fur stoles to make his costume.

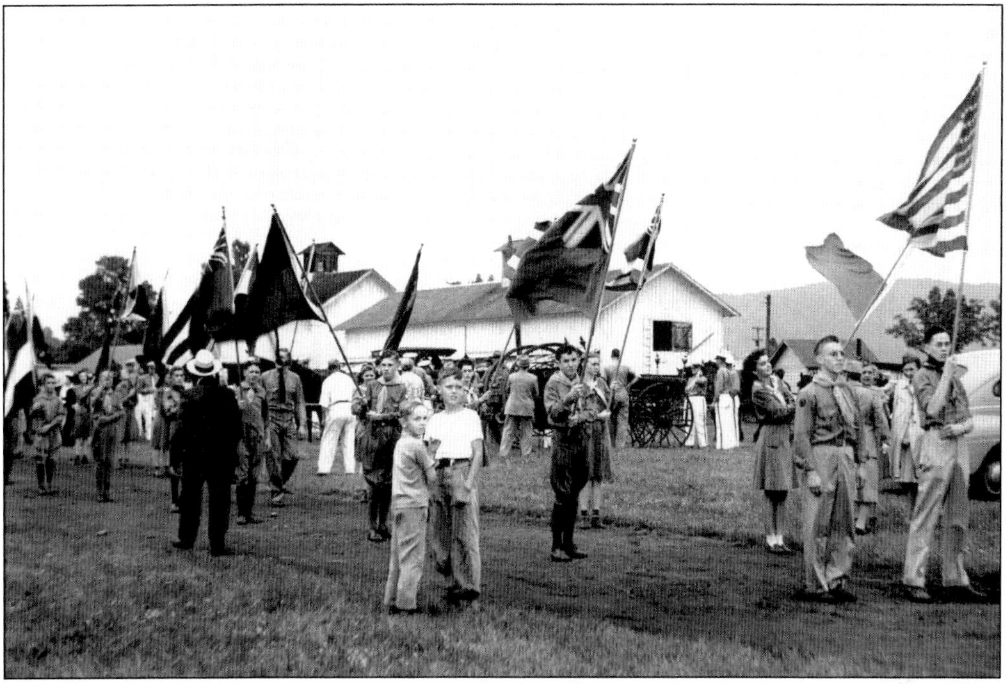

Sesquicentennial celebrations were staged out of the fairgrounds. The wartime Scouts fly flags of the Allies in addition to the national colors.

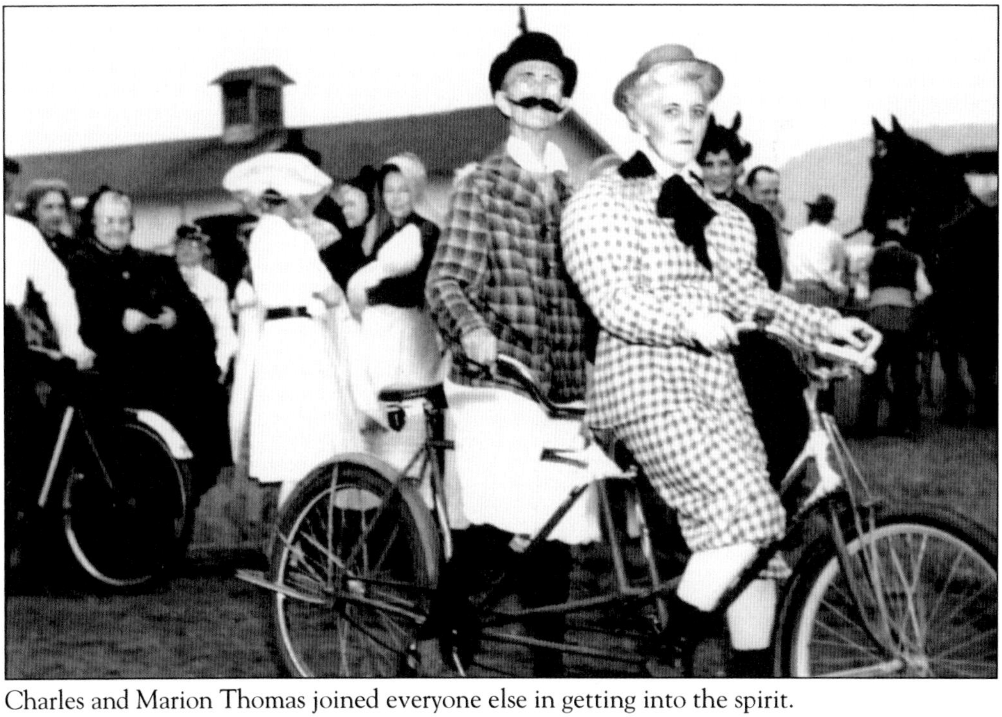

Charles and Marion Thomas joined everyone else in getting into the spirit.

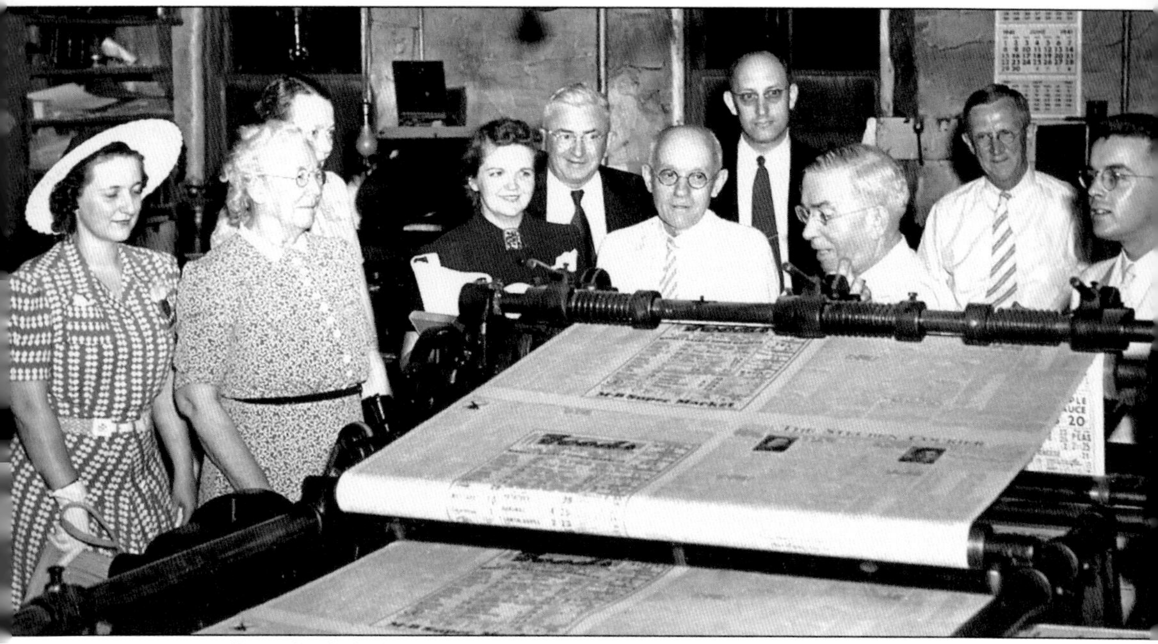

Henry O. Elkins (eighth from the left) was in his glory, celebrating his 50th anniversary as editor of the *Courier,* the 100th anniversary of the *Courier* itself, the 150th anniversary of Bath, and, as a good Presbyterian, the 300th anniversary of the Westminster Assembly.

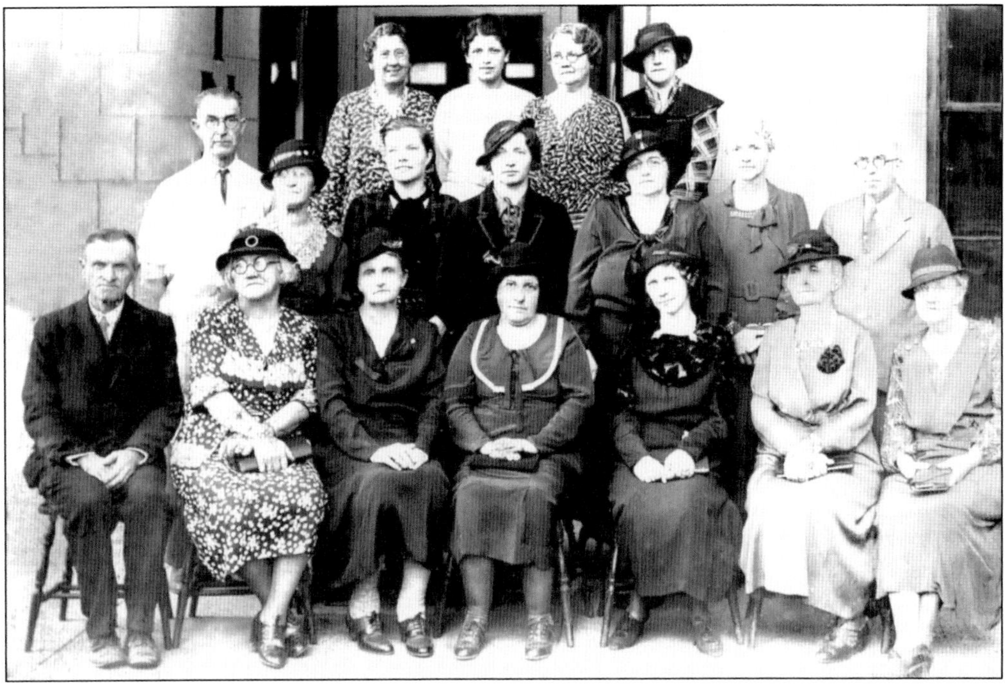

The *Courier* local correspondents, however, managed to restrain their excitement. Longtime Bath photographer C. D. deGroat captured this image.

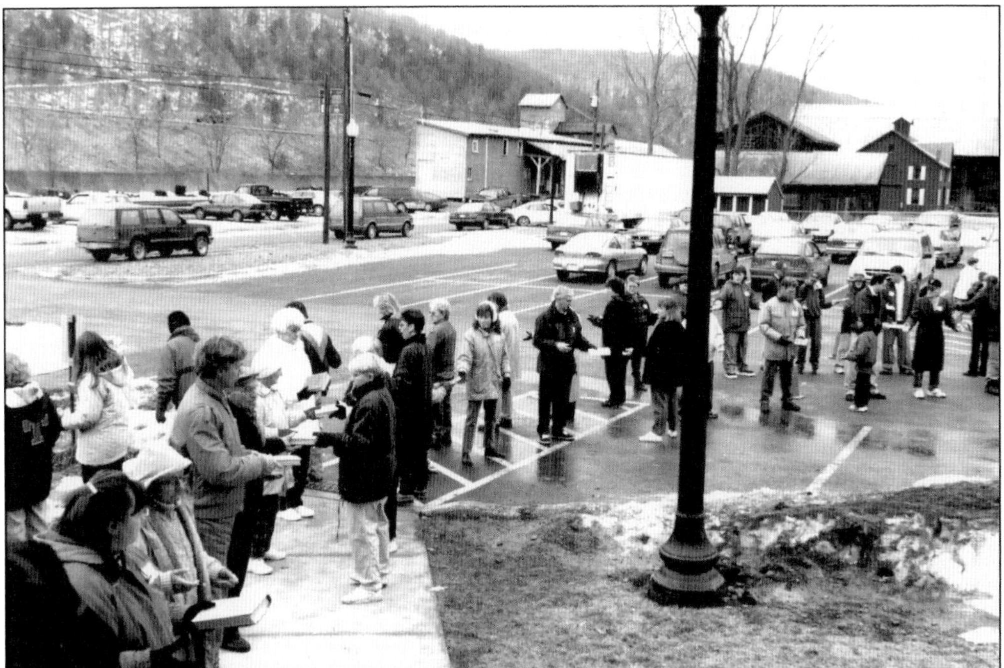

When the library moved across the parking lot from the 1831 Magee House to its new 1998 facility, enthusiastic patrons formed a human chain to move every book in the collection. Magee House then became host for such events as the annual History Fair.

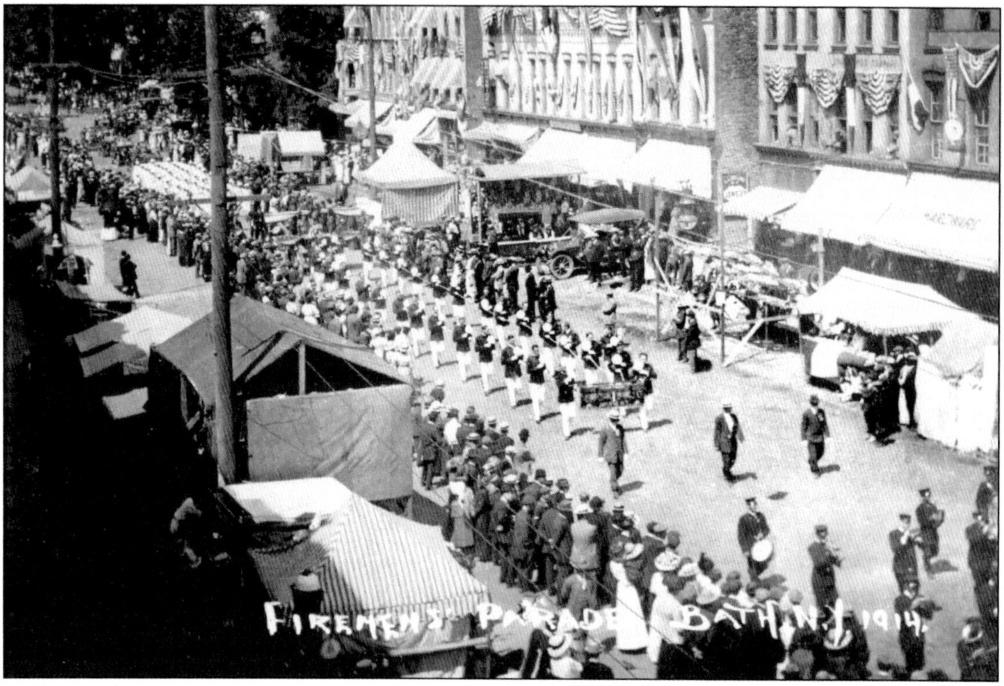

Bath somehow manages to turn the whole town into a celebration ground. The 1914 Firemen's Parade was obviously a major event.

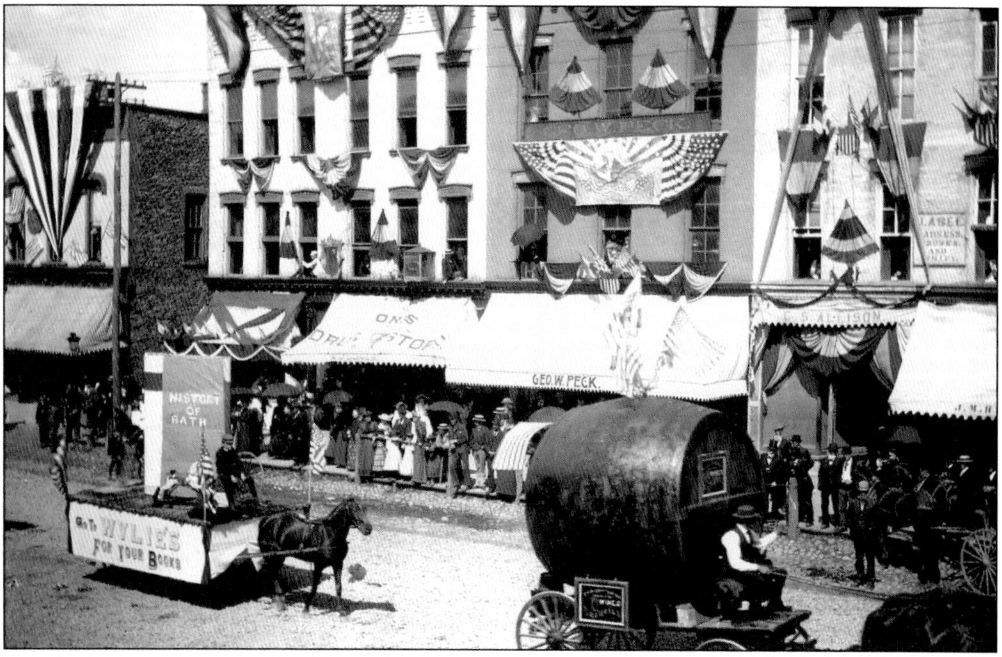

The Bath centennial parade shows that winemaking was already important back then . . . and so were books about Bath history.

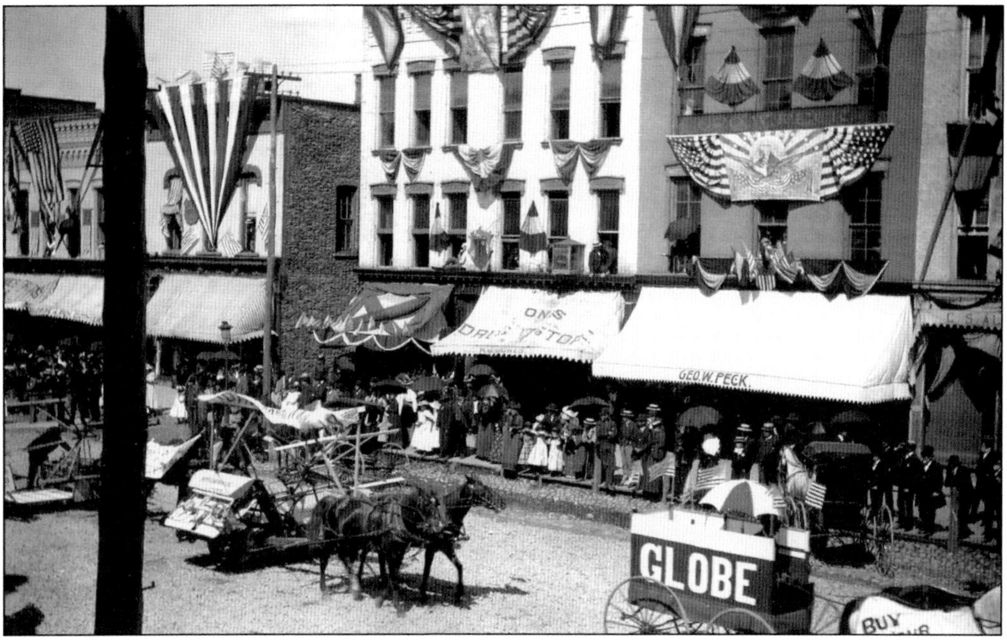

Parades offered a chance to showcase agricultural equipment.

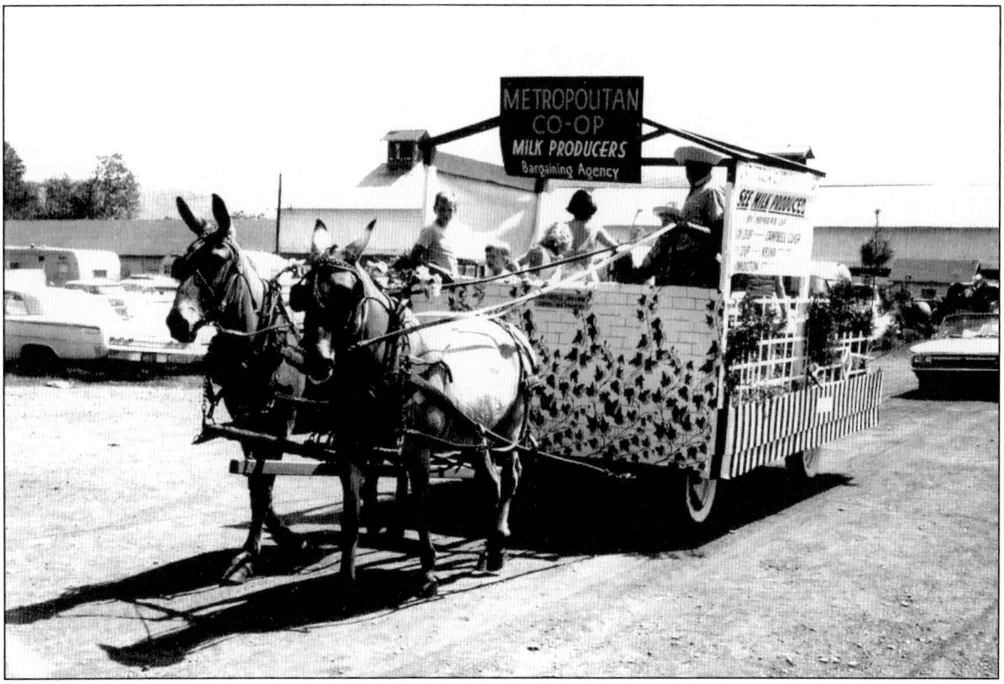

The June Dairy Festival has been a big event for decades. In the early 1960s, Irv Weaver, shown driving, and Levi Weaver imported a mule team for the day and won first prize in the Dairy Parade. In the 1990s, Bath's Warren Hopkins was the perennial winner in the mayor's milking contest. (Courtesy Levi Weaver.)

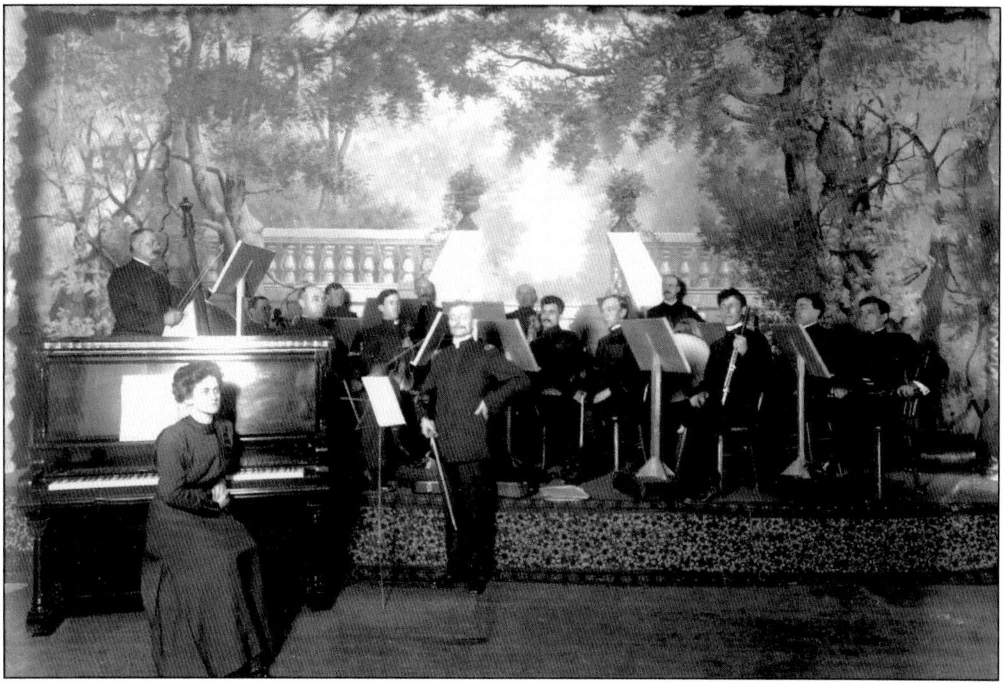

Bath, like many other towns of moderate size, had its own orchestra. (Courtesy Steuben County historian.)

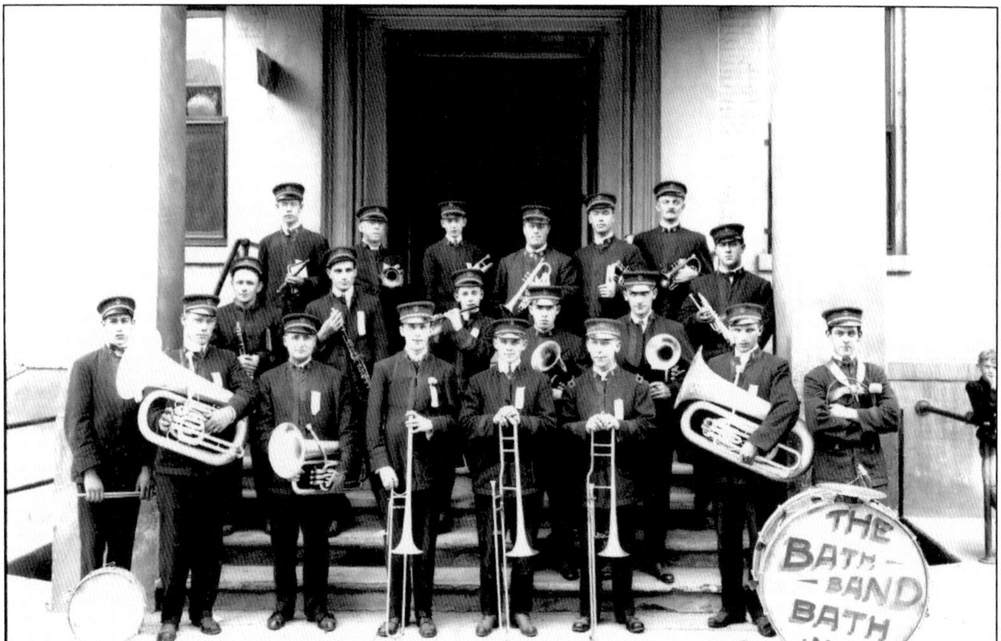

No town was complete without a band. (Courtesy Steuben County Historian's Office.)

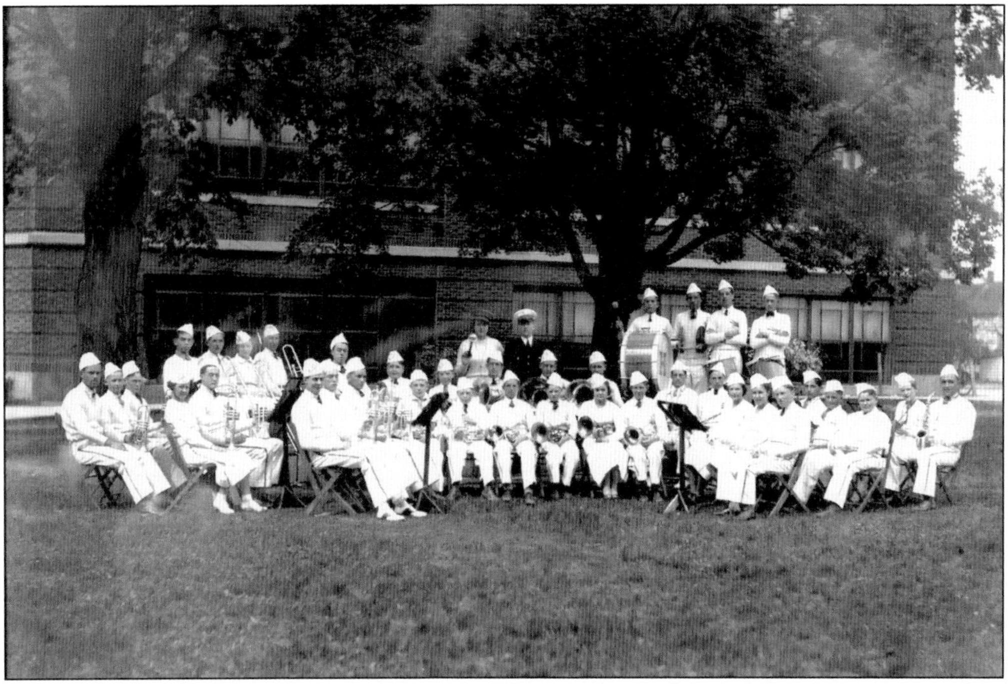

Haverling High created its own band, pictured here in front of the school. (Courtesy Steuben County Historian's Office.)

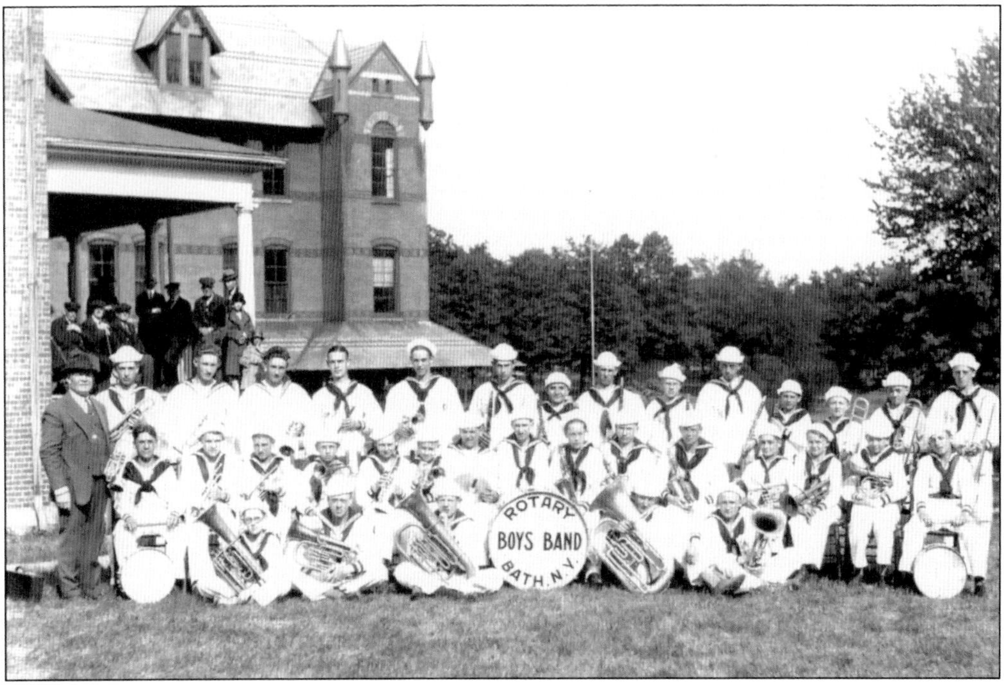

The Boys' Band is no more (perhaps those suits were too much), but the Bath Rotary Club still supports youth programs. (Courtesy Steuben County Historian's Office.)

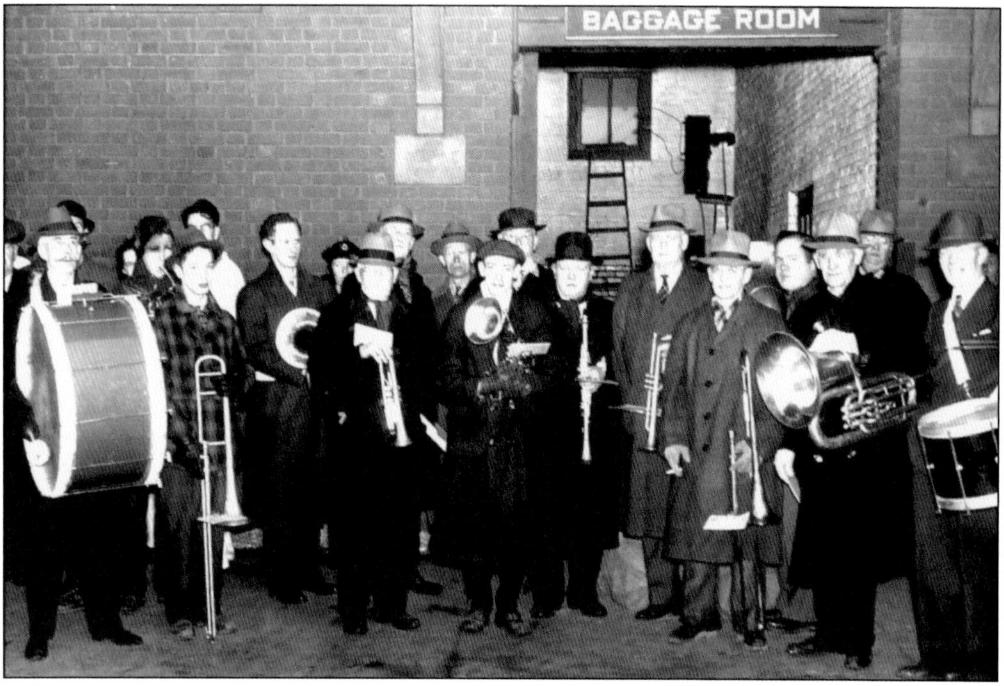

"They're either too young or too old." It was not fun exactly, but the Old-Timer's Band, helped out by a few callow youths, gathered this particular morning to see off Bath's first draft contingent in 1940. The band honored every other departing group for the rest of the war.

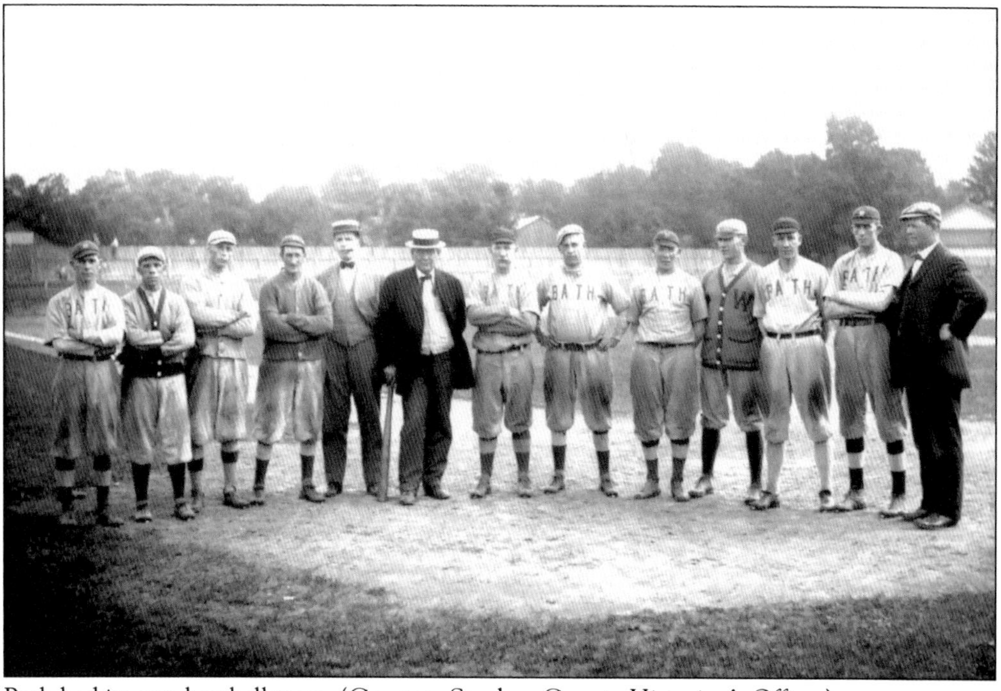

Bath had its own baseball team. (Courtesy Steuben County Historian's Office.)

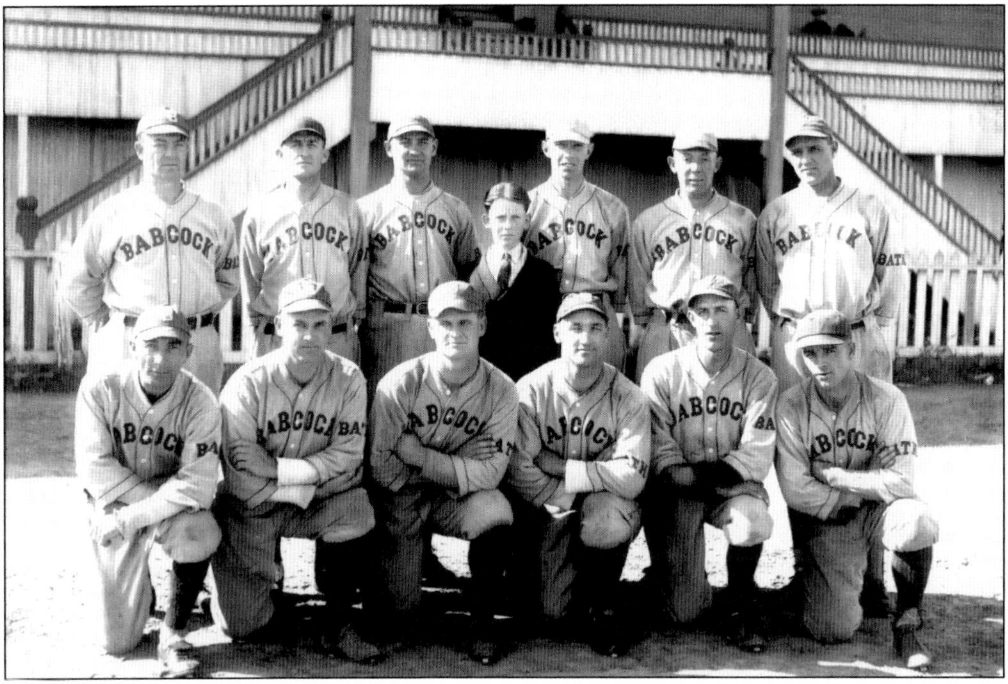

Babcock Ladder, like some other local businesses, sponsored a baseball team. (Courtesy Steuben County Historian's Office.)

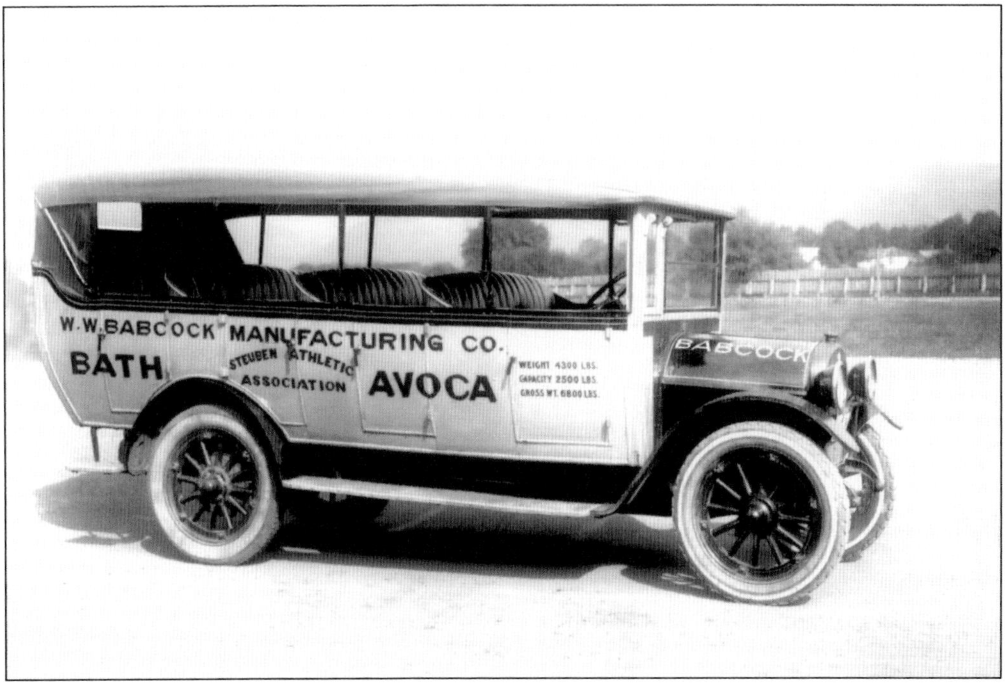

The Babcock Ladder team owned a bus. Not many sponsors were that generous. (Courtesy Steuben County Historian's Office.)

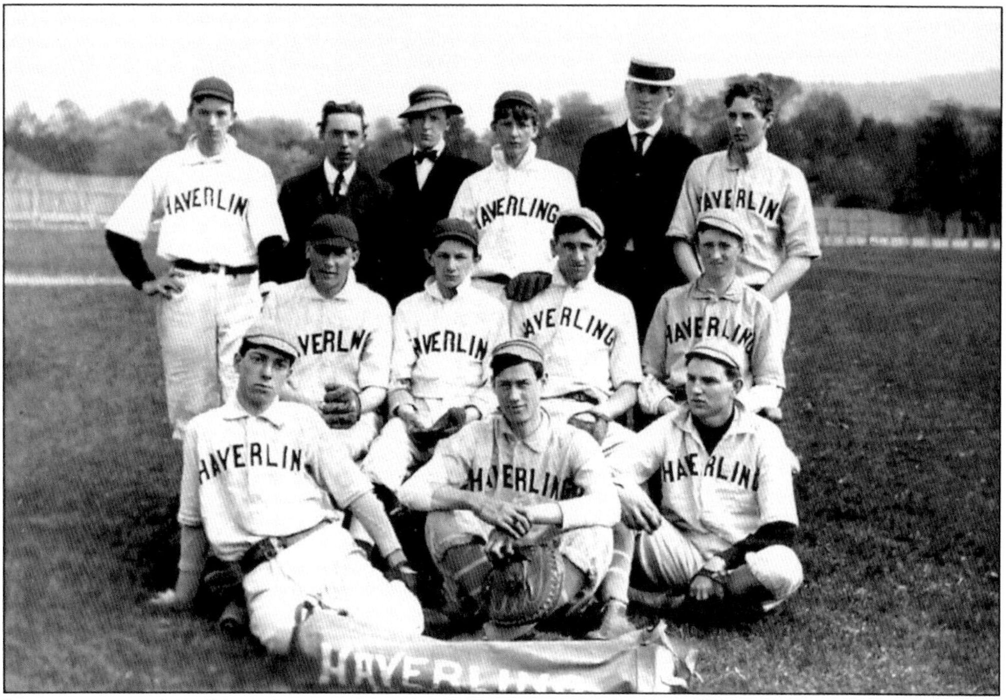

It is not unusual for Haverling sports teams to win sectional titles, although this particular squad seems pretty glum about its prospects.

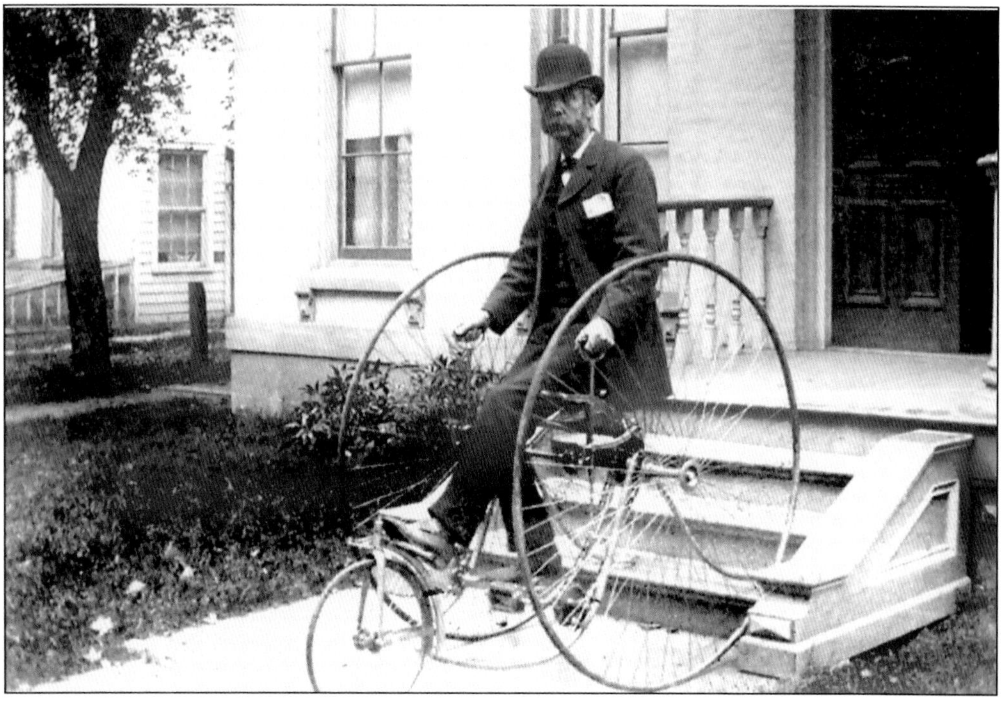
But after all . . . fun is where you find it.

Four

The Girls' Home and the Soldiers' Home

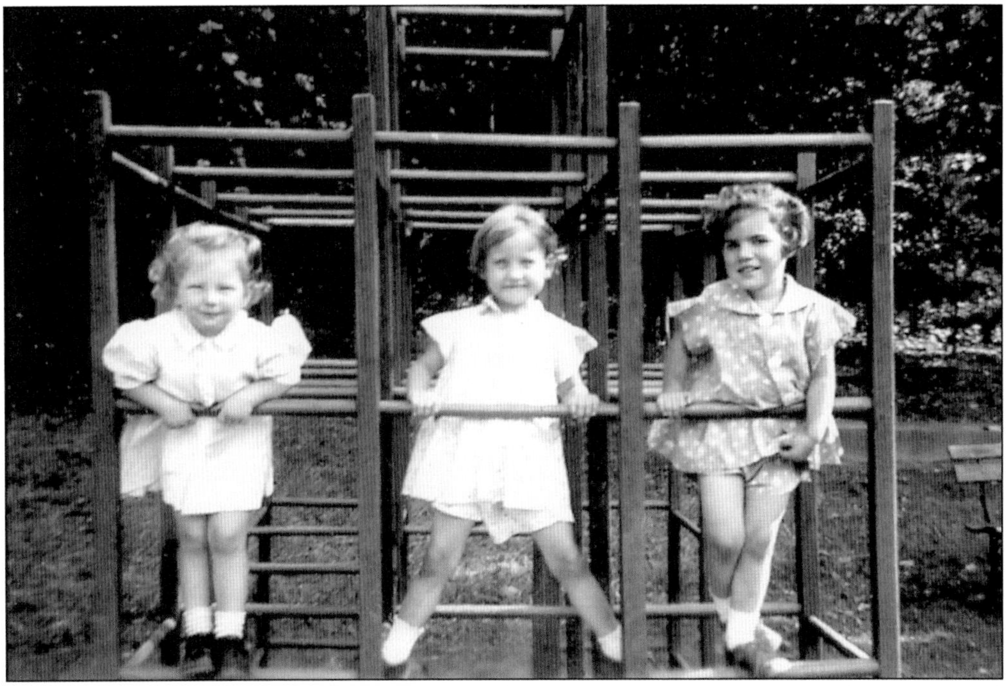

As the county seat, Bath is home to many social service agencies—governmental, religious, and private. Handicapped citizens, recovering veterans, and people in many kinds of need find help . . . and friendly faces . . . in Bath. However, two institutions in particular added special color to life in Bath: the New York State Soldiers' and Sailors' Home, or Bath Soldier's Home, which is now the Bath facility of the Veterans Administration serving veterans from across the Twin Tiers and western New York; and the Davenport Home for Orphan Girls, or the Girls' Home, which no longer exists except in memory and in the legacy left by the Davenport family.

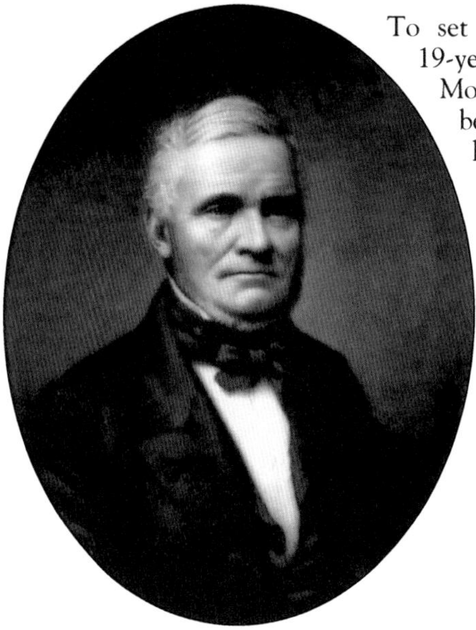

To set up as a Steuben County shopkeeper in 1815, 19-year-old Ira Davenport drove a wagon 300 miles. Moving to Bath 32 years later, he put his wealth to work bettering his community. In 1864, four years before his death, the Davenport Home for Orphan Girls opened its doors.

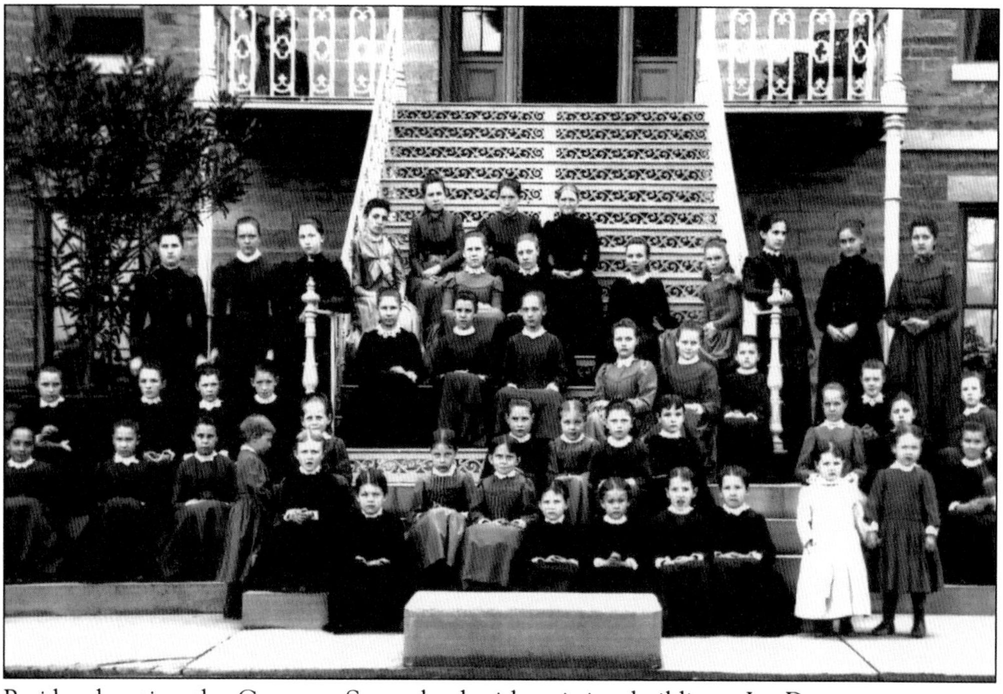

Besides donating the Cameron Street land with existing buildings, Ira Davenport set up a $100,000 endowment and left an additional $50,000 upon his death four years later. His brother Charles Davenport added $30,000 to the endowment. The institution was solidly established by the time these girls were photographed in 1892.

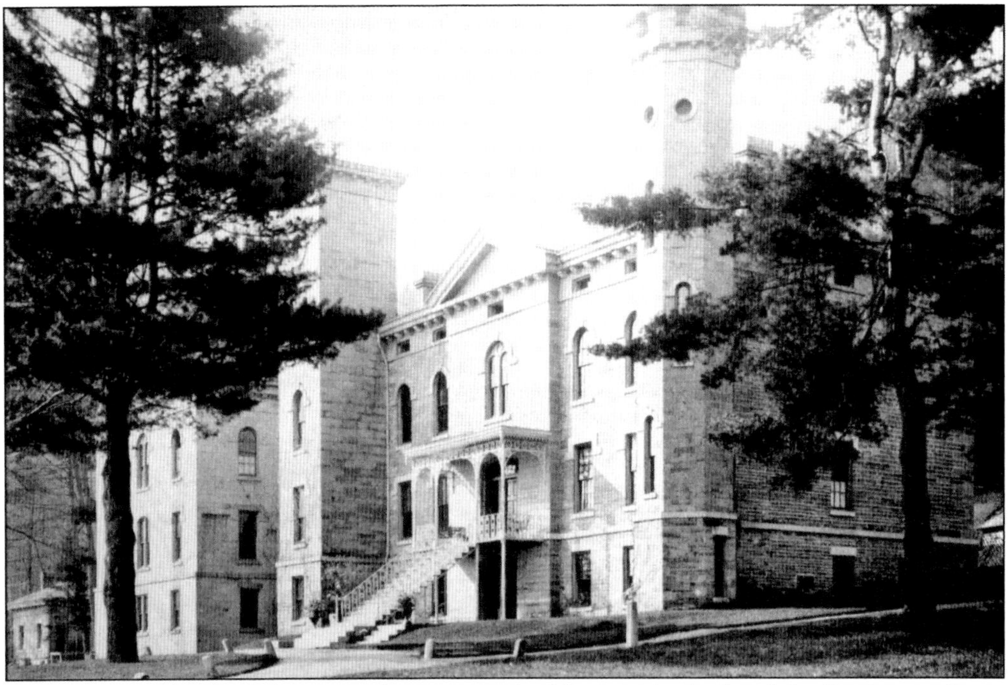

Ira Davenport also funded an entirely new main building on the banks of the Conhocton River near his estate.

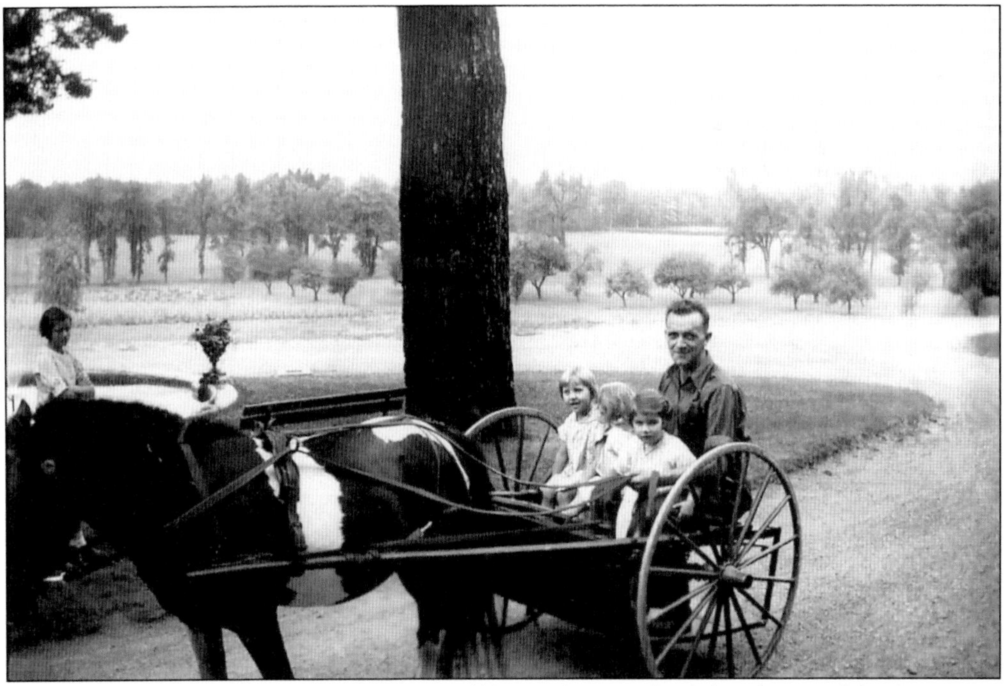

"Davenport girls" still living in the area recall happy lives with adults who cared for them.

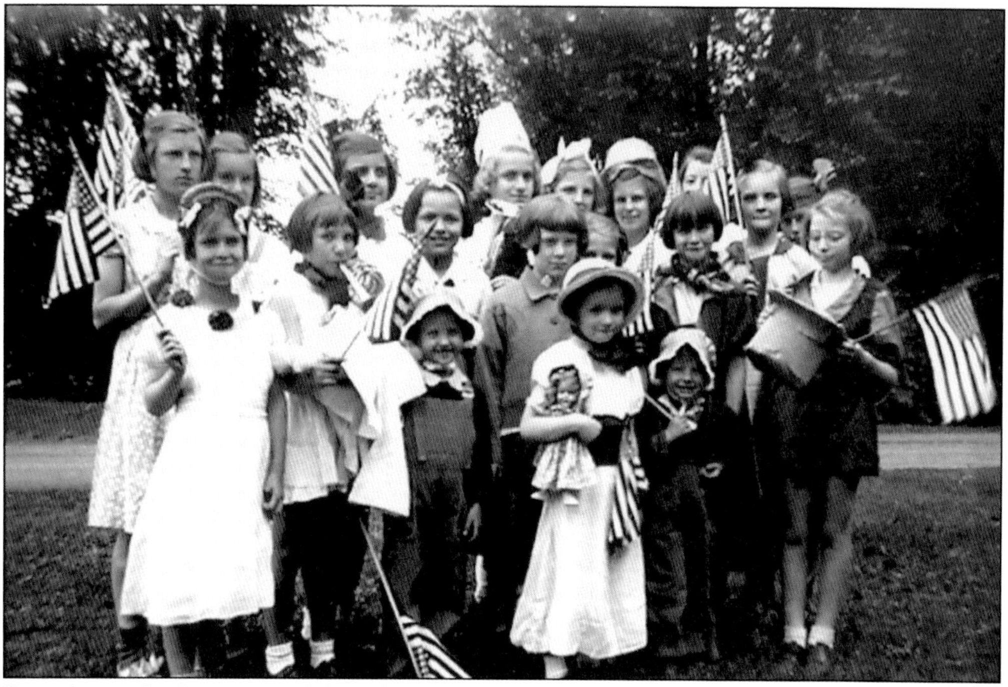

Even during the Depression, life at the Davenport Home included holiday celebrations.

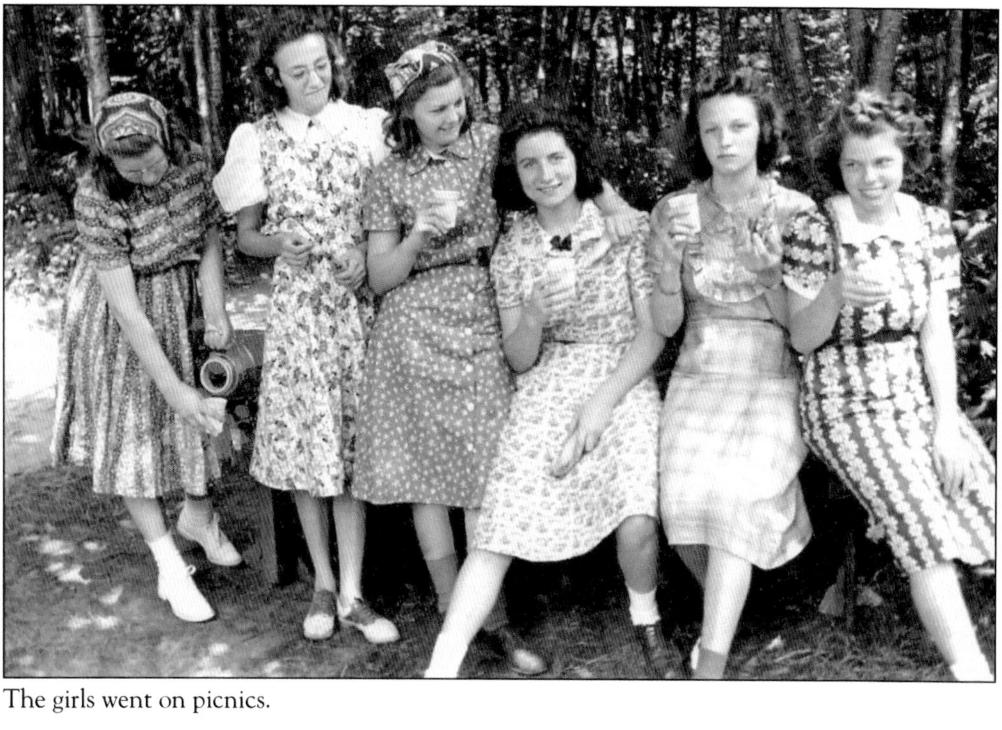

The girls went on picnics.

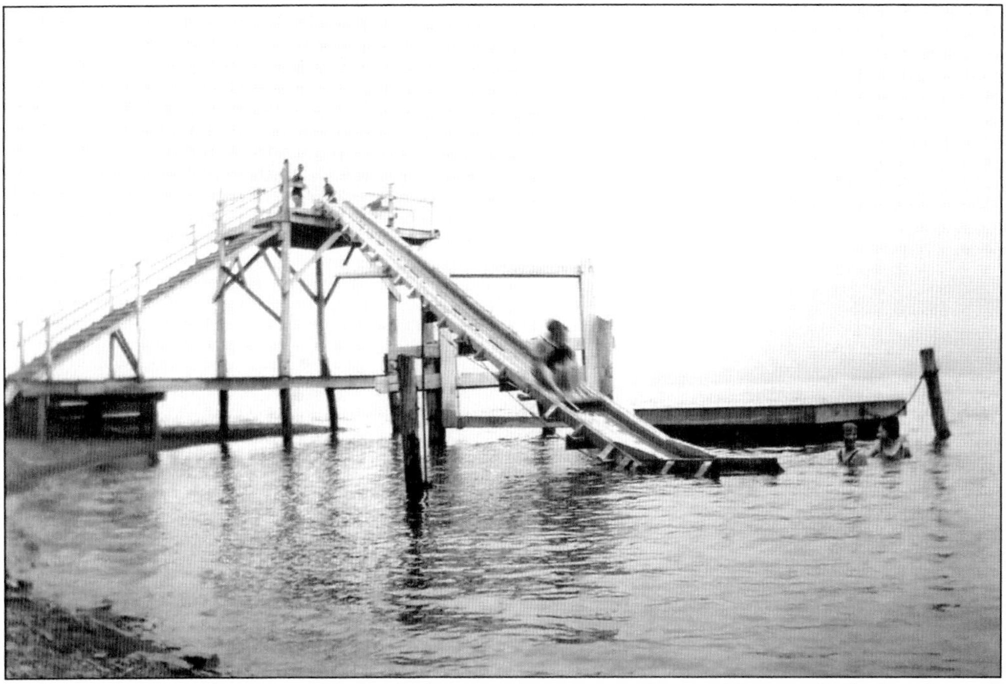

Davenport girls took trips to Keuka Lake, seen here, as well as to Niagara Falls, Letchworth Gorge, and the Thousand Islands.

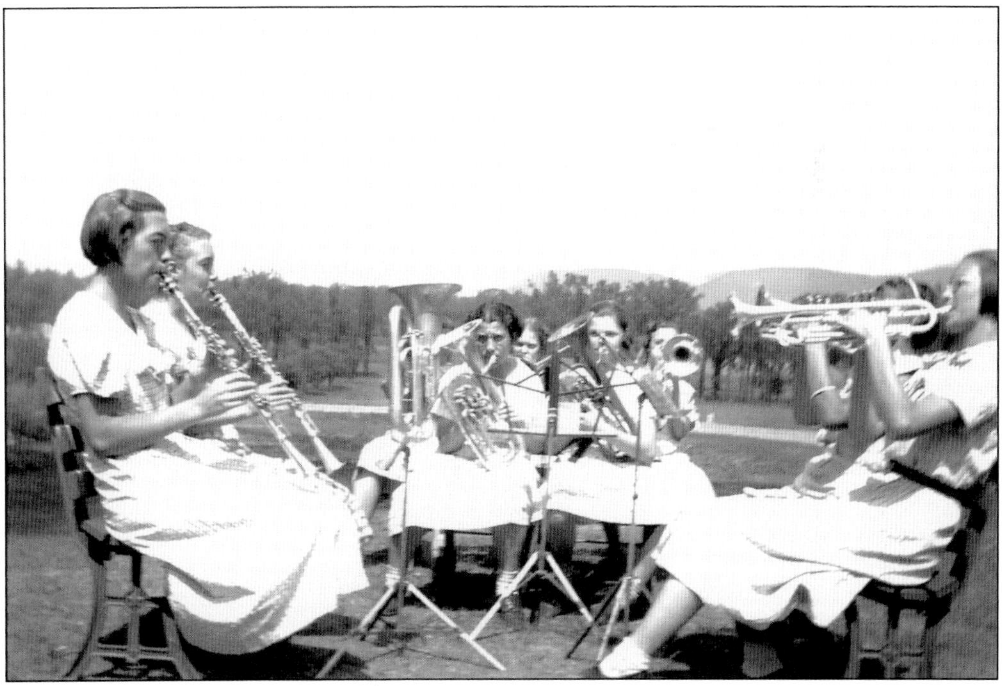

They performed in musical ensembles.

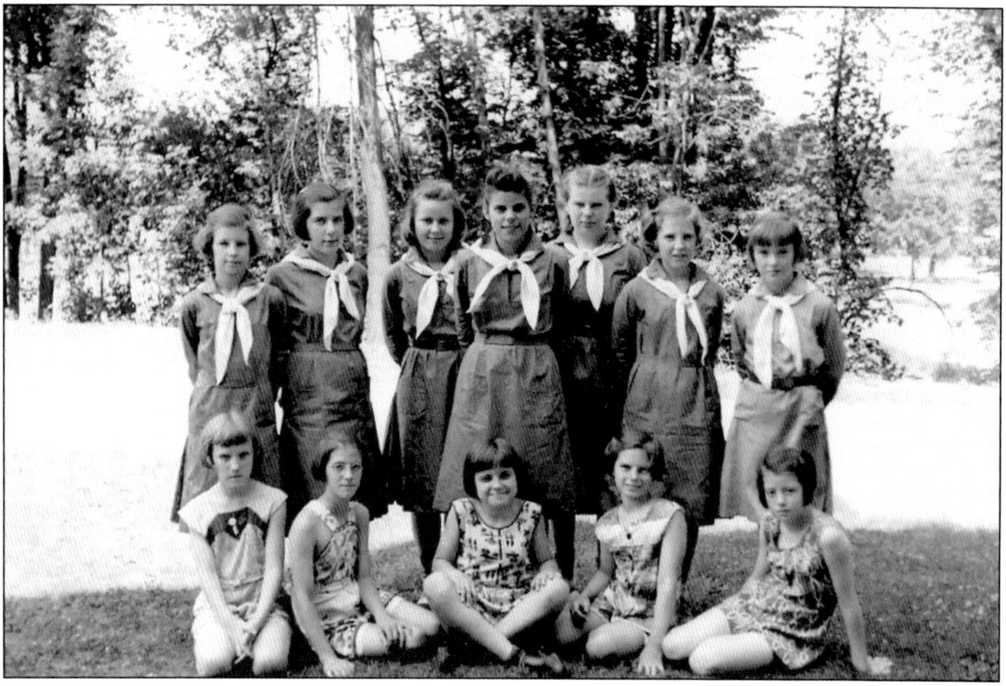

The Davenport Home sponsored Scouting activities for Silver Birch Troop 7139.

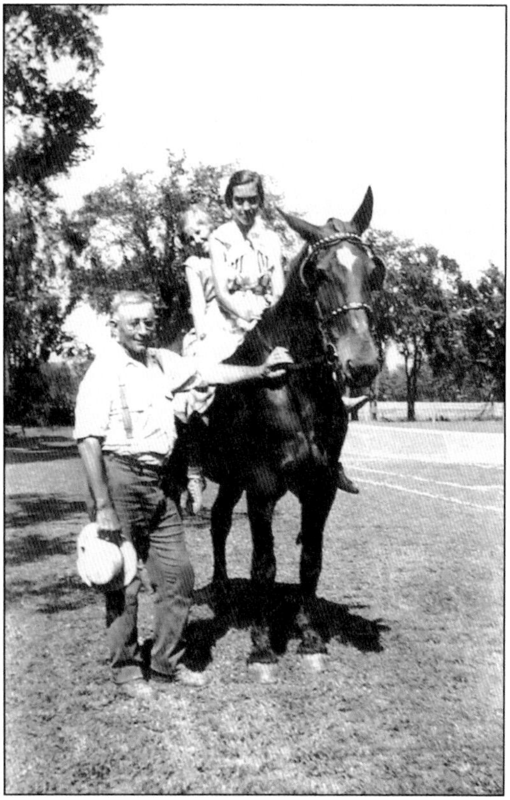

The girls went horseback riding.

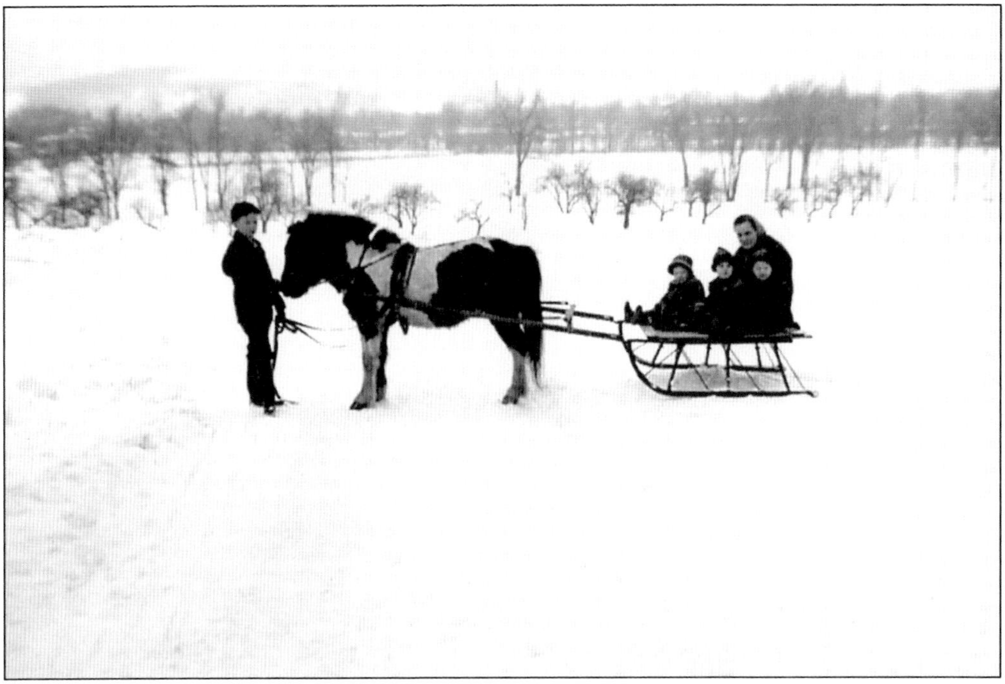

Davenport girls went for sleigh rides in winter.

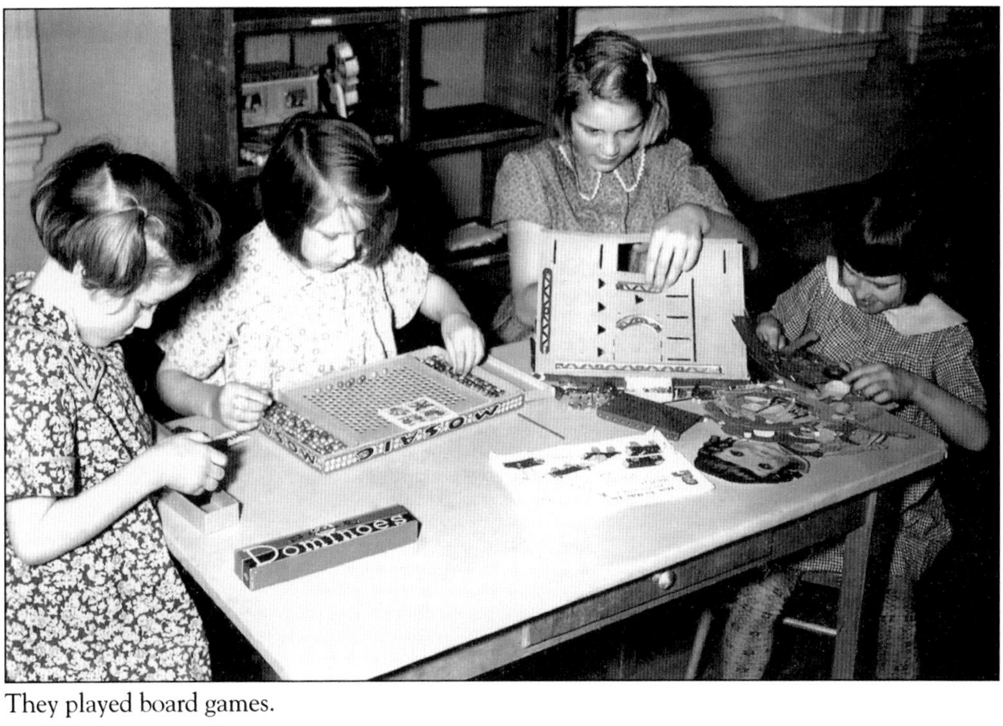

They played board games.

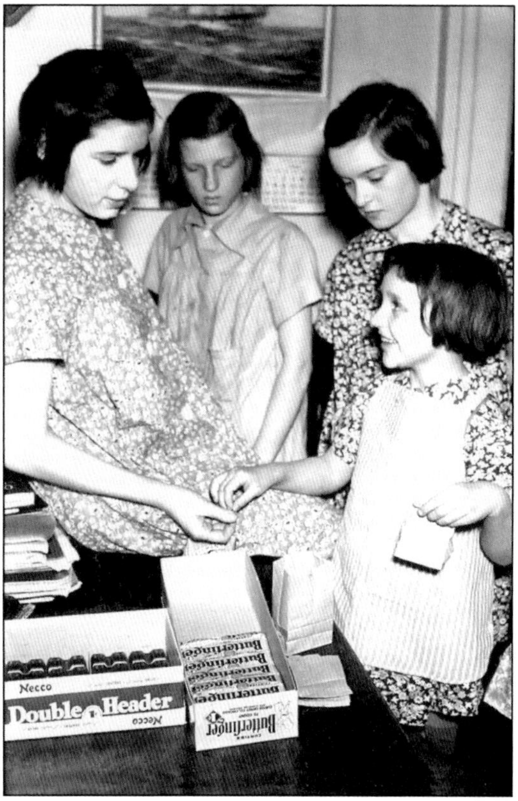

At the Davenport Home, girls learned business education.

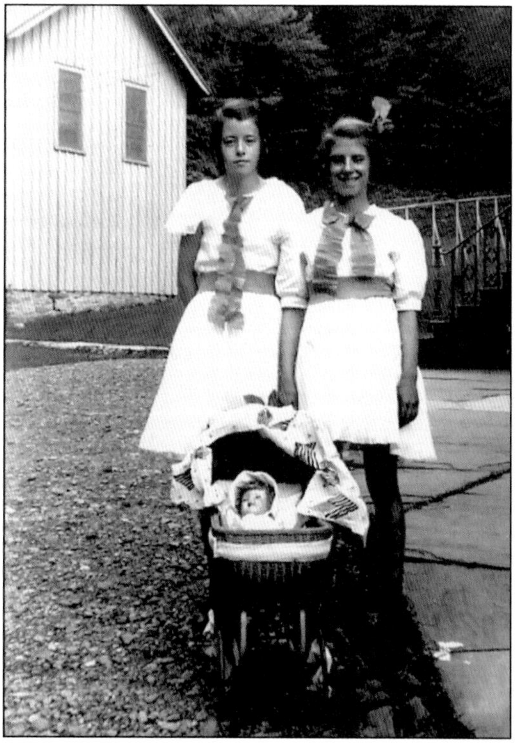

They enjoyed dressing up.

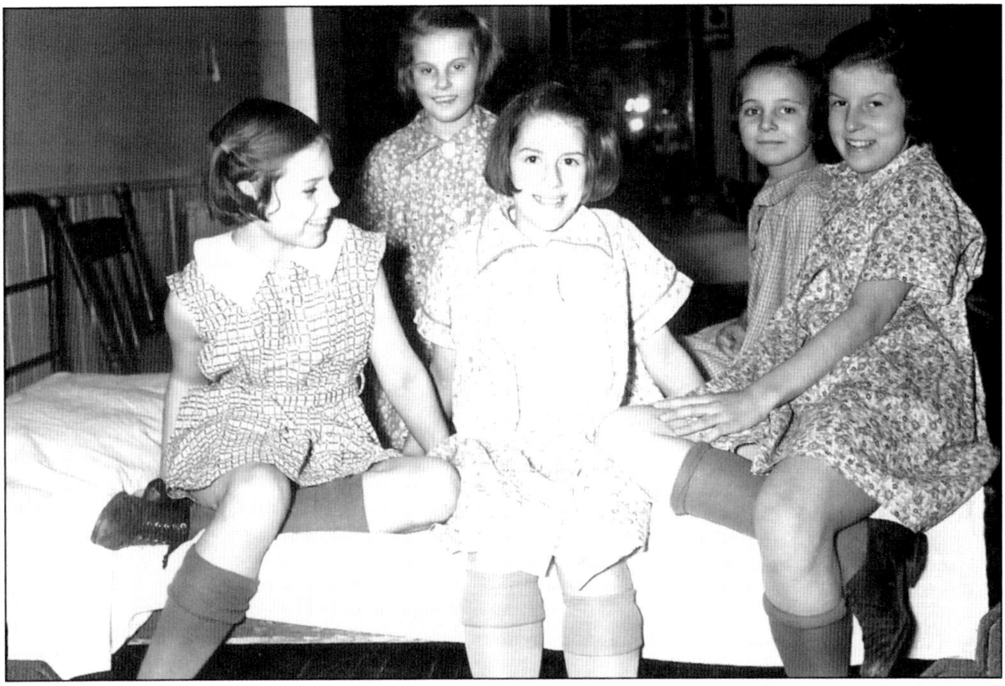

Girls at the Davenport Home made friends. Perhaps lights out was not always strictly observed.

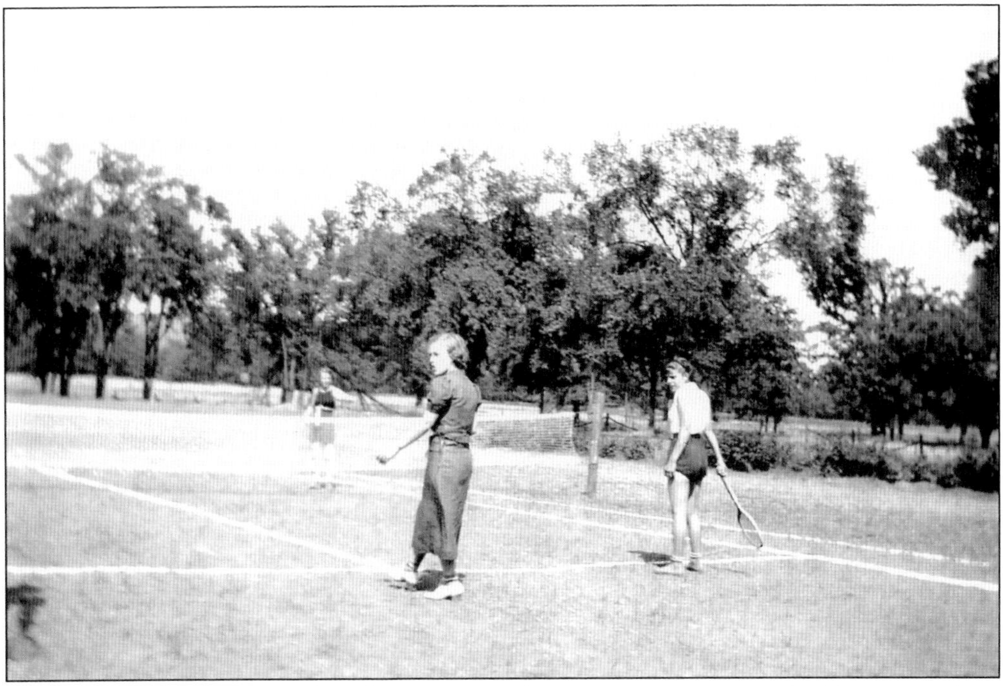

The girls and their teachers played tennis. Betty Daniels and her partner doubled against Miss Young (front left) and Hannah Mae Rozelle.

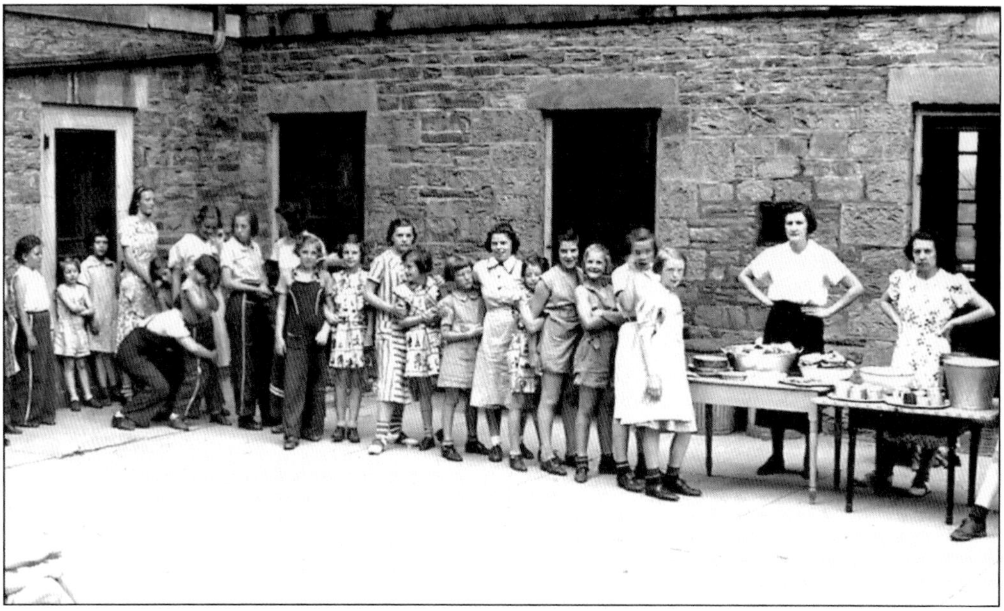

The girls remembered frequent visits from young men, not just because it is in the nature of young men to make such calls. The boys were acutely aware that everyone at the Davenport Home ate very well.

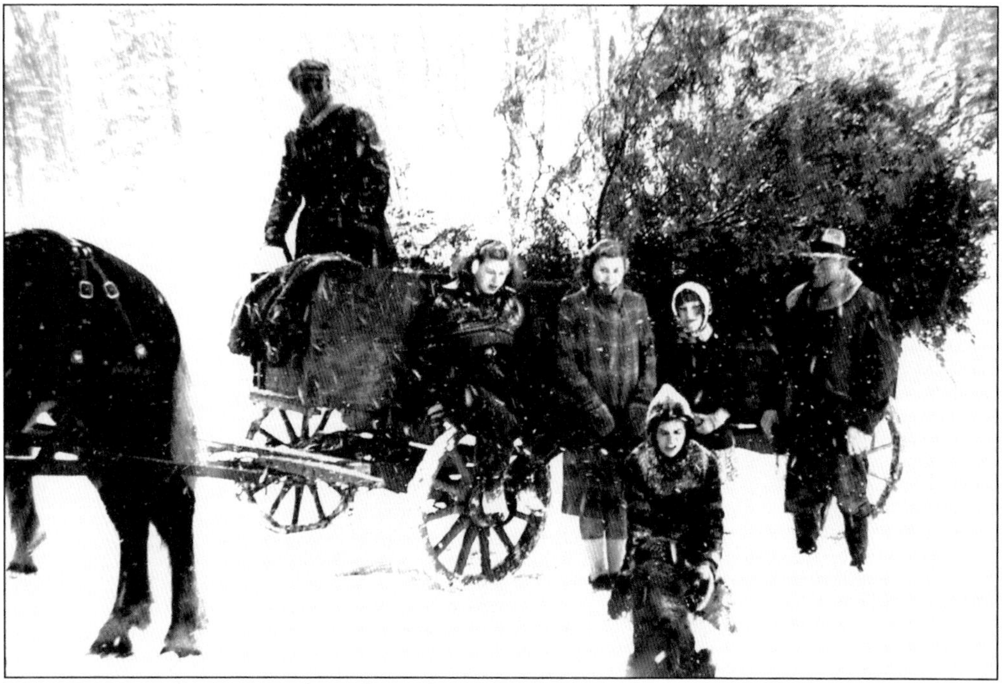

Mr. Kinsman and Mr. Frazier brought in the tree one year, assisted by Jean, Martha, Frances, and Hannah Mae. Christmas in an orphanage must have been tinged with a certain sadness.

Even so, the Davenport staff always did its best to ring in holiday cheer. Note that most of the girls received dolls for Christmas.

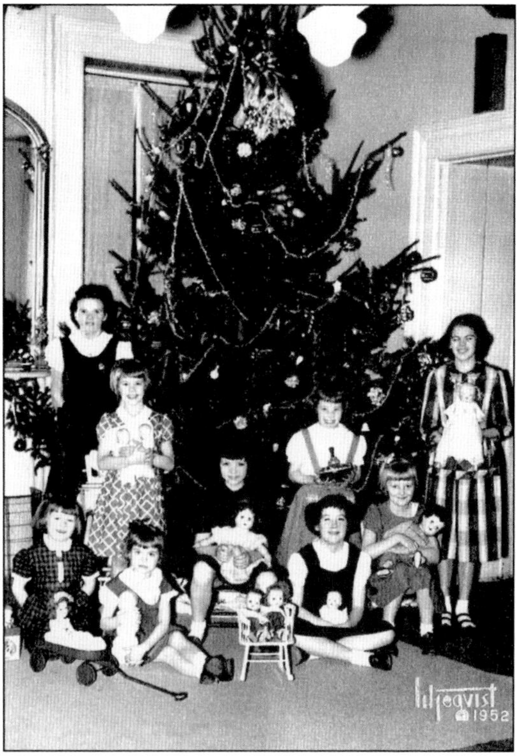

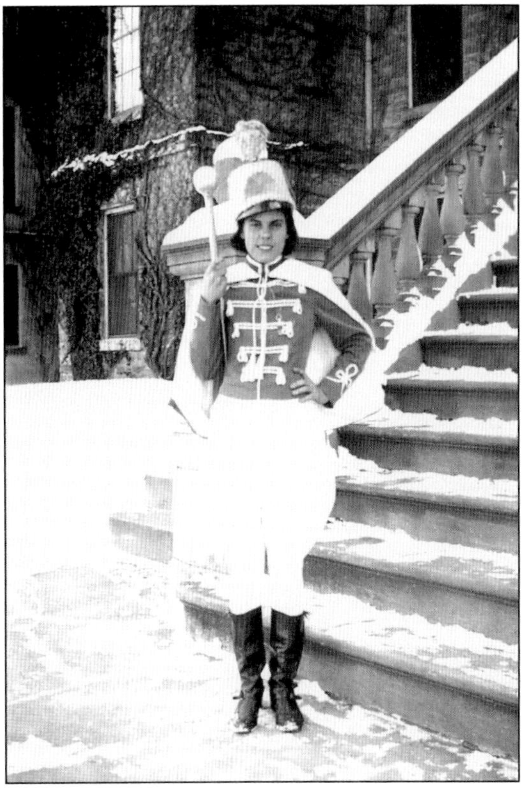

Strolling or riding across the bridge to the village, Davenport girls fit right in to school, church, and community life. Hannah Mae Rozelle was a Haverling drum majorette in 1939.

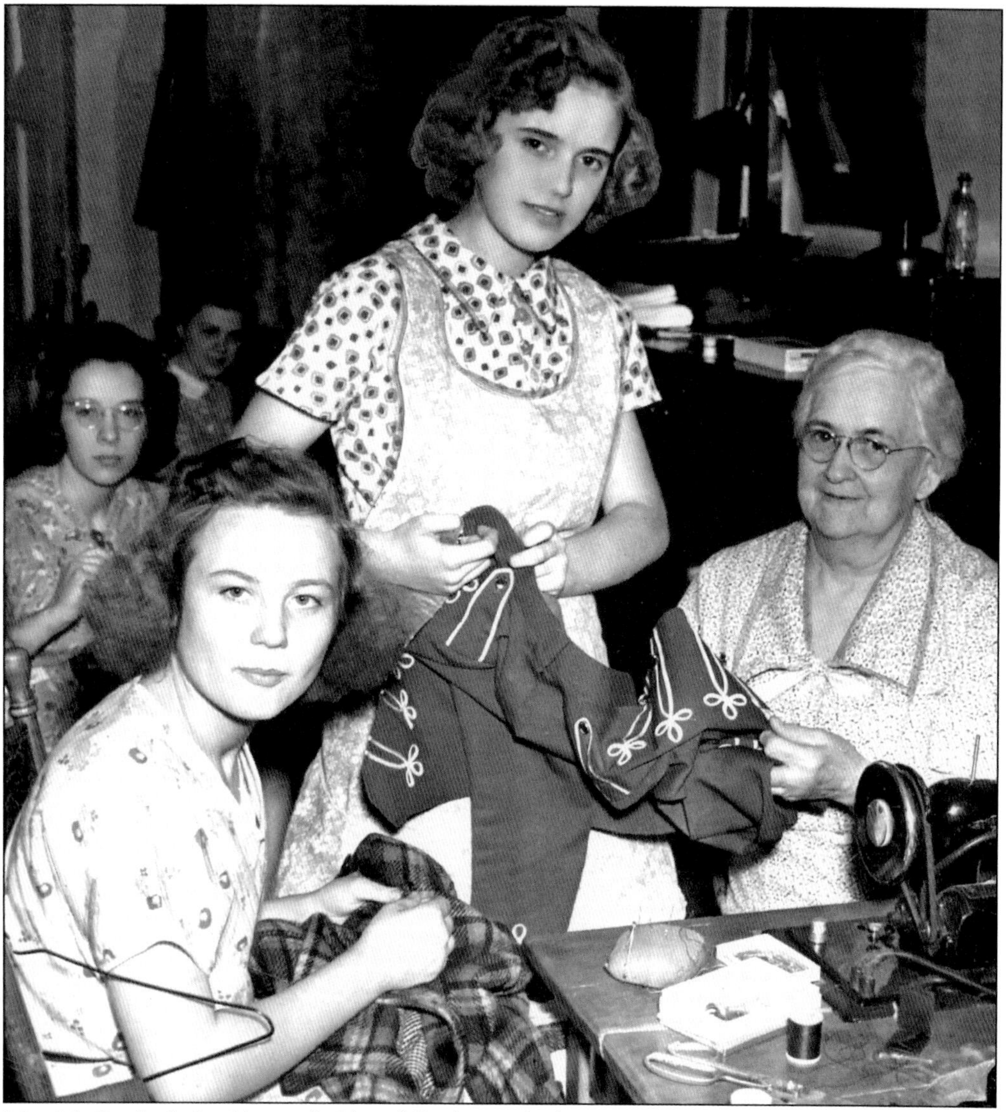

Miss McCarthy helps Vergie (left) and Roslyn with their sewing.

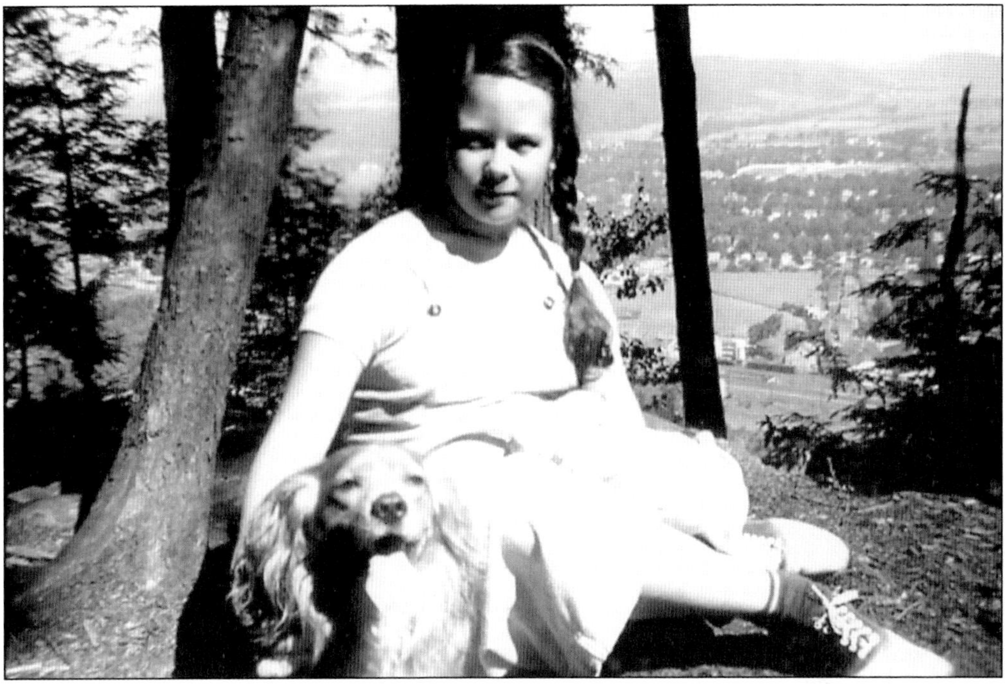

Mossy Bank was part of the Davenport estate.

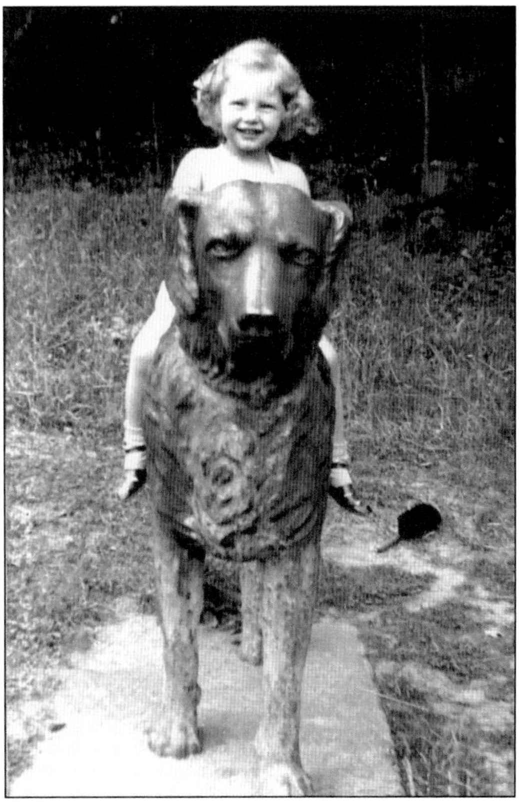

Even the newest girl found she was welcome.

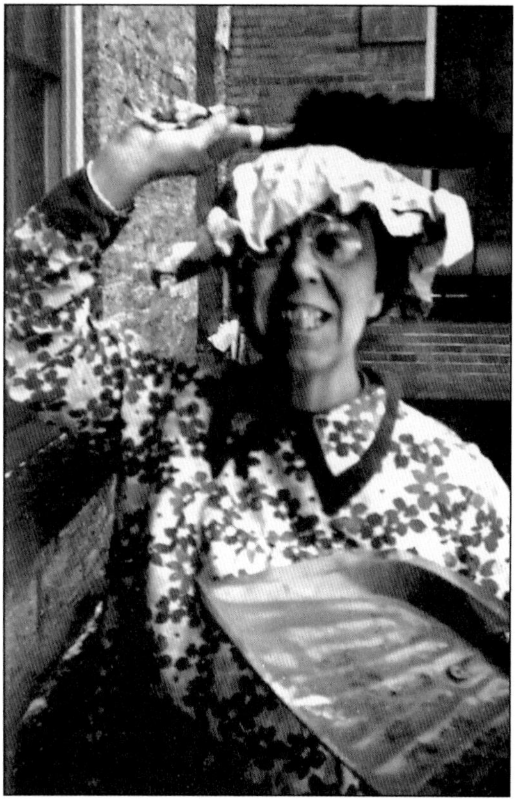

Staff members of the Davenport Home obviously maintained a sense of humor.

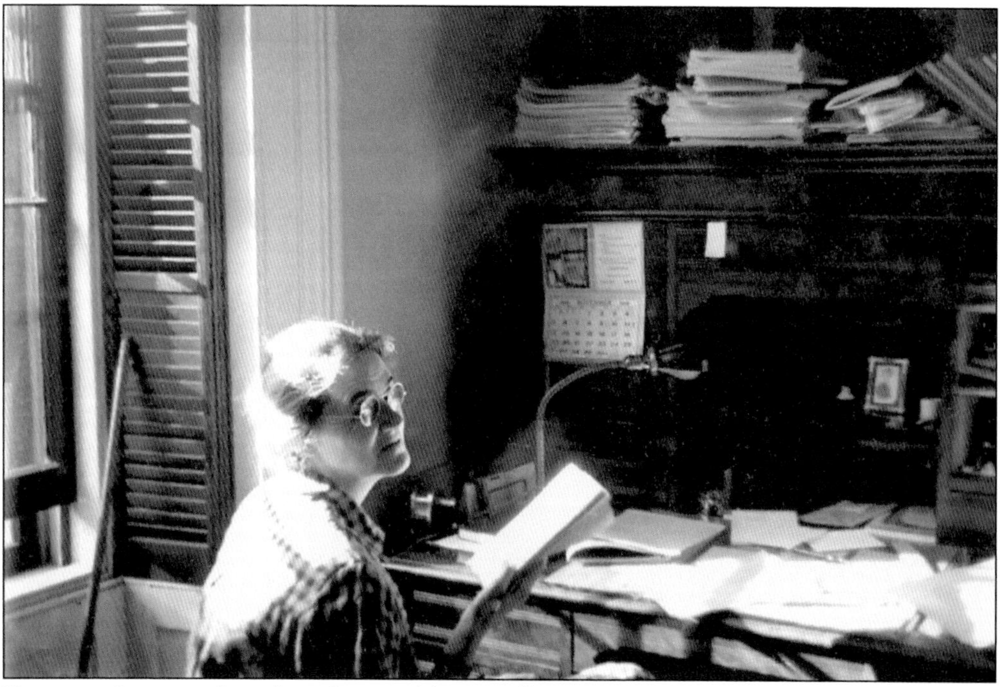

However, they must have been businesslike as well.

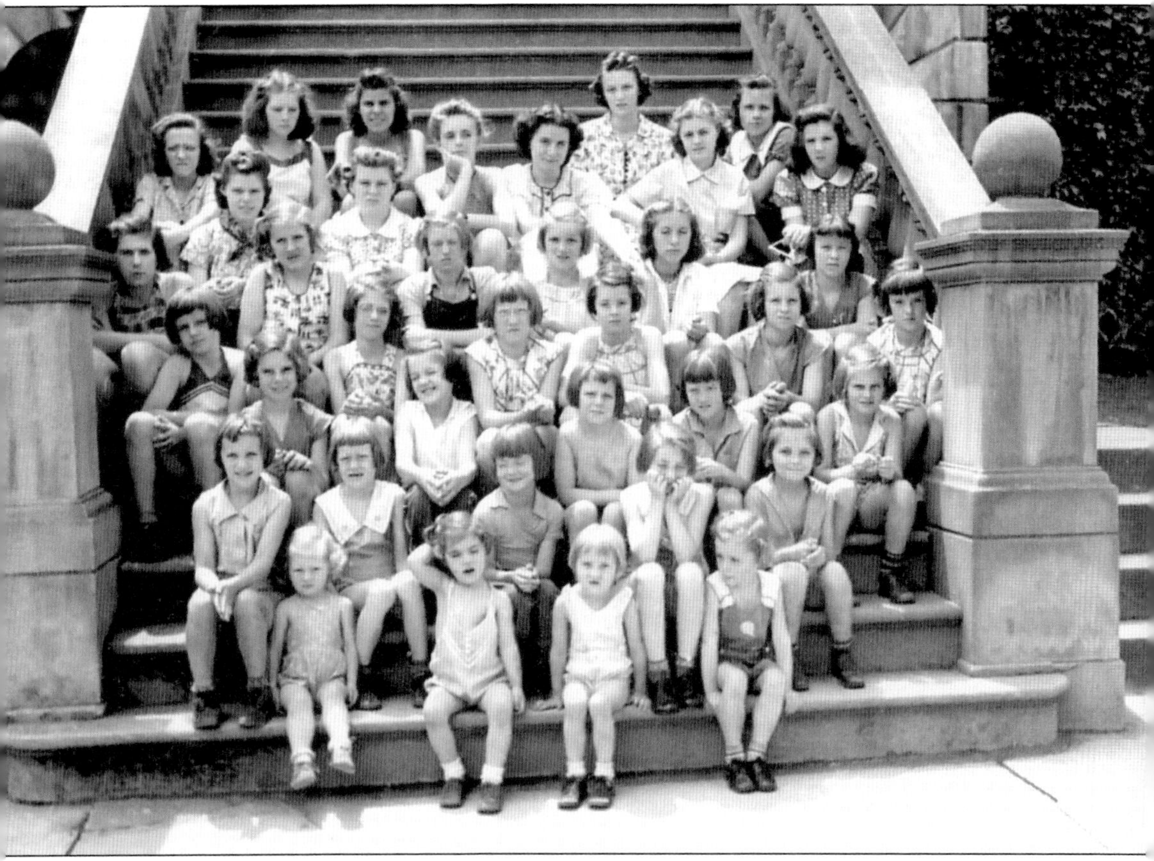

Compare this 1930s gathering with the 1892 photograph on page 90 to see how styles changed and how people became more relaxed in front of cameras.

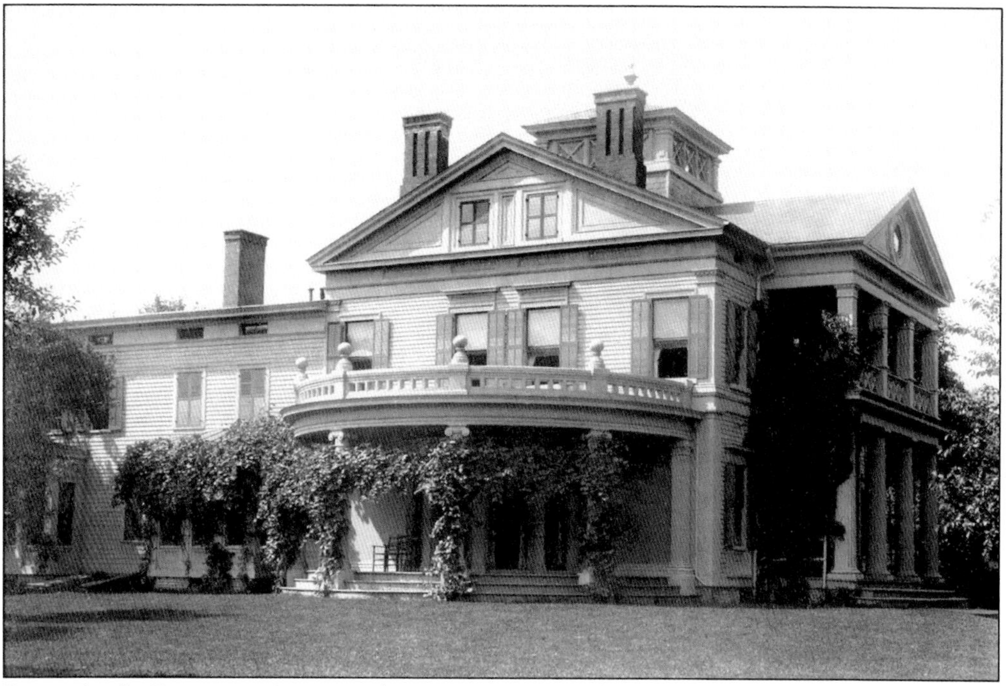
Riverside, the Davenports' own residence, was a remarkable mansion.

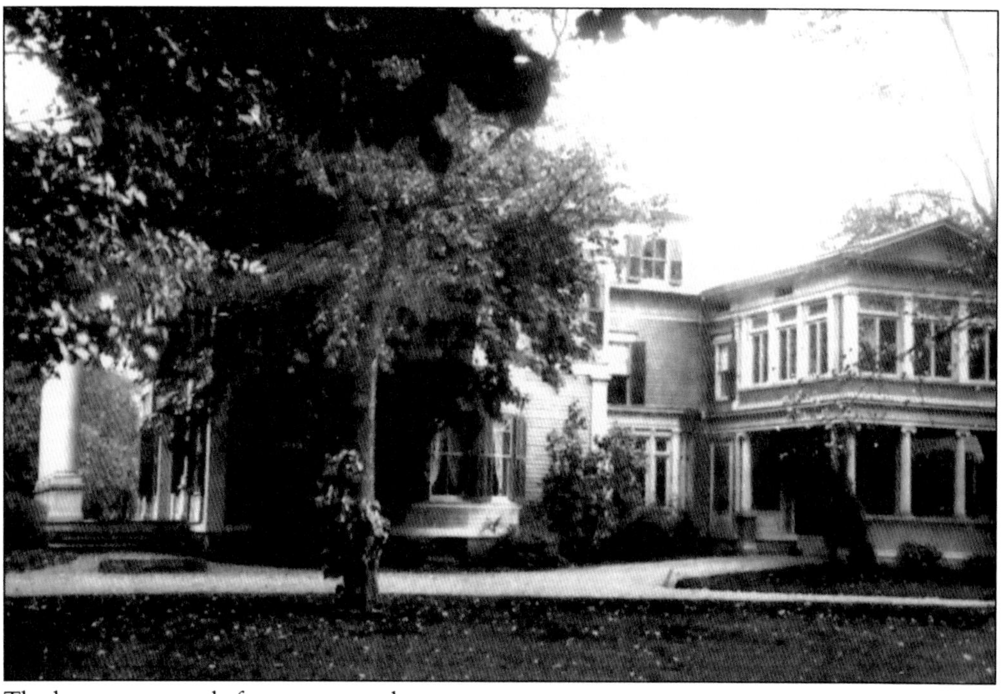
The house was stately from every angle.

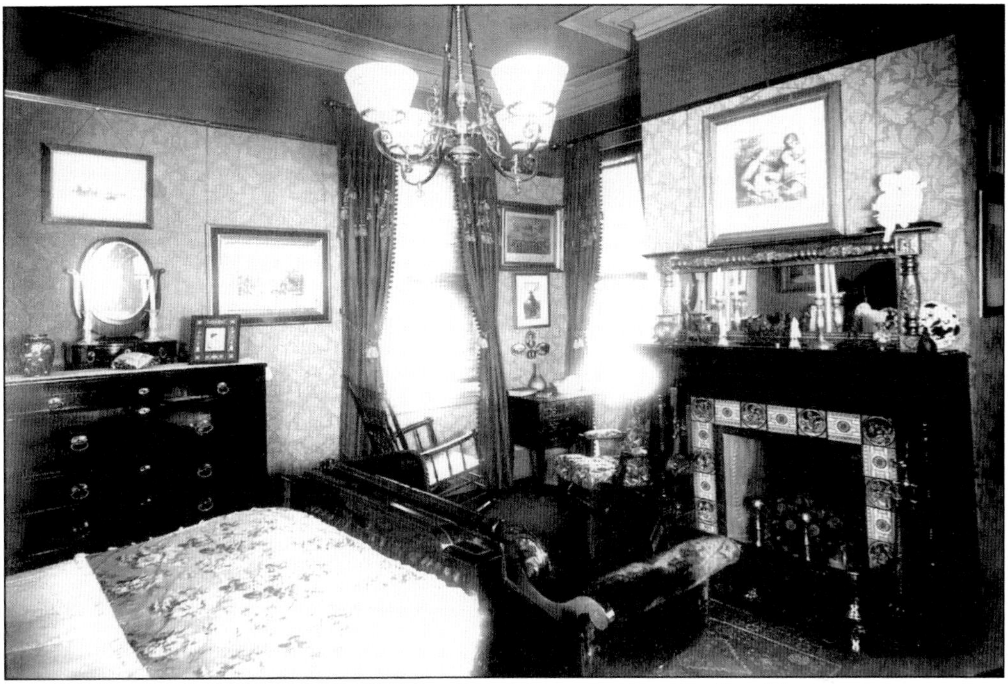

Interiors were predictably opulent and, in those Victorian days, predictably ornate.

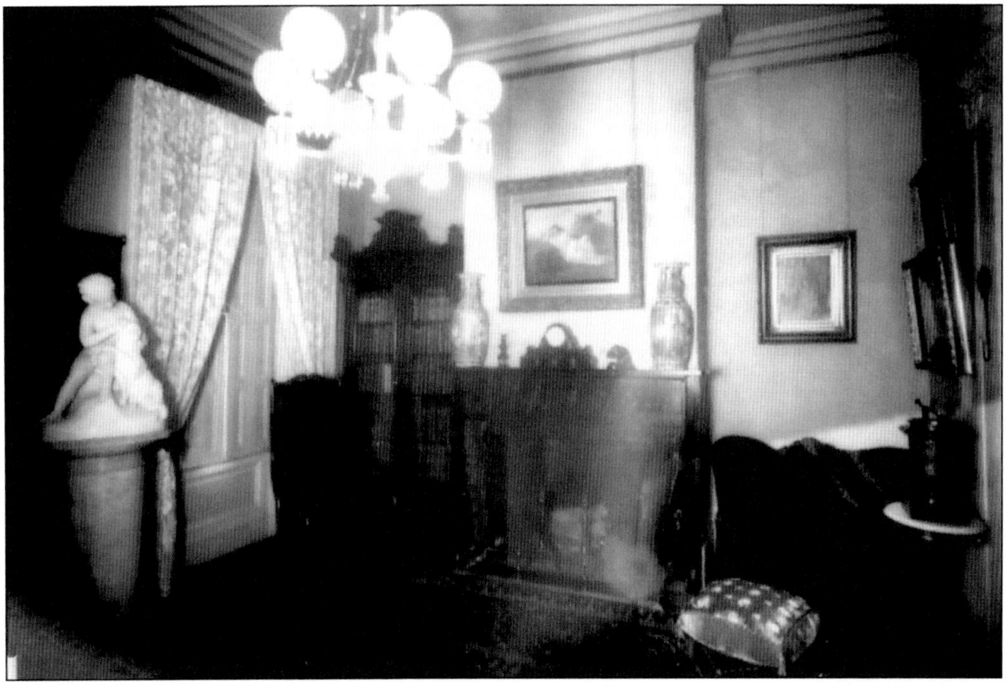

Some of the small statuary is now in the Davenport Hospital, where it memorializes the family that gave so much to Bath.

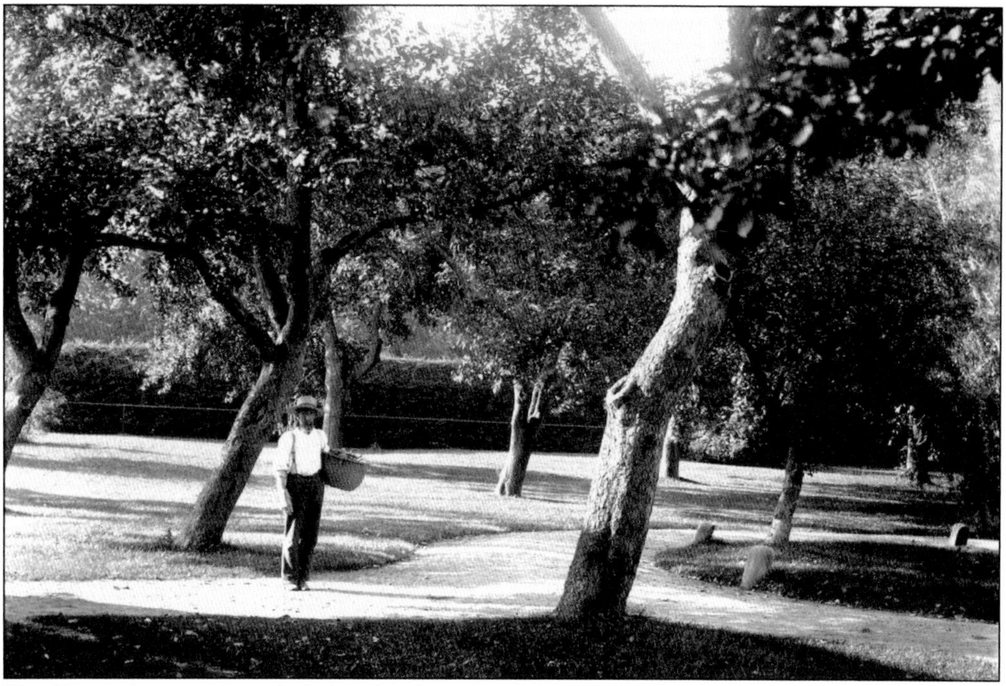

The Riverside grounds included orchards.

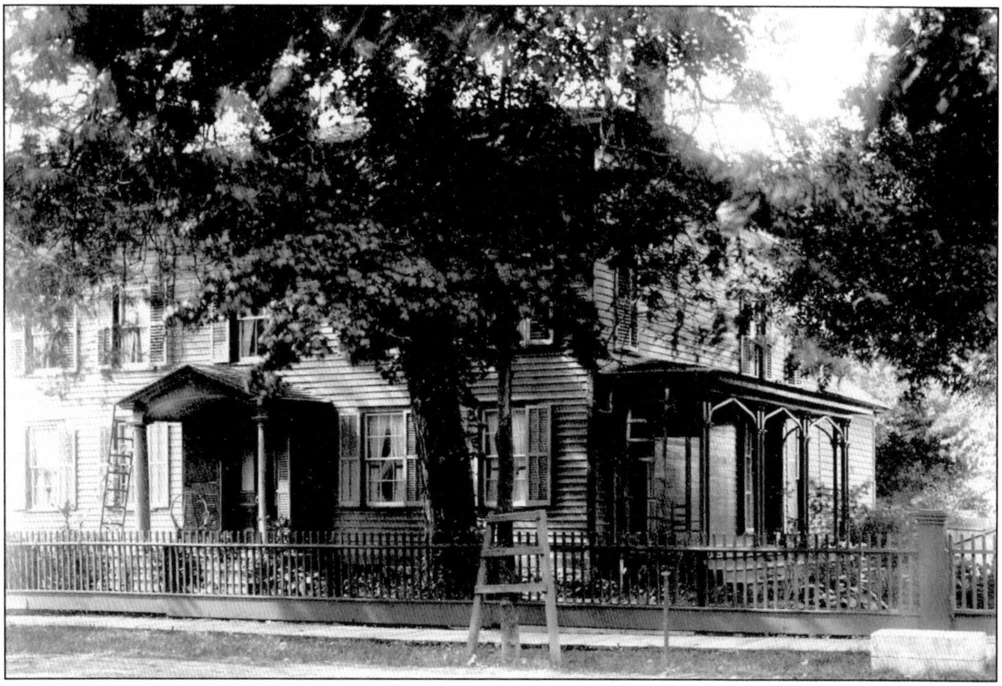

Elm Cottage was also located on the estate. The house is gone, but the name is preserved in the Steuben County Historical Society's museum, on the lowest level of the Magee House.

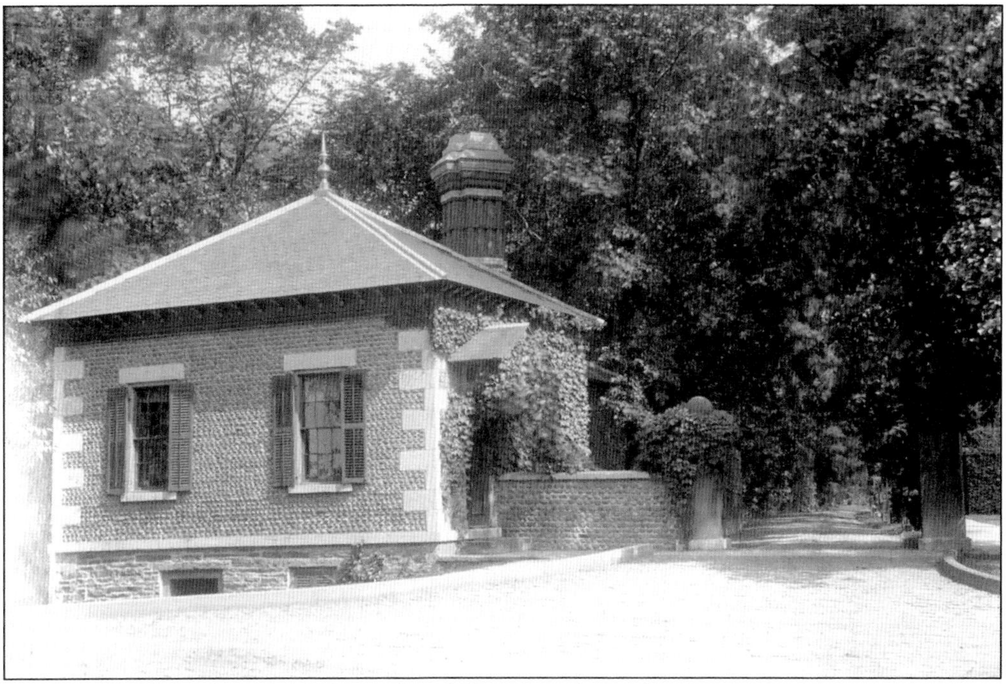

The Riverside gatehouse, made with cobblestones from the river, was once a prominent landmark.

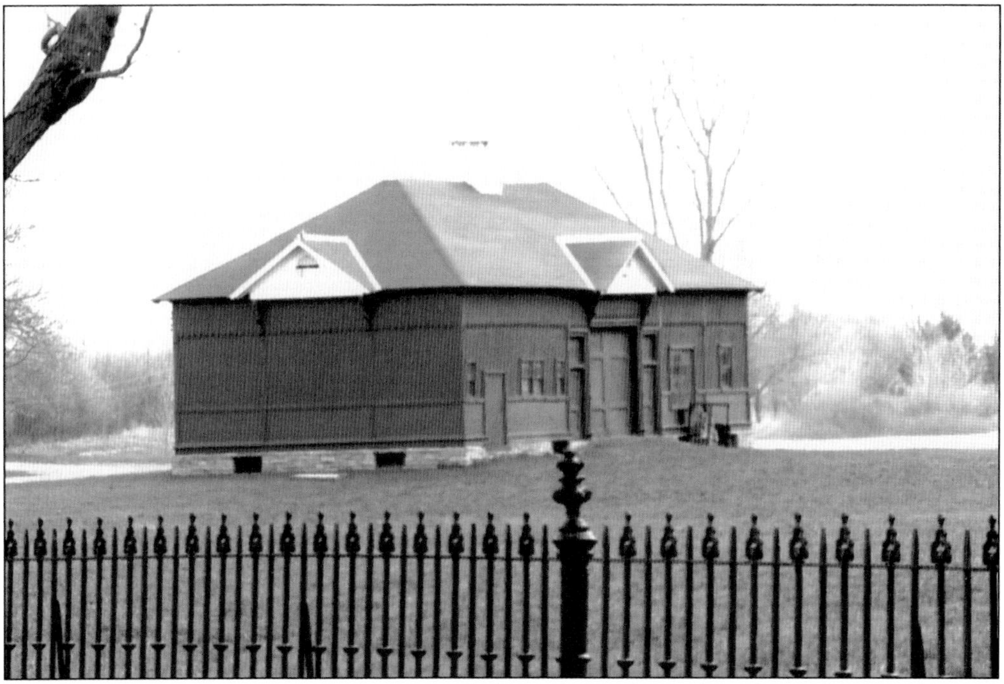

Times changed, and the carriage house is all that is left today. When the orphanage closed in 1959, trustees transferred the endowment to the proposed new Bath hospital, which changed its prospective name from Lakeview to Ira Davenport Memorial. The family's generosity preserves the name throughout the area.

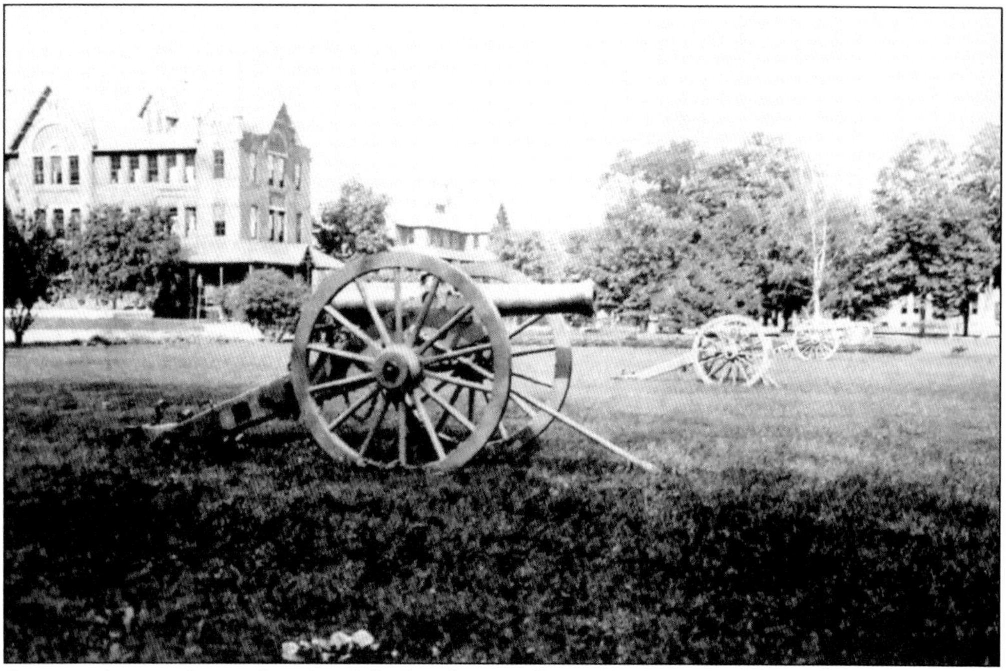

State residents indignantly refused the legislature's first attempt to set up an asylum for distressed Civil War veterans, insisting that they would care for their own. In 1878, however, the New York State Soldiers' and Sailors' Home was built on the Conhocton River at the edge of Bath. Local residents promoted the site by donating $23,000.

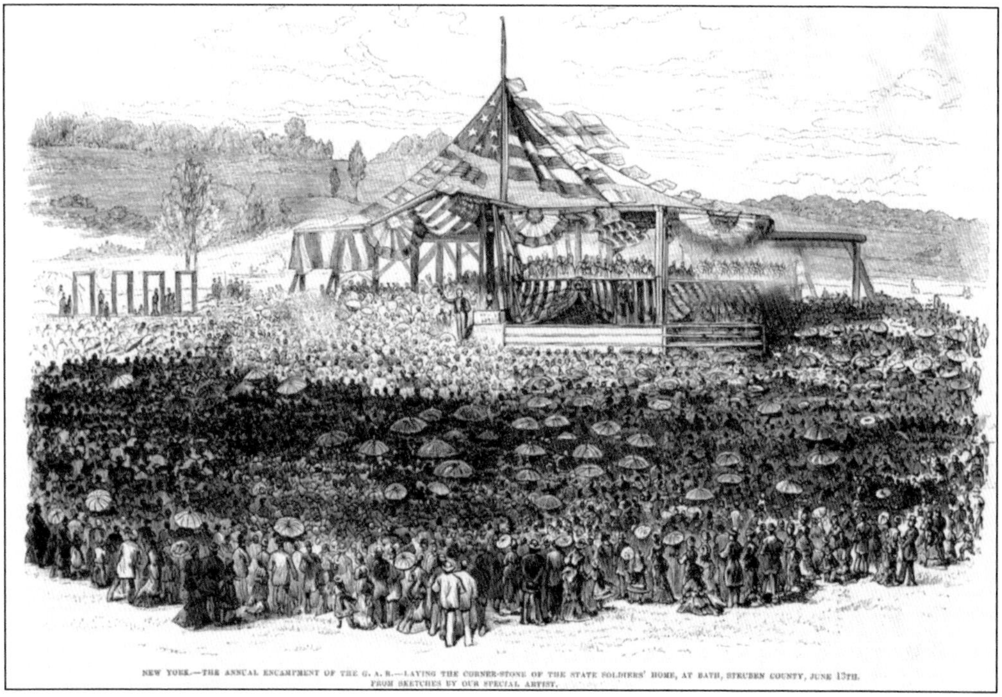

The event attracted national attention. *Leslie's Weekly* news magazine covered it in the June 30, 1877, issue.

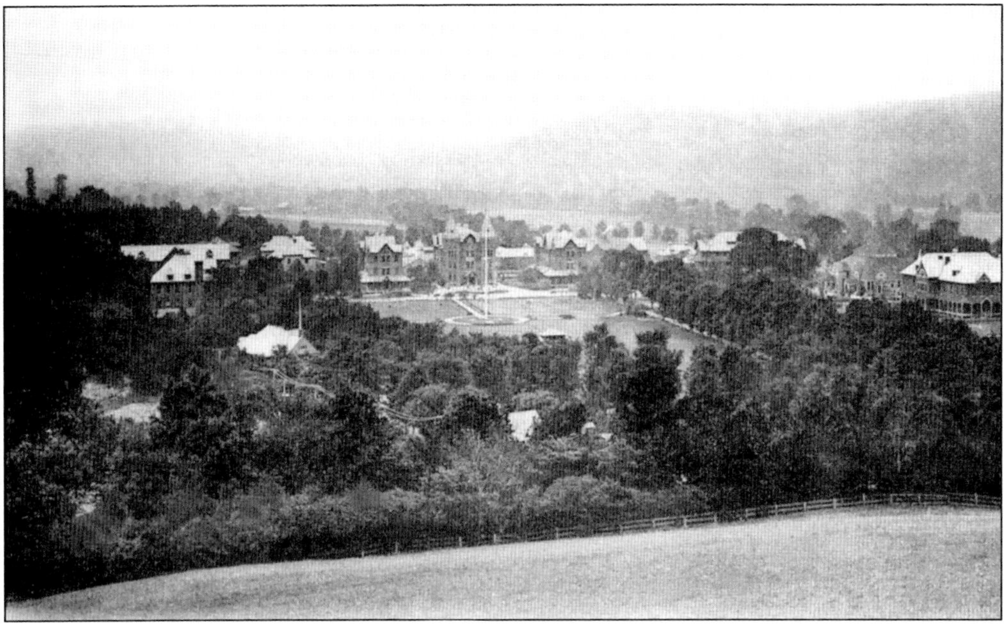

By late 1901, the Bath Soldiers' Home, as it was commonly known, had more than 1,700 residents. It is now a Veterans Administration (VA) facility, and veterans receiving care remain a part of daily life in Bath.

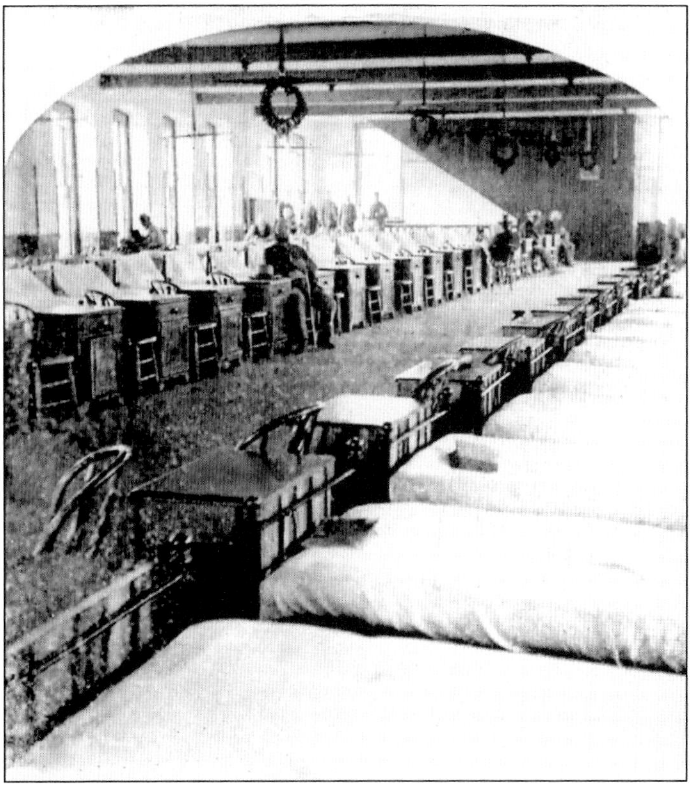

Although this stereograph shows Spartan facilities with no privacy, the accommodations were doubtless far superior to those that residents had endured during the Civil War.

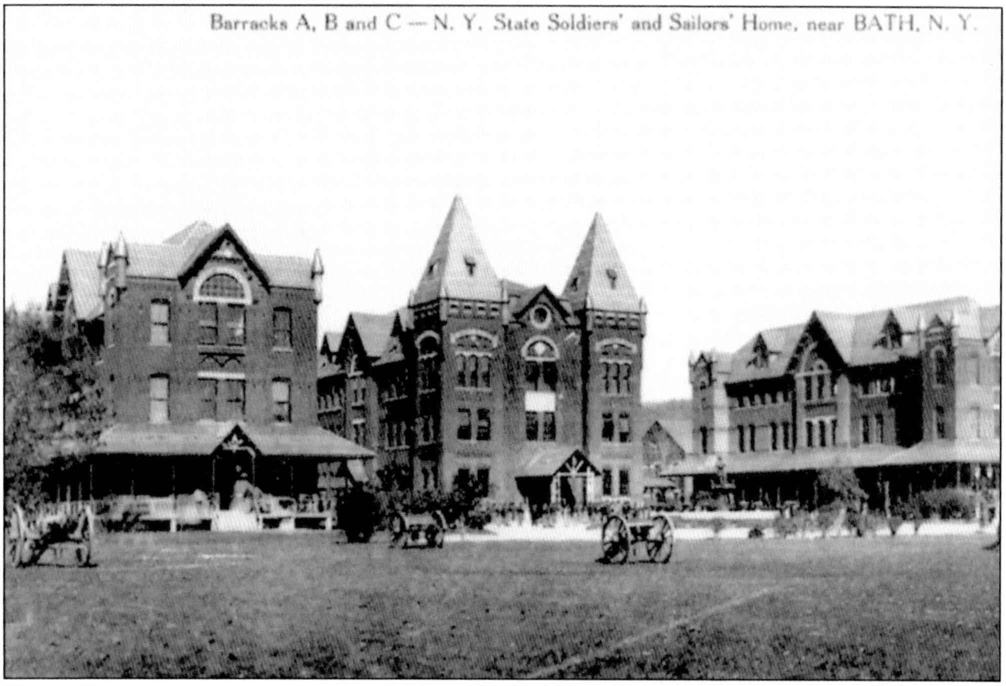

Certainly treatment was institutional, but care was also taken so that the Bath Soldiers' Home was attractive, as this view illustrates.

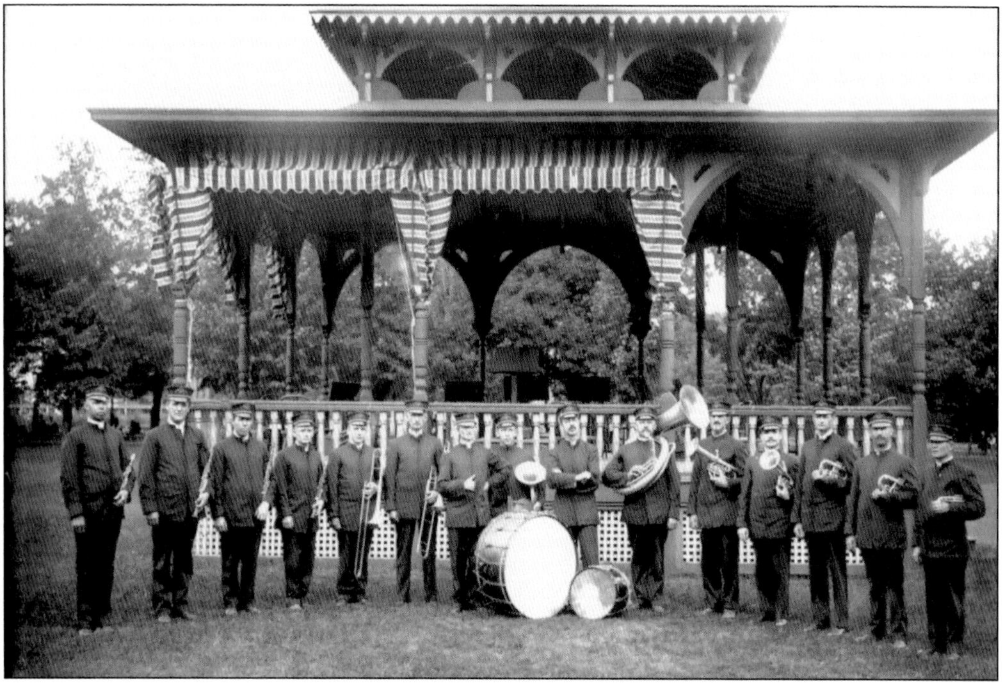

Homegrown bands were an important part of life in the days before even gramophones had appeared. (Courtesy Steuben County Historian's Office.)

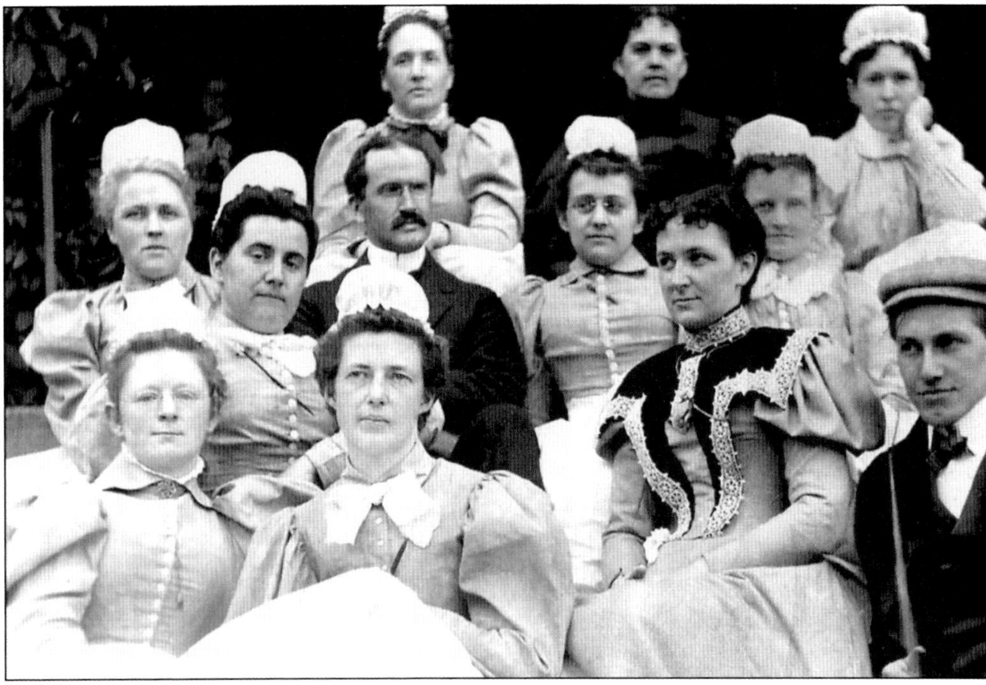

Female nurses first appeared around the beginning of the 20th century.

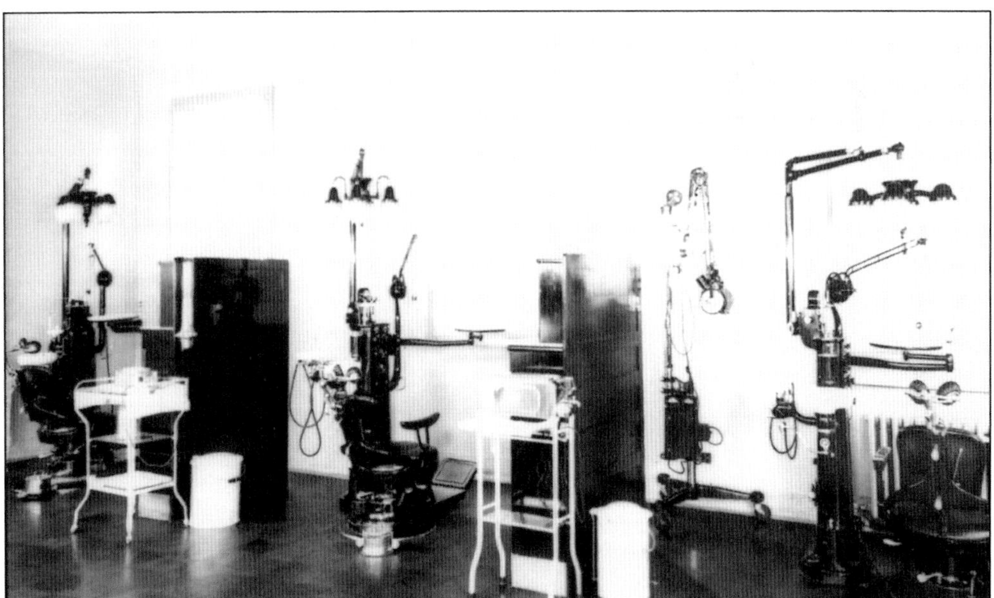

The Bath Soldiers' Home covered all aspects of care.

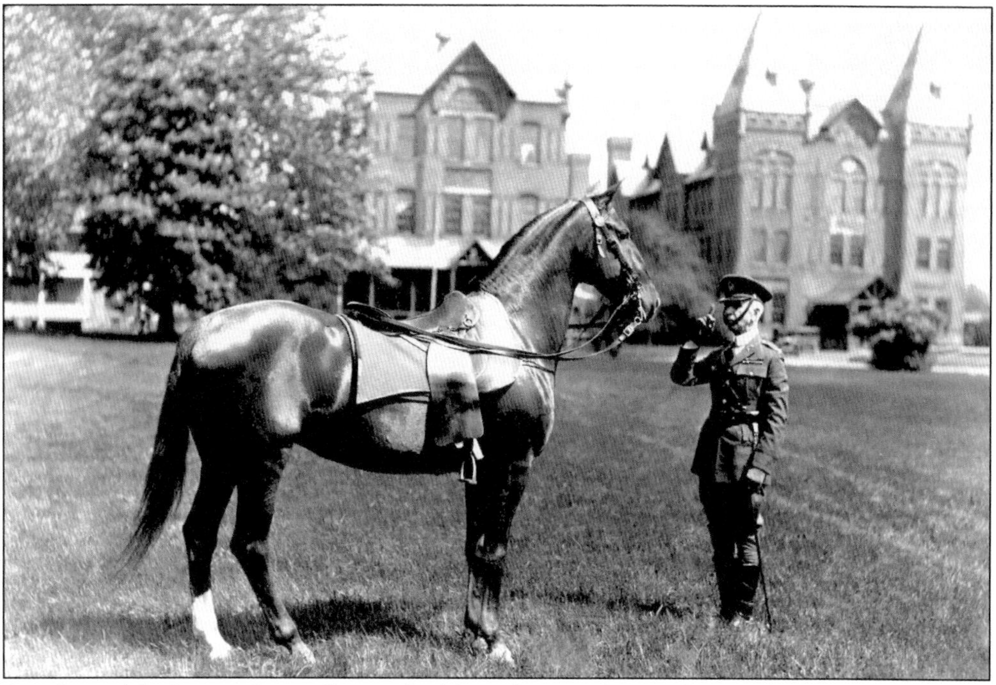

Cavalry and draft animals rapidly vanished from the U.S. forces after World War I. Maybe Bath should have made a home for them, too. (Courtesy Steuben County Historian's Office.)

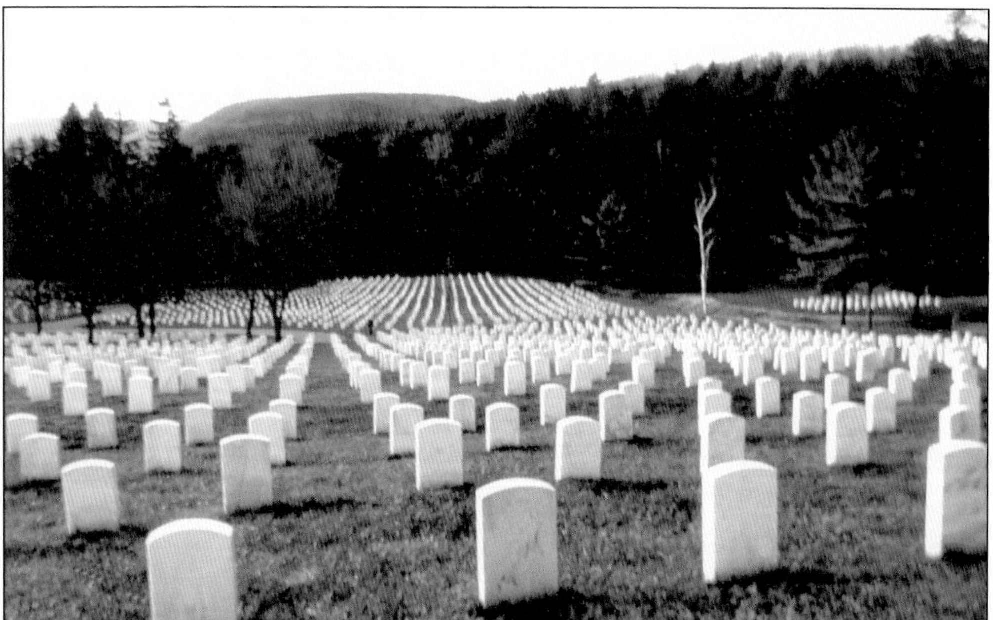

In 1988, the bodies of 28 unknown veterans of the War of 1812, recently discovered in Canada, were reinterred in the National Cemetery at the Bath Veterans Administration facility. The unknown veterans were honored by Bath citizens, veterans, and dignitaries from the United States and Canada. Their final resting place is a fitting one. Given the units involved, they were probably all Finger Lakes boys.

Five

Kanona, Savona, and All around Town

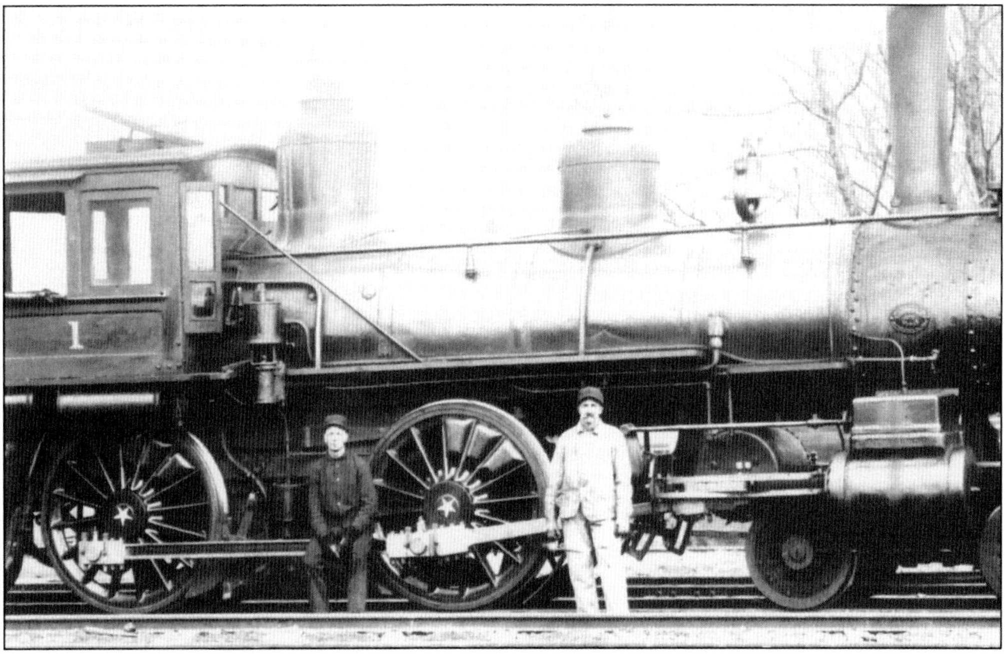

Beyond Bath village but still within the town of Bath lie settlements such as Savona and Kanona. These hamlets and the long stretches of rural countryside each have their own flavor. "The trains don't stop here anymore," and the ease of automobile traffic has turned them largely into bedroom communities, but each settlement has its own heritage and keeps its own character. Fewer and fewer Bath folk farm, but agriculture endures as a linchpin of local life. Steuben is famed nationally with an unbeatable reputation: New York's number one deer county. One colorful feature of Bath life through the late 19th and early 20th centuries was the Kanona & Prattsburg Railroad. The K & P (or "Kick and Push") was, like the Bath & Hammondsport Railroad a few miles farther east: a one-track, north–south short line. An automobile driver, stopped for not pausing at a K & P crossing, told the officer, "There's only one engine—and since I'm not driving it, it's not going anywhere!" Since the first engine was neither supplemented nor replaced for 50 years, the large numeral 1 on the cab shows either delectable whimsy or incurable optimism.

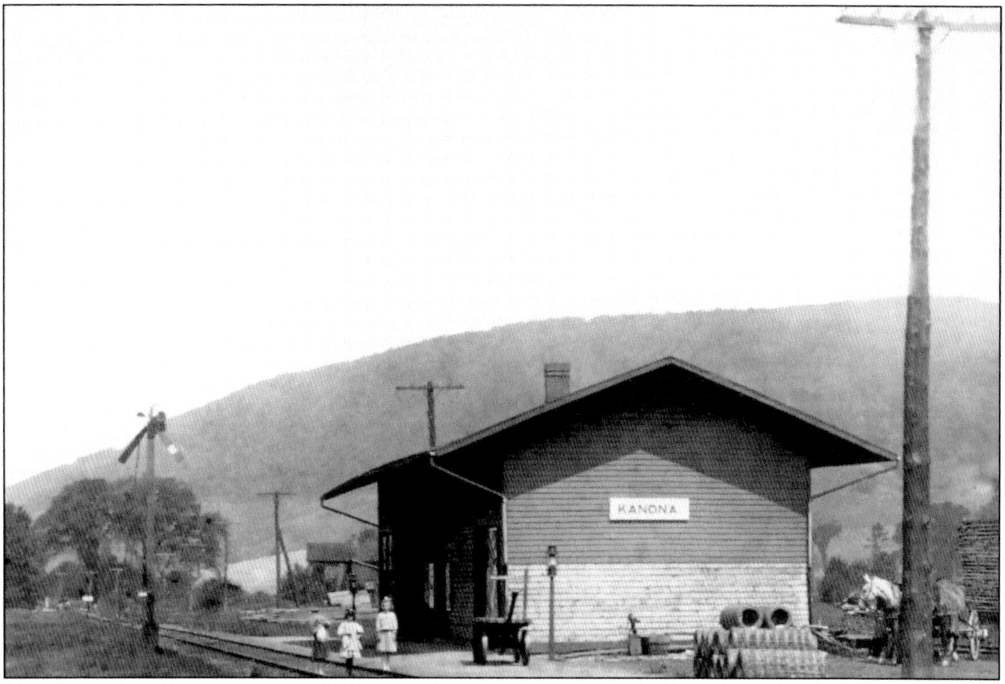

The Kanona & Prattsburg Railroad, which met the Erie Railroad in Kanona, carried more than 13,000 passengers in its peak year of 1892. These girls would have been in trouble if a mother had seen them on the tracks.

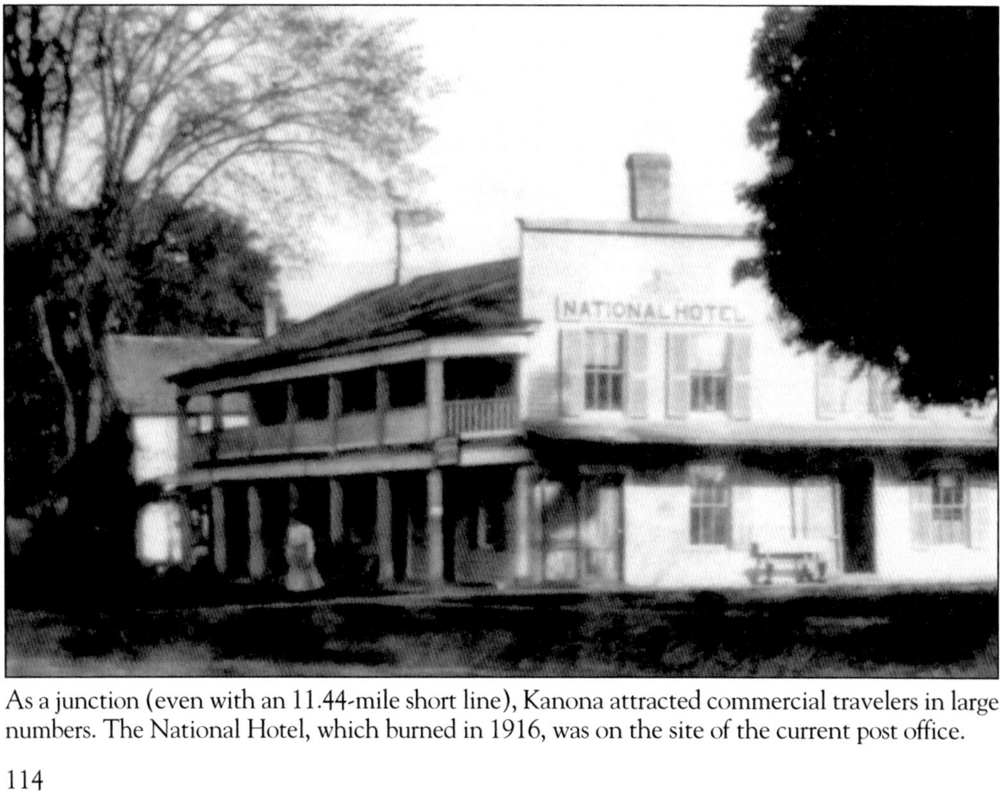

As a junction (even with an 11.44-mile short line), Kanona attracted commercial travelers in large numbers. The National Hotel, which burned in 1916, was on the site of the current post office.

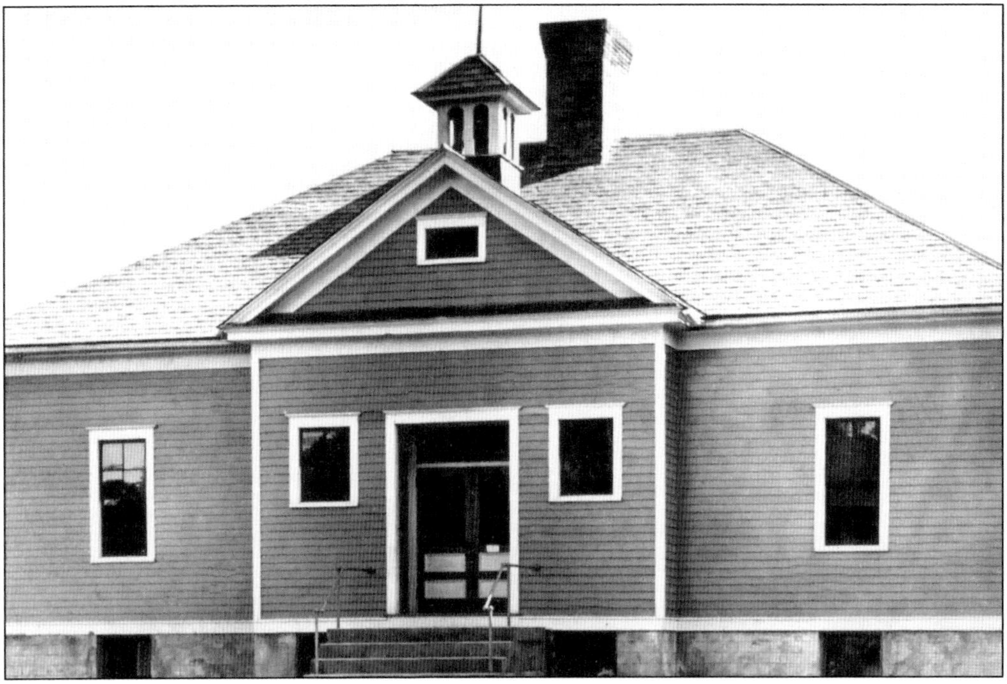

Kanona, west of Bath village, built an attractive school on Railroad Avenue in 1920. After the schools were centralized, this building was converted to apartments.

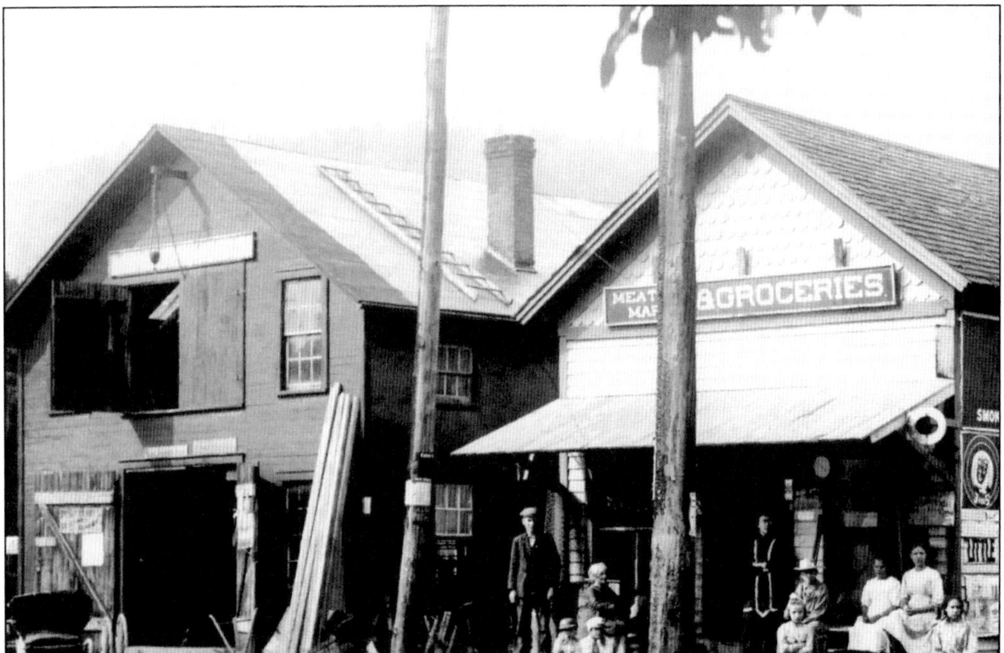

Even small communities in the 19th century had active industrial and mercantile lives.

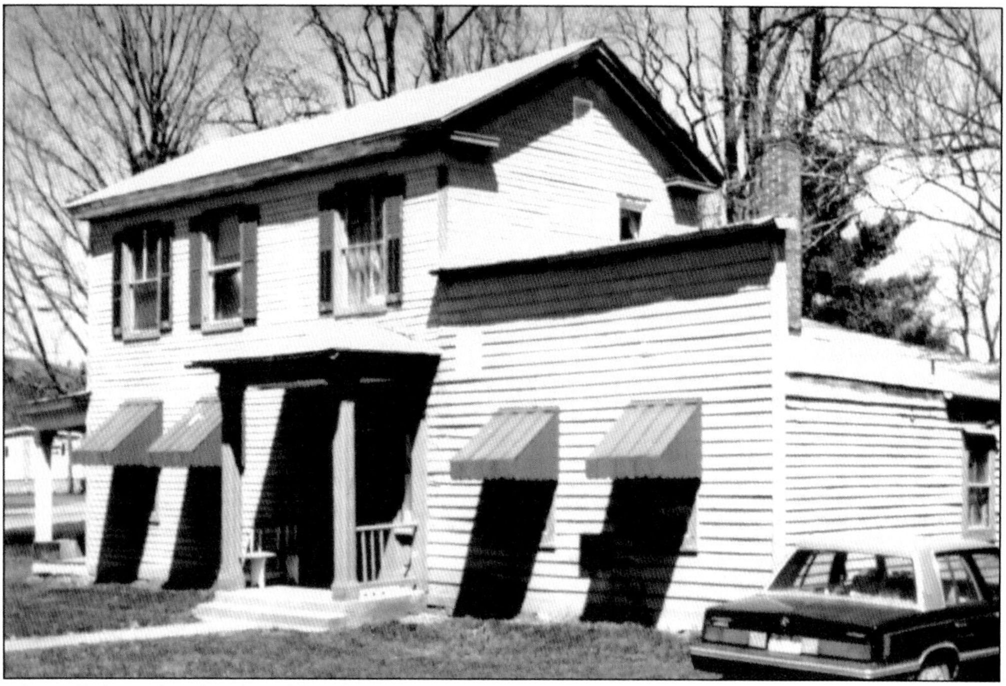

This is believed to be the oldest house in Kanona.

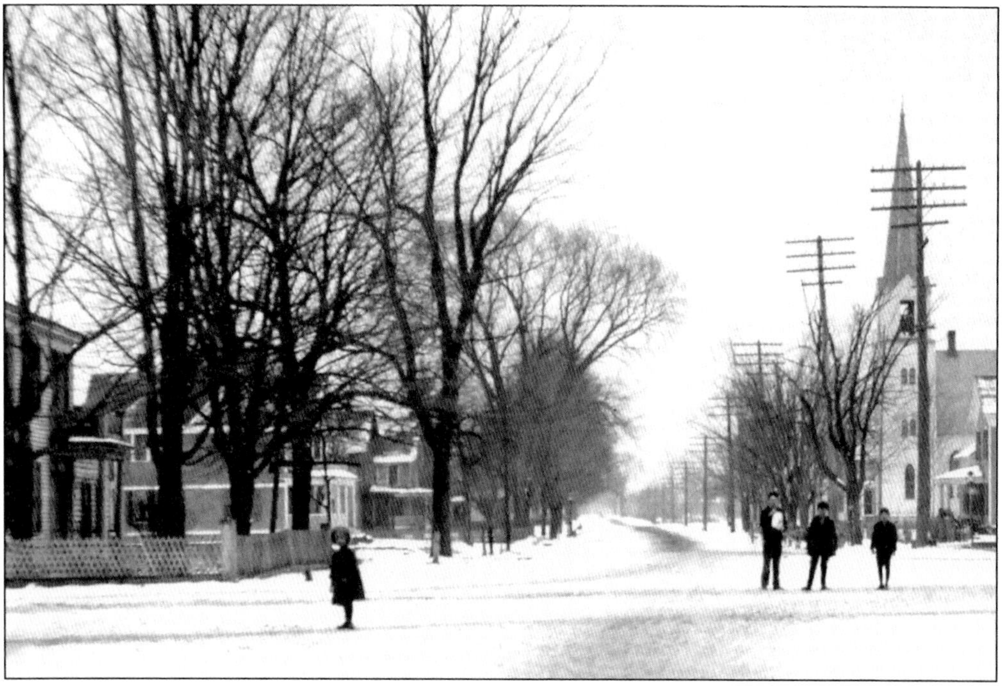

The Methodist church, like much of the unincorporated hamlet, was troubled from time to time by flooding from the Conhocton River.

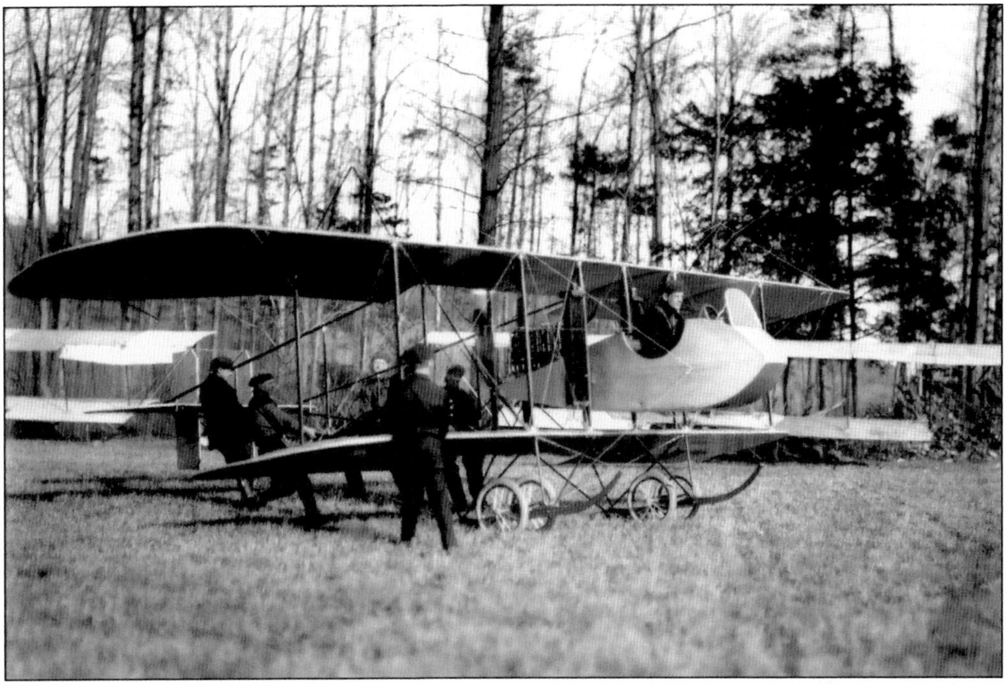

Some of the Thomas Brothers' flying took place near Kanona. (Courtesy Curtiss Museum.)

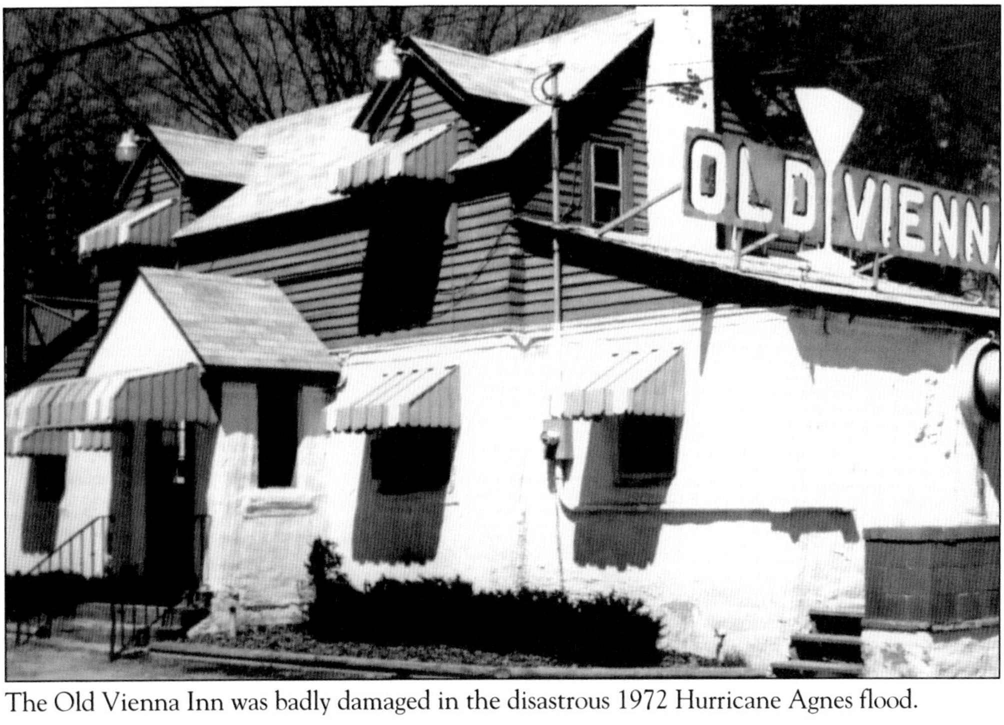

The Old Vienna Inn was badly damaged in the disastrous 1972 Hurricane Agnes flood.

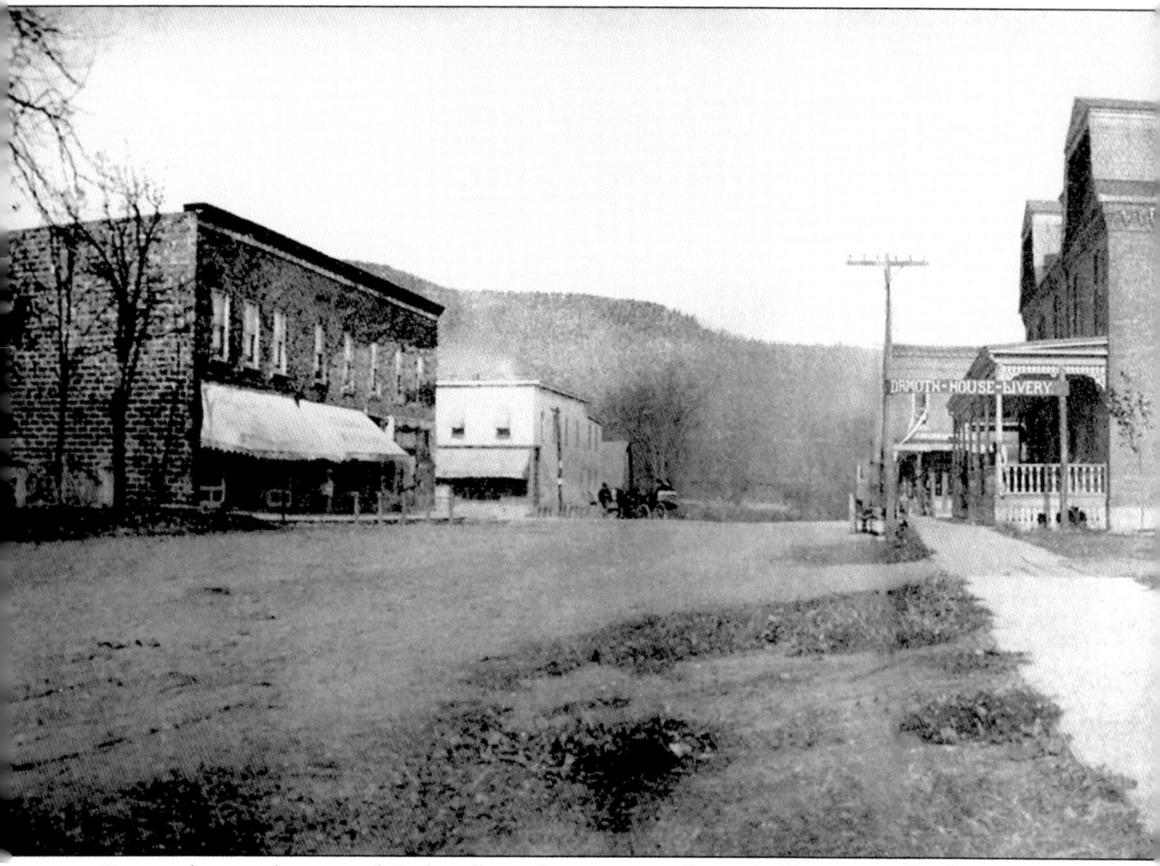

Savona lies to the east of Bath village. Its imposing Damoth House was finally dismantled in 2002, leaving three of the four corners empty. This panoramic view looks north up what

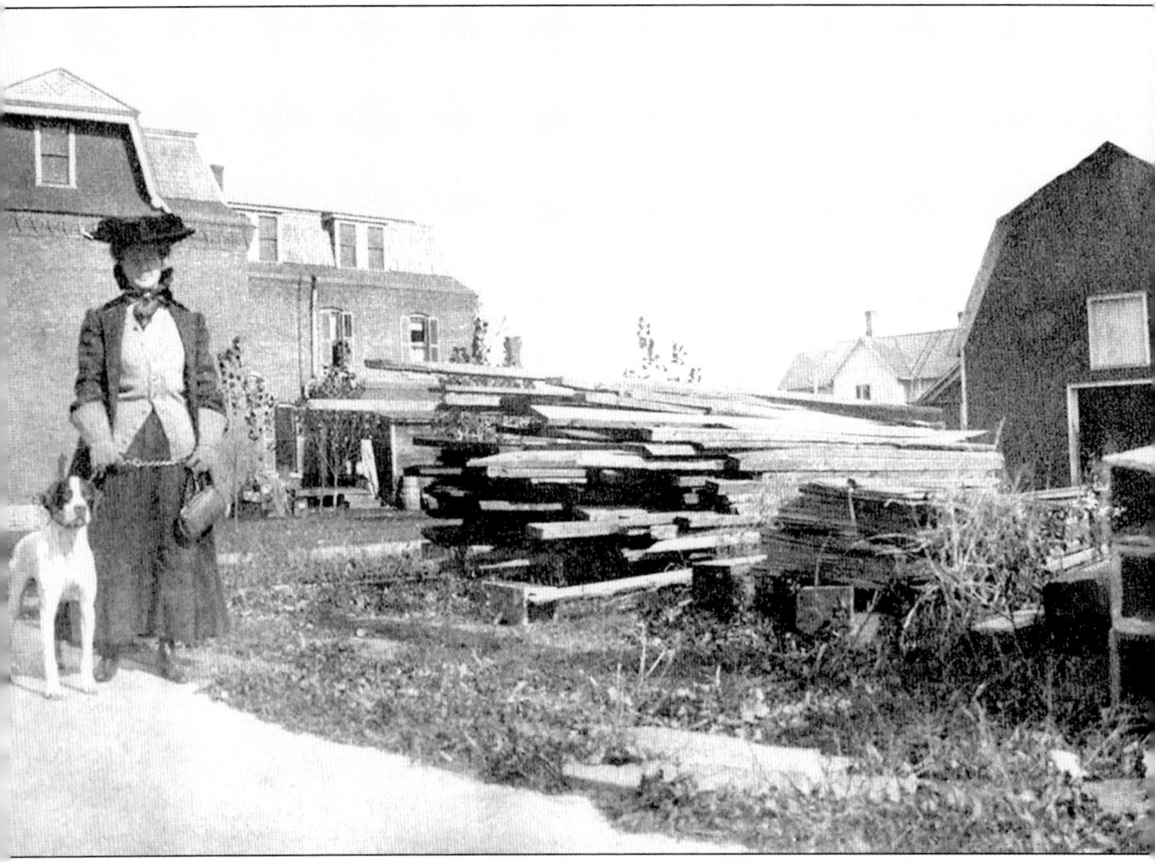

later became the original Route 15. Savona, although part of the town of Bath, had its own incorporated village government. (Courtesy Corning-Painted Post Historical Society.)

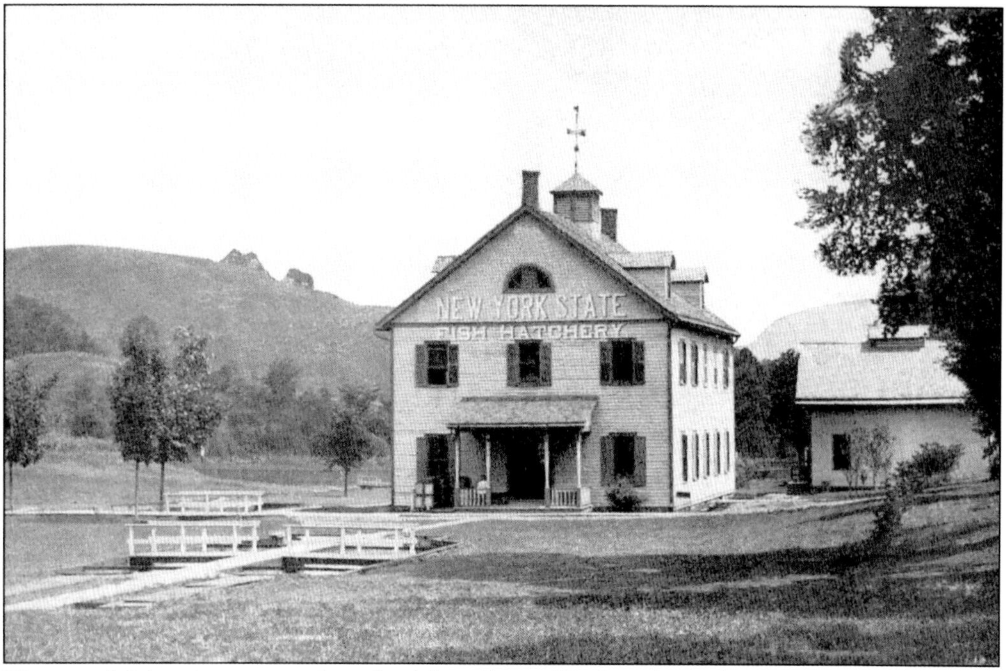

The state fish hatchery, opened north of the village of Bath in the 19th century, is still a thriving concern today, stocking fish in streams and lakes.

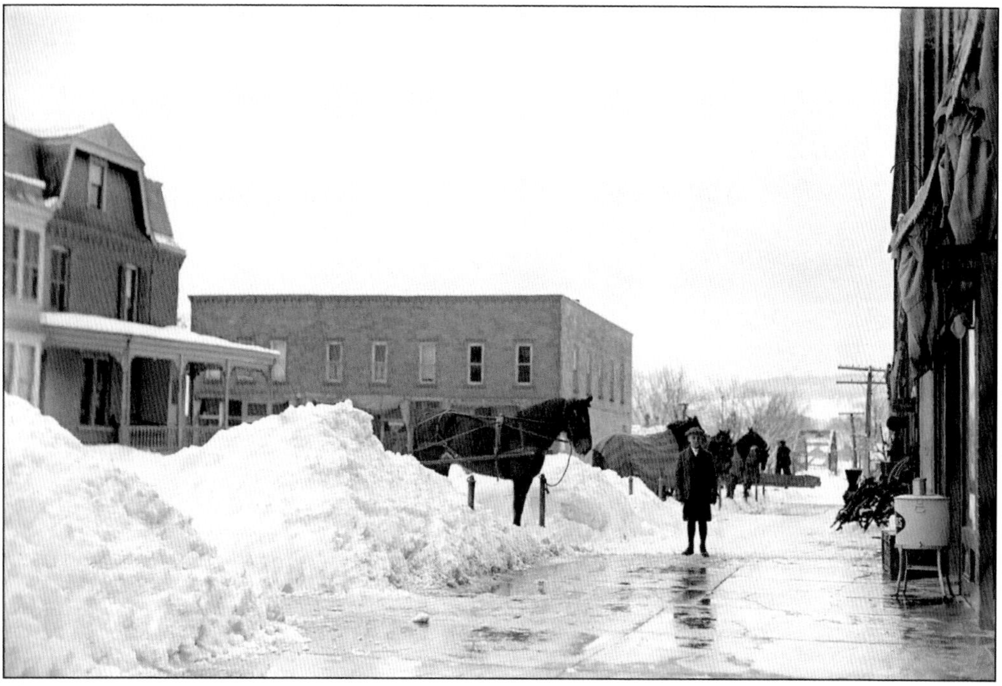

This snowstorm stopped Savona traffic at the corner of Church and Lamoka Streets. The shopkeeper is still hoping someone will drop in for a washing machine.

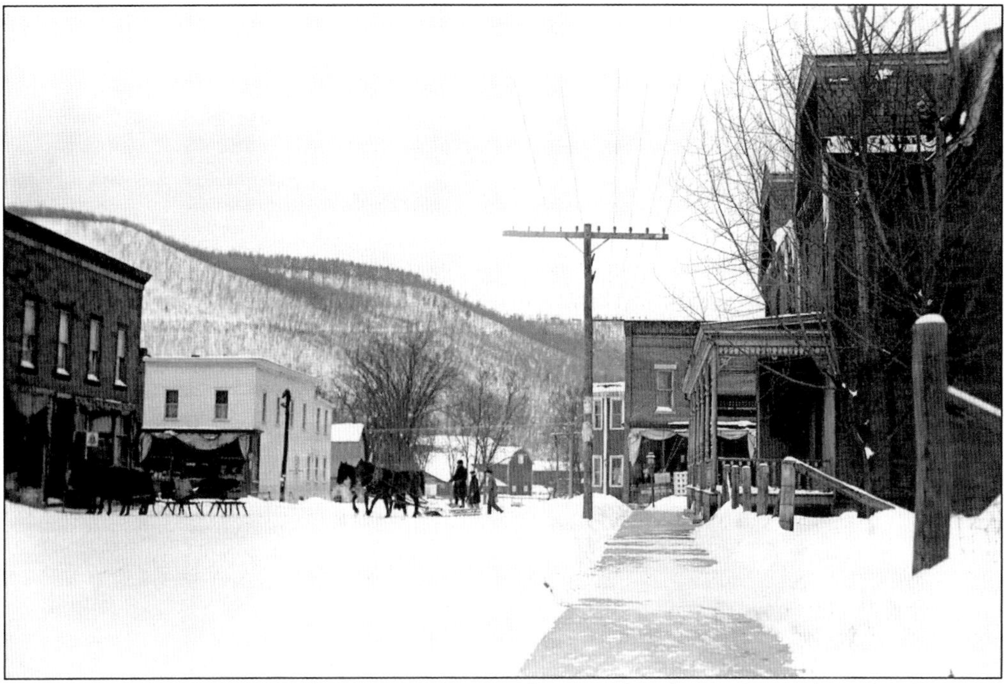

This photographer braved the snow to get a photograph of Lamoka and Orchard Streets in Savona.

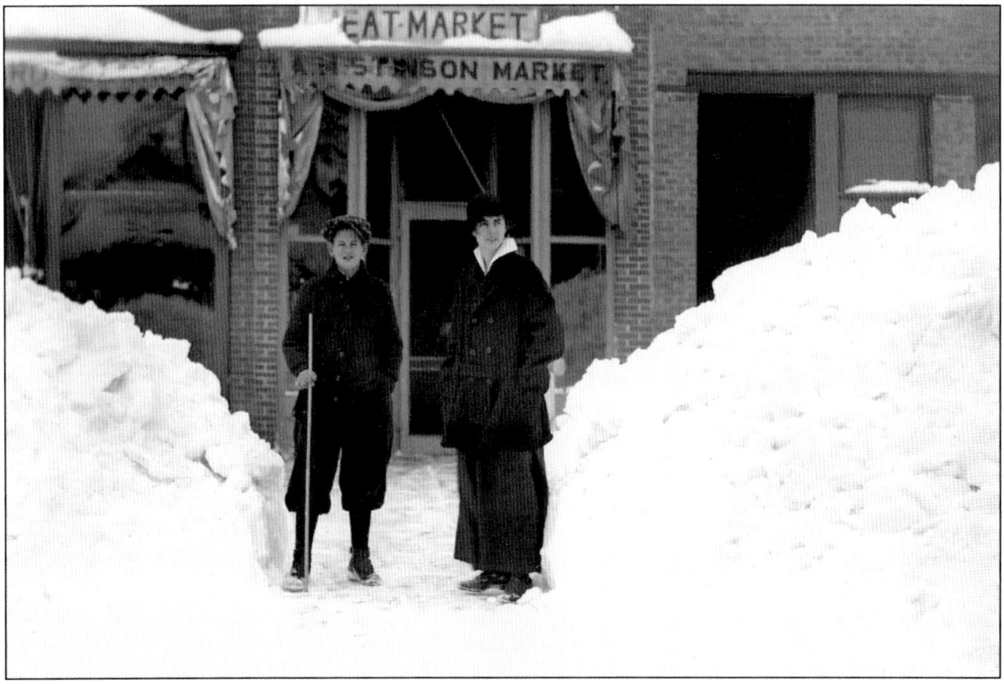

As usual, young people made a celebration from what their elders probably saw as a massive inconvenience. That cheery young fellow probably used his stick for measurements.

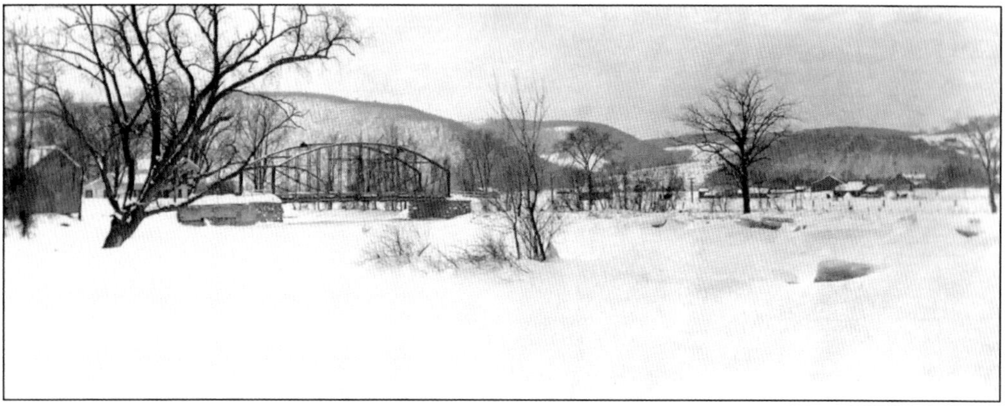

How many people remember Savona's old river bridge, shown in this panoramic image?

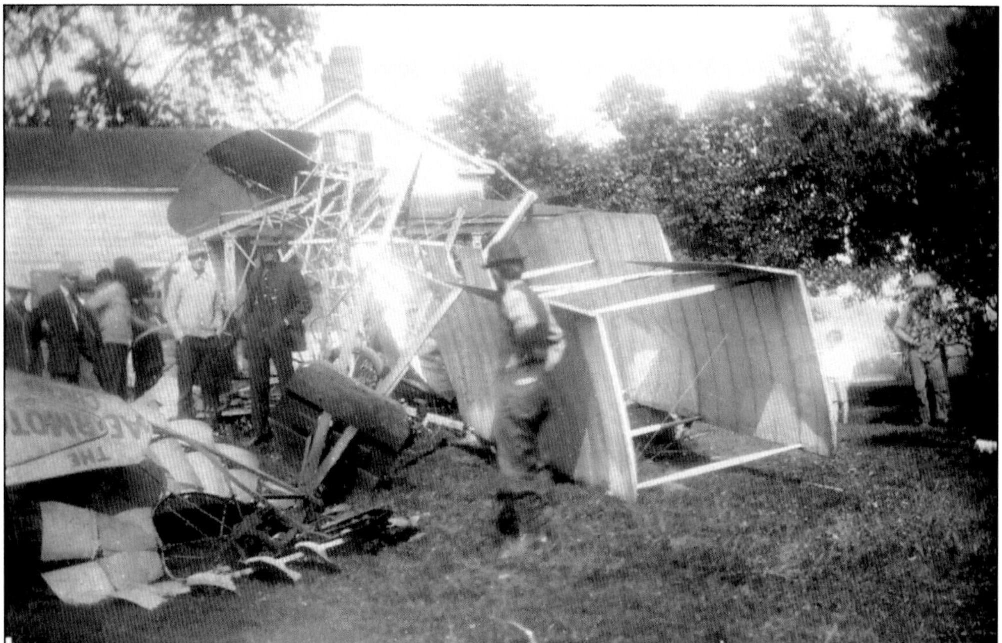

Japanese aviator Kondo Motohisa was killed test-flying a Kirkham airplane in 1912. The plane smashed into a windmill on Eagle Valley Road between Bath and Savona. Today, the broken propeller is in the Curtiss Museum. (Courtesy Curtiss Museum.)

"KIRKHAM" AVIATION POWER PLANTS FOR SEASON OF 1912

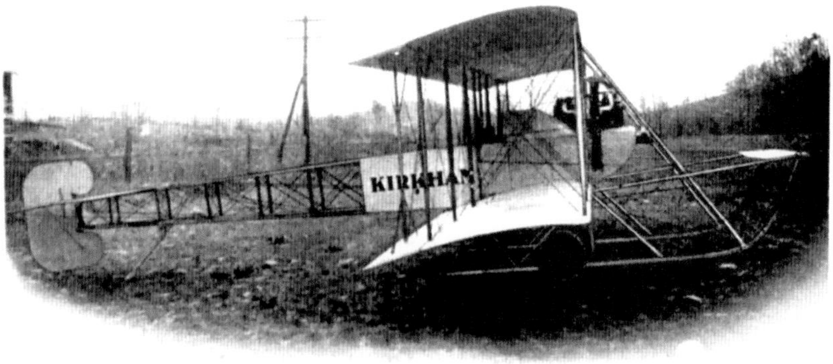

Model B-6 installed in "KIRKHAM" Tractor Biplane

THE "KIRKHAM" AVIATION MOTOR IS OFFERED IN FOUR DIFFERENT MODELS:

Model B-4,	**35 H-P.,**	**4-cyl.,**	**weight, 185 lbs.**
Model B-6,	**50 H-P.,**	**6-cyl.,**	**weight, 235 lbs.**
Model B-G-6,	**70 H-P.,**	**6-cyl.,**	**weight, 255 lbs.**
Model B-12,	**120 H-P.,**	**12-cyl., V.,**	**weight, 400 lbs.**

All of these models are sold as complete power plants or motor only, as desired.

THE universal success of every 6-cylinder, 50-H.P., "**KIRKHAM**" motor for season of 1911 has demonstrated their unquestionable reliability and efficiency; therefore the new models listed above contain not only all the features which have made the "**KIRKHAM**" Aviation motor noted for its reliability but in addition, all models for 1912 are to be equipped with the new Bosch 2-spark magneto, larger valves and special cooling tubes through oil tank, whereby the oil is always at a safe temperature no matter how hard or how long the motor is run.

Now is the time to get in your order if you want reasonably quick delivery as a large number of orders have been booked for spring delivery and there is sure to be a rush when the spring opens. Anyway, you better get acquainted with the only American motor that actually delivers what is claimed for it.

CATALOG FOR THE ASKING

CHARLES B. KIRKHAM, *Manufacturer*

SAVONA, NEW YORK

After breaking up his partnership with Fred Eells, Charles Kirkham started a new operation in Savona, where he created the highly advanced new airplane in which aviator Kondo Motohisa died. (Courtesy Curtiss Museum.)

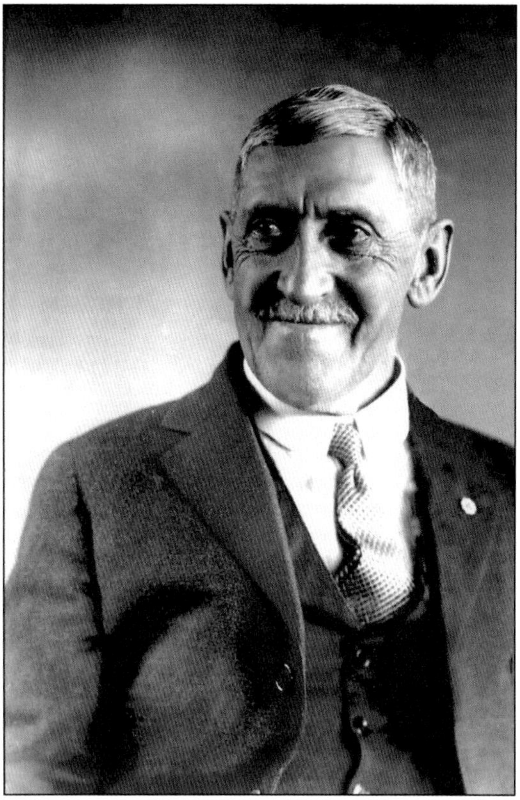

Throughout the two centuries and more since Bath was founded, agriculture has remained a significant part of the local economy. Edward Heineman, founder of the Farm Bureau, had the honor of being designated as one of 12 New York State Master Farmers.

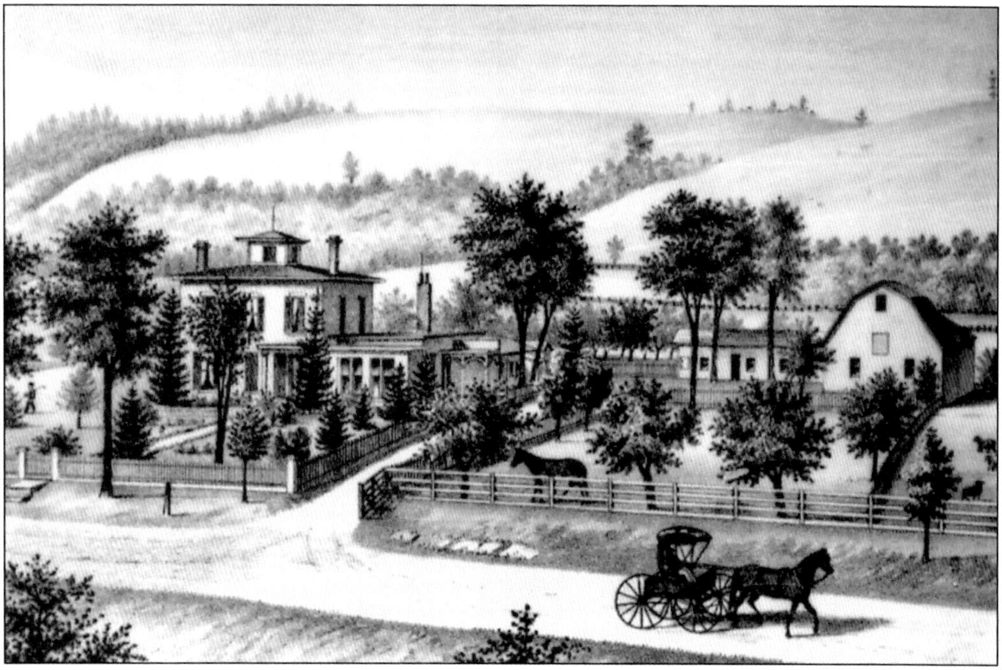

W. W. Clayton's 1879 history of Steuben County pictured the farm and home of George Haverling, the man who supervised construction of the Davenport Home for Orphan Girls.

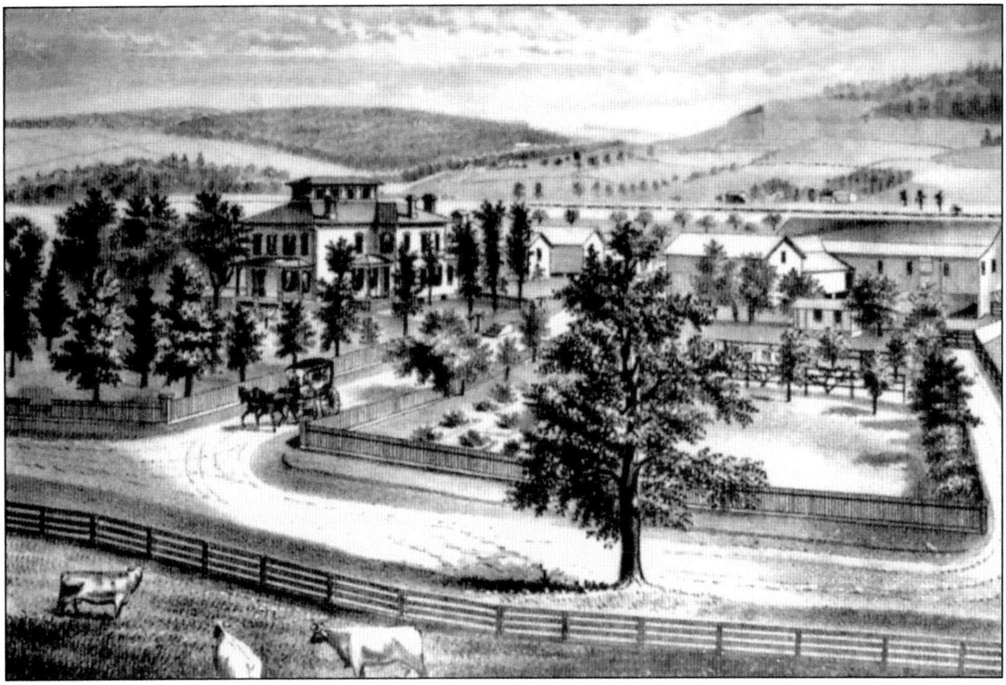

The home on the Smith farm, which stood near Route 415 and Telegraph Road, had more than 20 rooms, including a ballroom.

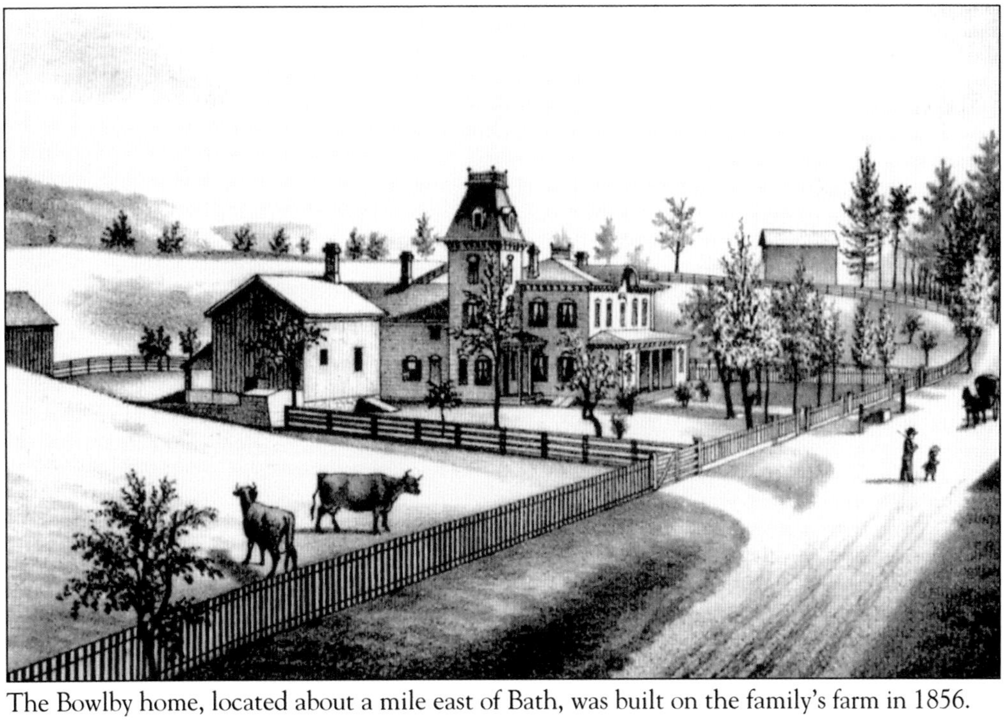

The Bowlby home, located about a mile east of Bath, was built on the family's farm in 1856.

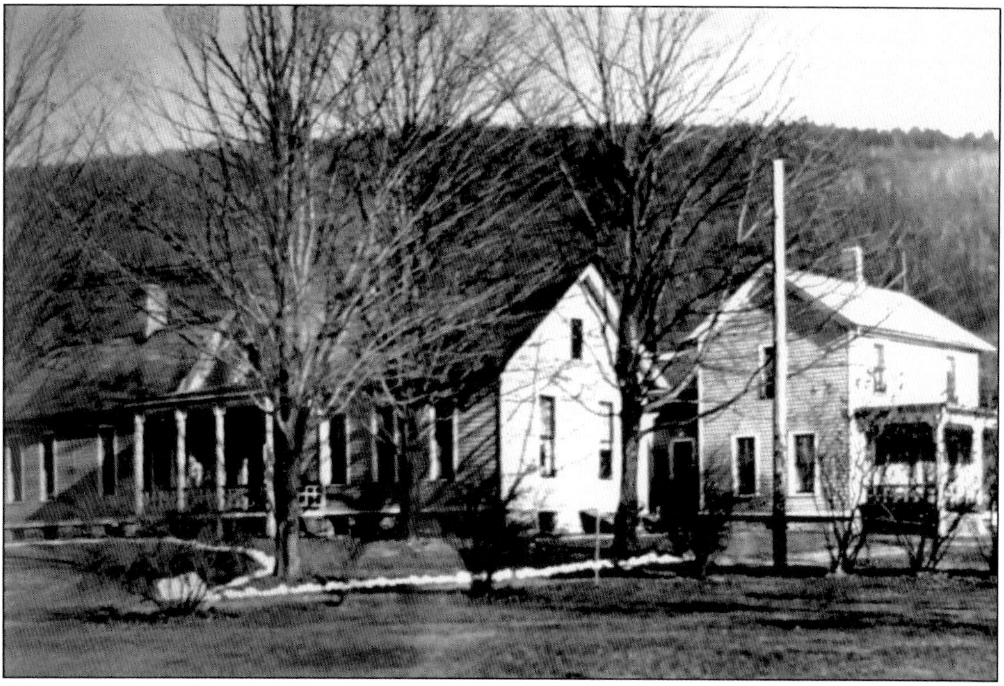

Along with agriculture, social services and county business have been major parts of life in Bath. The old county farm is still in use, although many of its original functions have been superseded by the county infirmary, across the road.

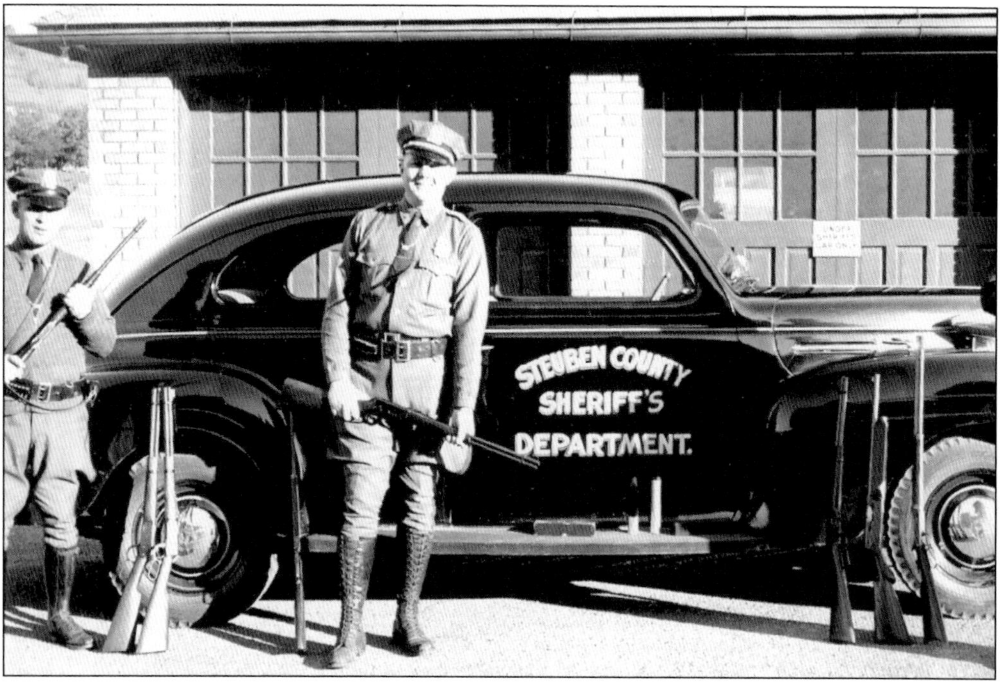

He had a number of able successors . . . but nobody could ever quite replace Sheriff Charlie Reynolds.

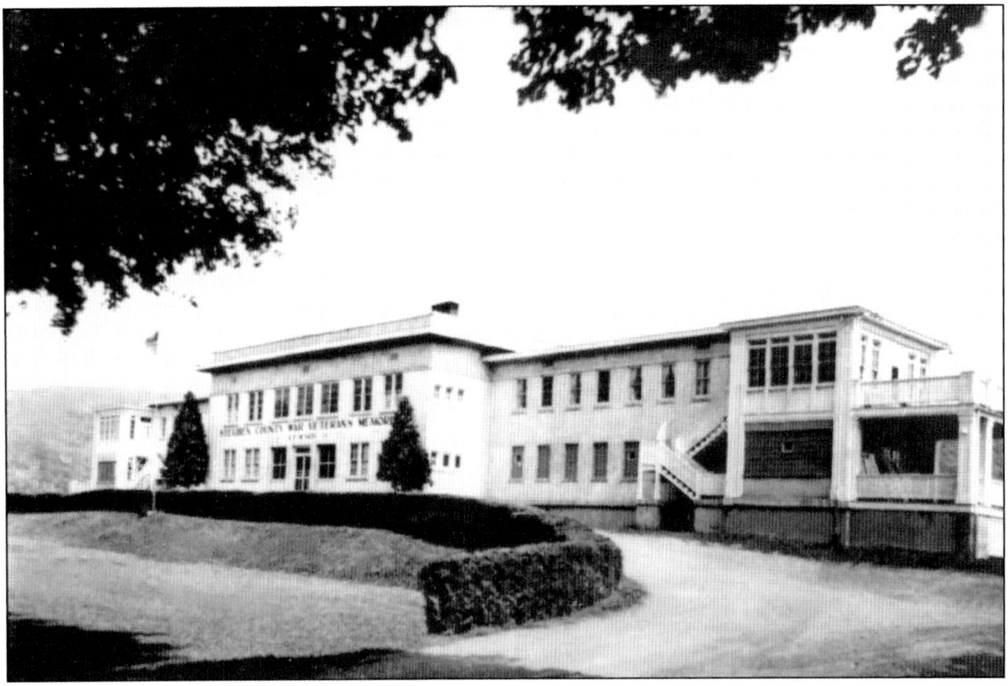

The Veterans of Foreign Wars Post building on Route 54 has since been replaced with a more manageable home.

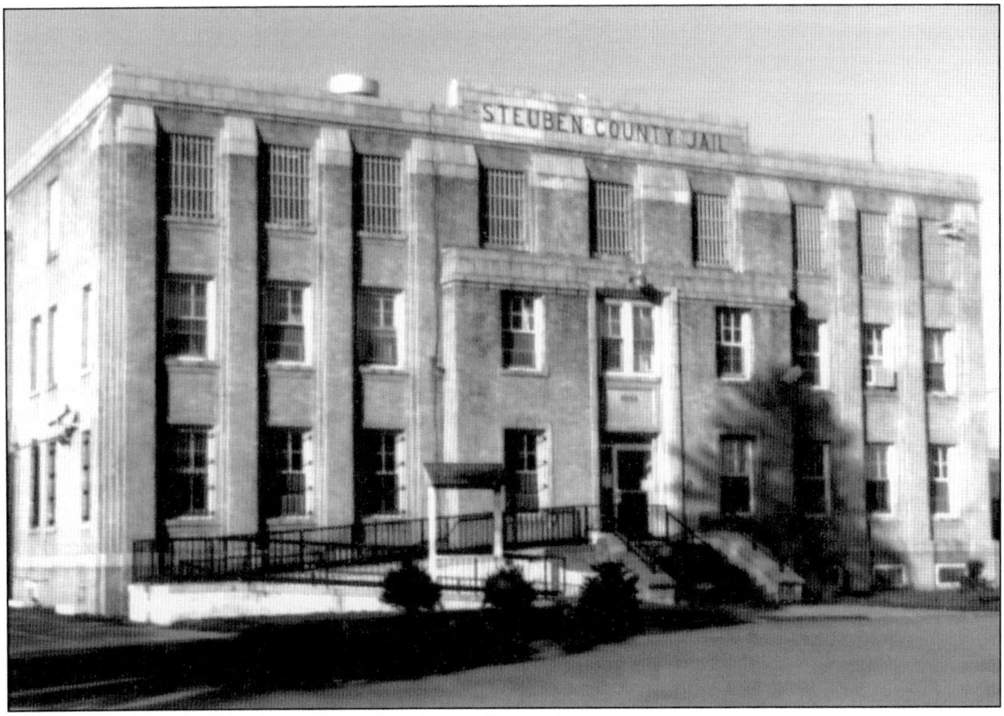

A more modern facility has taken the place of this old county jail.

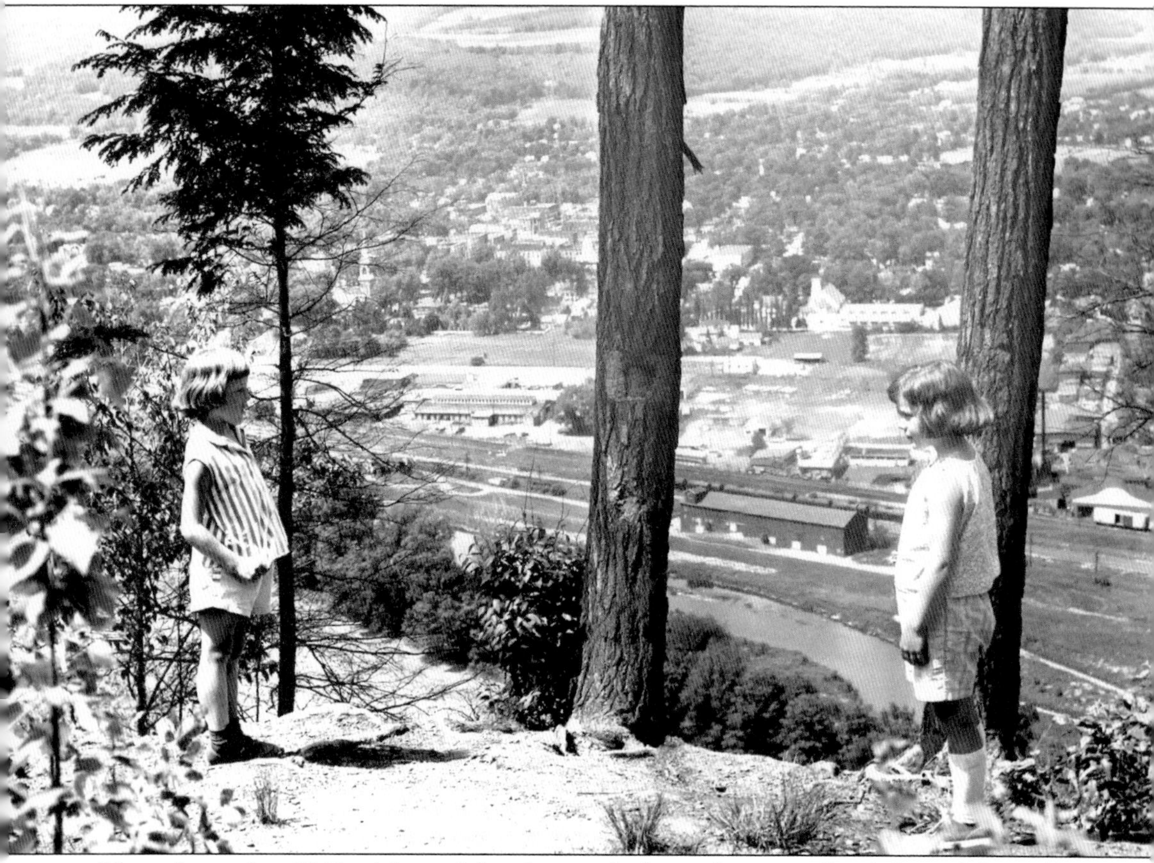

Throughout the 1960s, Mayor John Langendorfer enthusiastically dedicated himself to developing Mossy Bank as a public park. Daughters Joanne (left, now Hastrich) and Carol (now Mozes) shared his vision, and now everyone profits from his legacy. From Colonel Williamson to Mayor Wallace . . . from the 18th century to the 21st . . . from the banks of the river to the heights of the cliff . . . Bath remains, in the words of Arch Merrill, "the Grand Dame of the Southern Tier." (Courtesy Betty Langendorfer.)